Special Education Law

Peter S. Latham, J.D.
Latham & Latham, Washington, DC

Patricia Horan Latham, J.D.
Latham & Latham, Washington, DC

Myrna R. Mandlawitz, J.D.
MRM Associates, Washington, DC

PEARSON

Boston   New York   San Francisco
Mexico City   Montreal   Toronto   London   Madrid   Munich   Paris
Hong Kong   Singapore   Tokyo   Cape Town   Sydney

Executive Editor : *Virginia Lanigan*
Editorial Assistant: *Matthew Buchholz*
Senior Marketing Manager: *Kris Ellis-Levy*
Production Editor: *Janet Domingo*
Editorial Production Service: *Pine Tree Composition, Inc.*
Composition Buyer: *Linda Cox*
Manufacturing Buyer: *Linda Morris*
Electronic Composition: *Pine Tree Composition, Inc.*
Cover Administrator: *Linda Knowles*

For related titles and support materials, visit our online catalog at www.ablongman.com.

Between the time website information is gathered and then published, it is not unusual for some sites to have closed. Also, the transcription of URLs can result in typographical errors. The publisher would appreciate notification where these errors occur so that they may be corrected in subsequent editions.

ISBN-13: 987-0-205-47975-7
ISBN-10:   0-205-47975-8

Library of Congress Cataloging-in-Publication Data

Latham, Patricia H.
    Special education law / Latham, Latham, Mandlawitz.—1st ed.
        p. cm.
    ISBN 0-205-47975-8
    1.   Special education—Law and legislation—United States. 2.   United States.
Individuals with Disabilities Education Act. 3.   United States. No Child Left Behind Act
of 2001.   I. Latham, Peter S. II. Mandlawitz, Myrna. III. Title.

    KF4209.3.L38 2008
    344.73'0791—dc22

                                                                    2007022252

Printed in the United States of America

10   9   8   7   6   5   4   3   2   1   11   10   09   08   07

ABOUT THE AUTHORS

Peter S. Latham

Peter S. Latham, J.D. is a partner in the Washington, DC law firm of Latham & Latham and is the co-author of eight books on legal issues in employment and education, including *Learning Disabilities and the Law* and *Attention Deficit Disorder and the Law,* as well as a contributor to nine additional books. He has authored an extensive text on disputes involving government contracts, has produced four videos on disability legal topics, has over twenty years experience in alternative dispute resolution, has served on the professional advisory board of Learning Disabilities Association of America, and served as a U. S. Navy officer during the war in Vietnam. He served at the U. S. Naval Support Activity, Da Nang, Vietnam (1968-69) and then as Trial and Defense Counsel, U. S. Naval Station, Washington, DC. He was awarded the Navy Achievement Medal (Combat "V") in 1969.

He is a member of the District of Columbia Bar and is admitted to practice before the U. S. District Courts for the District of Columbia and Maryland and the U. S. Court of Appeals for the District of Columbia. He also is admitted to the U. S. Court of Appeals for the Federal Circuit and the General Courts Martial of the Armed Forces of the United States. He is a graduate of Swarthmore College, B.A. and the University of Pennsylvania Law School, J.D.

Patricia Horan Latham

Patricia Horan Latham, J.D. is a partner in the Washington, DC law firm of Latham & Latham and is the co-author of eight books on legal issues in employment and education, including *Learning Disabilities and the Law* and *Attention Deficit Disorder and the Law,* as well as a contributor to nine additional books. She is a member of the panel of arbitrators and mediators of the American Arbitration Association serving as arbitrator and mediator in a wide range of commercial, employment, and international cases, serves on the panel of arbitrators of the New York Stock Exchange, has lectured at the Columbus School of Law, Catholic University of America, and has appeared on programs, including Court TV, to discuss legal topics. She has served on an advisory committee of the GED Testing Service and on the Board of Directors of Learning Disability Association of America.

She is a member of the District of Columbia Bar and is admitted to practice before the U. S. Supreme Court, the U. S. District Courts for the District of Columbia and Maryland, and the U. S. Court of Appeals for the District of Columbia. She is a graduate of Swarthmore College, B.A. and the University of Chicago Law School, J.D.

Myrna R. Mandlawitz

Myrna Mandlawitz, J.D., has been involved in the field of education for the past 30 years and is the author of a number of books on special education, including most recently *What Every Teacher Should Know About IDEA 2004 Laws and Regulations*. She has worked as a classroom teacher, in project development in state government, and as an education advocate in Congress. She is recognized as a national expert in special education law and policy. Ms. Mandlawitz provides training and writes extensively on special and general education and has provided representation for education administrators, related services providers, and parents of children with disabilities. She serves as the co-chairman of the National Alliance of Pupil Services Organizations, the major national coalition representing related services providers.

She is a member of the Pennsylvania Bar and is a graduate of Boston University, B.A., M.Ed., and Temple University Law School, J.D.

CONTENTS

Introduction   xv

PART ONE   The Constitutional Framework

1 The Judicial System   1

   A. In General   1

   B. State Courts   1

   C. Federal Courts   2

   D. Administrative Litigation   3

   E. Alternative Dispute Resolution (ADR)   3

   F. Sources of Law   3

   G. Summary   5

2 The Constitution   7

   A. Basic Principles   7

   B. Statutory Measures   8
      1. The Rehabilitation Act of 1973   8
      2. The Individuals with Disabilities Education Act   9
      3. The Americans with Disabilities Act of 1990   11
      4. The Reconstruction Civil Rights Acts   12

   C. Due Process   12
      1. Substantive Due Process   12
      2. Procedural Due Process   13
      3. Due Process Protection   13

   D. Equal Protection: Rational Basis Review Required   13
      1. Basic Principles   13
      2. Sovereign Immunity   14
      3. Rational Basis   14

E. Equal Protection: Intentional Discrimination Barred   15
1. Overview   15
2. The RA and ADA Must Be Interpreted Similarly   16
3. Fundamental Right   16
4. Denial of the Right Must be Deliberate and Knowing   18

F. What is the Status of Regulations Issued Under the RA/ADA?   19
1. Overview   19
2. Regulations: Alexander v. Sandoval   19
3. Title II Regulations   20

G. Summary   20

3   Statutory Overview   23

A. Introduction   23

B. IDEA: Meeting the Need for Special Education   23

C. The Rehabilitation Act of 1973   26

D. The Americans with Disabilities Act of 1990   26

E. The Relationships among the RA/ADA and the IDEA   26
1. Two Approaches to One Goal   26
2. The RA/ADA Mandate Access for Individuals with Disabilities   27
3. The IDEA: Access Through Funded Special Education   29

F. State Law   31

G. Summary   32

PART TWO   The IDEA

4   The IDEA: Coverage   33

A. In General   33
1. The Special Education Population   33
2. The Philosophy of the IDEA   35
3. The 2004 Reauthorization of the IDEA   36
4. The IDEA Works through Funding   37

B. Statutory Language and Coverage   37
1. Child with a Disability   37
2. Specific Learning Disability   38
3. Severe Discrepancy   38
4. Students With ADHD and Asperger's Syndrome   40

C. **The Duty to Evaluate**   **43**
1. Child Find   43
2. Evaluations   43
3. Initial Evaluation   44
4. Content of Evaluations   44
5. Failure or Refusal to Evaluate   45
6. Comment on the Duty to Identify and Evaluate   45
7. The Problem of Comorbidity (Co-occurring Disorders)   47

D. **Summary**   **48**

5 **IDEA: FAPE**   **49**

A. **In General**   **49**

B. **Definition of FAPE**   **51**
1. Statutory Language   51
2. Board of Education v. Rowley   52
3. Failure to Furnish FAPE   52

C. **The Individualized Education Program (IEP)**   **55**
1. The IEP Team   55
2. Planning For the IEP Meeting   57
3. The IEP Document   58
4. Some IEP Defects Deny a FAPE   60
5. Some IEP Defects Do Not Deny a FAPE   60
6. The 2004 IDEA   61

D. **Placement**   **61**

E. **Related Services**   **62**

F. **Inclusion**   **63**
1. The IDEA and Least Restrictive Environment   63
2. Cases—Inclusion   63

G. **Private School**   **66**
1. Private School Placement   66
2. Public Services; Private Setting   69

H. **Summary**   **71**

6 **Discipline**   **73**

A. **Overview**   **73**
1. Discipline Is a Fundamental Requirement   73
2. The IDEA Approach to Discipline   74

B. School Code Violations 75
1. School Codes 75
2. Basic Rule 75
3. Manifestation Determinations 76
4. Cases on School Code Violations and Disabilities 77
5. Consequences of Manifestation Determinations 78
6. Children Who Might Have Disabilities 79

C. Selected Serious Criminal Misconduct 79
1. Crimes 79
2. Consequences of Certain Criminal Conduct 80

D. Continued Services 82

E. Disputes 83

F. Relationship to RA/ADA 84

G. Summary 84

7 Mediation 85

A. In General 85
1. Arbitration 85
2. Mediation 86
3. State Educational Agency Complaint 86
4. Agreements That Determine Civil and Statutory Rights 87

B. Mediation Under IDEA 88
1. Congressional Preference 88
2. Proper Subjects of Mediation 88
3. Improper Use of Mediation Prohibited 88
4. Mediators Must be Impartial and Expert? 89

C. The Mediation Process 89
1. Notice of Hearing 89
2. Parents Decide Whether to Mediate 89
3. The Mediator is Selected 89
4. Mediation Confidentiality 90
5. Mediation Confidentiality Agreement 90
6. Settlement Agreements that Result from Mediation 91
7. Attorneys' Fees in Mediation 91

D. Summary 92

8 The Due process Hearing 93

A. In General 93
1. Notice and Pre-Hearing Matters 93
2. Due Process Hearing Requirement 93
3. The Complaint and Response 94
4. The Resolution Conference 96
5. Disclosure of Key Documents 96
6. Right to a Hearing 96

B. Preparing for a Hearing 97

C. The Hearing 98
1. Time and Location 98
2. Statute of Limitations 98
3. Representation 98
4. Behavior 98
5. Rules Governing the Conduct of the Hearing 99
6. Burden of Proof 99
7. Opening Statement 99
8. Introduction of Documents 99
9. Evidence of Facts 99
10. Opinion Evidence 100
11. Decision 100

D. Administrative Review 101

E. Judicial Review 101

F. Summary 101

9 Court Proceedings 103

A. In General 103

B. Contesting Administrative Decisions in Federal Court 103
1. What May be Litigated 103
2. Are States Immune From Suit? 103
3. A Suit That Cannot Be Brought 104
4. Exhaustion of Administrative Remedies 104
5. Futile to Resort to Due Process 105
6. General Policy That Violates the Law 106
7. Administrative Remedies Do Not Provide Adequate Relief 108
8. Statute of Limitations 108

9. Injunctions   109

10. Stay-Put Provisions   109

11. Rules of Procedure   110

12. District Court Evidentiary Proceedings   110

13. The Limited Approach   111

14. The Broad Approach   111

C. **Contesting Administrative Decisions in State Court   112**

D. **Summary   112**

10 Attorneys' Fees and Costs   113

A. **In General   113**

B. **Defining Prevailing Party   113**

C. **Conduct Which Limits Recovery of Attorney's Fees by Parents   114**

D. **The Educational Agency as Prevailing Party—Special Considerations 114**

1. Parents   115

2. Parents' Attorneys   115

E. **Other Provisions Regarding Attorney's Fees   115**

1. Sanctions and Misconduct Under Federal Rule of Civil Procedure (FRCP) 11   115

2. Unproductive Litigation—IDEA and Federal Rule of Civil Procedure (FRCP) 68   116

3. Specific Activities That are Nonreimbursable   117

4. Unreasonable Rates and Hours   117

F. **Summary   118**

PART THREE   The Rehabilitation Act of 1973 and the Americans with Disabilities Act of 1990

11 RA/ADA: Individual with a Disability   119

A. **Introduction   119**

1. The Rehabilitation Act of 1973   119

2. The Americans with Disabilities Act of 1990   119

3. A Common Language   120

B. **Statutory Language   120**

C. Impairments Covered   **121**

D. Substantially Limits   **121**
1. Measuring the Severity of the Disability   122
2. Scope of Impact: Toyota v. Williams   122
3. Impact of the Supreme Court's Rulings   123

E. Major Life Activities   **124**
1. Learning   124
2. Reading   124
3. Working   124
4. Concentrating and Thinking   125

F. Otherwise Qualified   **125**

G. State Law Definitions of Disability   **126**

H. Summary   **126**

12   RA/ADA: Coverage   127

A. In General   **127**

B. The RA   **127**

C. The RA Applies to the Federal Government   **128**
1. Coverage   128
2. Basic Policies   128

D. The RA Applies to Most Government Contractors   **129**

E. The RA Applies to Federal Grant and Aid Recipients   **129**
1. Statutory Language   129
2. Grants and Aid are Broadly Defined   129

F. Overview of the ADA   **129**

G. ADA, Title I (Employment)   **130**

H. ADA, Title II (State and Local Governments)   **131**

I. ADA, Title III (Public Accommodations)   **132**
1. General Rule   132
2. Private Schools   132
3. Hospitals   132
4. Public Sports Events and Entertainment   133

J. Summary   **133**

13 RA/ADA Enforcement   135

A. In General   135

B. Enforcement of the RA   135

C. Enforcement of the ADA   135
1. Title I   136
2. Title II   136
3. Title III   136

D. Attorney's Fees and Costs   137

E. Office for Civil Rights (OCR)   138
1. Organizational Structure   138
2. Complaint Resolution   139
3. Evaluation of the Complaint Resolution Process   140
4. Compliance Reviews, Monitoring, and Technical Assistance   140
5. OCR Case Resolutions   140

F. Department of Justice   141

G. Summary   142

14 Elementary and Secondary Education   143

A. In General   143

B. Discrimination   143
1. Basis for Public Education   143
2. FAPE under the RA   144
3. Comment on the RA Regulations   146
4. Private Schools   147
5. Testing   148

C. Otherwise Qualified   148
1. Public Schools   148
2. Private Schools   149

D. Summary   150

15 Postsecondary Education   151

A. In General   151

B. Duty of Non-Discrimination   151

1. The Long Arm of the RA in Education   151
2. General Duty Under the RA/ADA   152

C. **Otherwise Qualified   152**

D. **Reasonable Accommodations   154**
1. Testing and Fundamental Academic Requirements   154
2. Delivery of Classroom and Other Educational Materials   157
3. Selecting the Appropriate Accommodation   158
4. Accommodations Must Be Requested   159
5. Documentation Requirements   159
6. Specific Accommodations   160
7. Required Accommodations Are Free   161
8. Programs for Students Who are Not "Qualified"   161

E. **Summary   162**

16   Employment   163

A. **In General   163**

B. **Basic Requirement   163**

C. **The Major Life Activity of Working   164**

D. **Otherwise Qualified   164**
1. Basic Rule   164
2. Essential Job Requirements   164

E. **Testing   165**

F. **Reasonable Accommodations   165**

G. **Selecting the Accommodation   165**

H. **Limitations on the Duty to Accommodate   166**

I. **Individualized Inquiry   166**

J. **"By Reason of"   166**

K. **Constructive Discharge and Hostile Work Environments   166**

L. **Disclosure   167**

M. **Confidentiality   167**
1. Preemployment Inquiries   167
2. Medical Examinations   167
3. Performance-Based Medical Examinations   168
4. Job Accommodation Information   168

5. Drug Testing Information   168
6. Admissions   168

N. Summary   169

PART FOUR   Other Legal Issues

17 Other Legal Issues   171

A. No Child Left Behind   171
1. Overview   171
2. Stronger Accountability for Results   171
3. More Freedom for States and Communities   171
4. Proven Education Methods   172
5. Options for Parents   172
6. Report Cards   172
7. Just Education   172
8. Cases Filed   172

B. FERPA   174

C. Civil Liability of Educators   175
1. Overview   175
2. Tort   175
3. Common Law Torts   176
4. Constitutional Torts   179
5. Cases   180

D. High Stakes Testing   181

E. Summary   183

Index   185

INTRODUCTION

Federal education and employment laws relating to individuals with disabilities are the subject of considerable litigation in the courts. The goal of these laws generally is to prohibit discrimination against individuals with disabilities and to provide access to the public elementary and secondary education offered to all children and to reasonable accommodations in postsecondary education and employment. While the goal is simple, the laws designed to achieve that goal are quite complex. There are many misconceptions about these laws and disagreements as to their interpretation. Even the courts do not always agree.

The purpose of this book is to provide a clear explanation, both analytical and practical, of the primary laws that pertain to individuals with disabilities in education and employment. Statutes and court cases are examined in relation to the underlying reasons for the laws and the court decisions. It is the authors' hope that clearer understanding of the laws and the court decisions interpreting those laws will help to facilitate the proper application of these laws in the future.

We would like to thank our reviewers: Alice A. Dickinson, Johnson Bible College; Dr. Anne Gallegos, New Mexico State University; Veda Jairrels, Clark Atlanta University; Kristina Krampe, University of Kentucky; Darcy Miller, Washington State University; and Renee D. Nash, Governors State University.

1

The Judicial System

A. In General

It is important, at the outset, to cover some basics about the American legal system. The American judicial system includes two types of courts, state courts and federal courts. Each operates independently of the other in areas assigned it by the U.S. Constitution and the constitutions of the states. The U.S. Supreme Court has the final authority for interpreting the Constitution.

B. State Courts

Most states have three types of courts: trial courts, appellate courts, and a single state supreme court. State courts have all of the powers that are generally given to courts. These powers include those traditionally possessed by the courts of England before the American Revolution, as well as those expressly conferred by state constitutions and statutes. Because they are thought to have the broadest powers, state courts are called courts of general jurisdiction. Most disputes are determined by state courts.

State courts generally have the authority to award monetary damages, decide whether laws have been violated, and issue orders requiring that governmental officials and others refrain from taking illegal actions. These orders are called injunctions or restraining orders, and they are backed by the courts' contempt powers. Courts have other powers that we have not discussed; however, those powers are not pertinent to our topic.

Trial courts generally decide cases by receiving relevant evidence, determining what happened factually on the basis of that evidence, and applying rules of law to the pertinent facts. Generally speaking, the trial court is the only type of court that is authorized to receive evidence and make findings of fact. The power to receive evidence and make findings of fact is called original jurisdiction. Generally, each state has a number of trial courts, each of which serves its own district.

Cases may be tried before a judge, and in appropriate cases, a judge and jury. Generally, jury trials are allowed in criminal cases and in the types of civil case that were permitted under English law before 1776. Most actions of the types we consider are tried by a judge.

Appellate courts have the powers of appeal and review of lower court decisions. They make sure that decisions of trial courts are based on sufficient evidence and that the law is applied correctly. They do not receive evidence. Generally each state has several appellate courts, each of which supervises several trial courts.

State supreme courts supervise the state's judicial system. Generally they represent the final word on state law. However, the state courts sometimes decide federal law questions, for example, when a state court litigant alleges that his or her rights under federal statutory or constitutional law have been violated. In these cases, it is sometimes possible to appeal from a state supreme court to the U.S. Supreme Court.

C. Federal Courts

The federal system was created by Article III of the U.S. Constitution. Section 1 states that "The judicial power of the United States shall be vested in one Supreme Court, and in such inferior courts as the Congress may from time to time ordain and establish." Similar to the state court systems, there are three types of federal courts: trial courts, appellate courts, and the U.S. Supreme Court. The trial courts generally are organized into districts by state or part of a state. For example, there is a U.S. District Court for the Eastern District of Virginia. The appellate courts (with two exceptions) cover groups of states. The U.S. Supreme Court governs them all.

The federal trial, appellate, and supreme courts have the same general functions as their state counterparts. However, unlike state courts, the federal courts have only the powers and authority that are expressly conferred on them by statutes enacted by the Congress and those inherent powers that are necessary to carry out their expressly assigned duties. Because they are considered to have limited powers, the federal courts are called courts of limited jurisdiction.

Congress has expressly provided the federal courts with the authority to award damages, determine the lawfulness of certain acts, and issue injunctions. All these powers are used in civil rights cases, and they have been extended to cover the rights of individuals with disabilities.

The general organization of state and federal courts are illustrated in Figure 1.1.

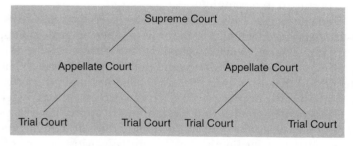

FIGURE 1.1   American Judicial System Paradigms (State and Federal)

D. Administrative Litigation

Tax claims, zoning exemptions, public assistance benefits, school admissions, school transfers, unemployment compensation, and countless other disputes are generated daily by the activities of government. These are technically civil disputes. In order to reduce the volume of regular court litigation and to ensure that governmental agencies are as free from judicial interference as possible, the states and the federal government have established a series of administrative procedures, and in a few cases special courts, for each agency or program to resolve claims, short of going to a regular court.

The administrative procedures usually consist of a hearing supervised by an administrative law judge with the authority to decide cases arising under a particular statute. An administrative hearing is like a trial before a judge, where evidence is introduced, witnesses may be presented, and cross-examination is allowed. The administrative law judge then issues an opinion based on the evidence presented. The decision is final, unless it is overturned on appeal.

Only a court has the authority to overturn an administrative determination, specifically, if the court determines that findings of fact are not adequately supported by the evidence or the ruling is incorrect as a matter of law. Where administrative procedures have been established, claimants may not sue in court until they have obtained an administrative ruling. This limitation on suing in court is known in legal parlance as exhaustion of administrative remedies.

E. Alternative Dispute Resolution (ADR)

In recent years, with an increased awareness of the cost of litigation, parties have turned to the use of alternative dispute resolution (ADR) techniques as a means of resolving disputes without resorting to traditional civil litigation. In ADR, the parties choose experienced professionals to help them resolve the dispute through the use of mediation or arbitration, an expedited and streamlined trial. ADR can be useful in settling disputes under the Individuals with Disabilities Education Act (IDEA) and the Americans with Disabilities Act (ADA). The IDEA specifically provides for mediation, and the ADA encourages the use of ADR techniques to the extent they are "appropriate" and "authorized by law." 42 U.S.C. §12212

The U.S. Supreme Court has ruled that arbitration of claims under the ADA is permissible, provided that the agreement to arbitrate uses language that shows a "clear and unmistakable" intention to do so. An arbitration agreement that is "very general" and provides only for arbitration of "matters under dispute," however, is not sufficiently clear. *Wright v. Universal Maritime Service Corp., 525 U.S. 70 (1998)*

F. Sources of Law

One hundred fifty years ago the distinctions between state and federal law were relatively clear. State law was administered by state courts, and federal law by federal courts. However, today those distinctions are not always as clear. Some state statutes supplement rights given by federal law, and some federal statutes require federal courts to apply state law in interpreting them. To complicate matters, many federal civil rights statutes permit suit in either state or federal court. This book concerns itself primarily with rights granted by federal statutes, which generally are enforced by suit in federal courts, after the exhaustion of all required administrative remedies.

A major source of law, in addition to statutes, is the vast number of regulations, which are issued by federal, state, and local governments. These regulations implement statutes in two basic ways. First, the regulations may provide definitions for statutory terms which are not clear in the statute itself. Second, the regulations may explain just how a particular program is to be administered. Federal regulations are set forth in the Code of Federal Regulations or CFR. They are cited by volume and section number, for example, 45 CFR § 84.1. The regulations are updated periodically, and amendments are printed in the *Federal Register,* a daily publication of the U.S. government.

While the techniques of legal research are a topic better addressed by law school courses and seminars, following are some suggestions for accessing legal information.

Most legal material may be found at no charge by using one of the following Internet search engines: Google, Alltheweb, Mamma, and Dogpile.

Constitutional provisions, statutes, and regulations may be found at the following legal-specific Web sites:

The Library of Congress:	http://www.loc.gov/
FEDLAW	http://www.thecre.com/fedlaw/default.htm
Findlaw	www.Findlaw.com
Government Printing Office	http://www.gpoaccess.gov/
GSU College of Law	http://www.gsulaw.gsu.edu/metaindex/
FirstGov: Government Search	http://www.firstgov.com

FIGURE 1.2   Web Sites Containing Legal Information

Federal Case Law

Federal court case law consists of district court opinions, appellate court opinions, and those of the Supreme Court.

District court opinions are not generally available on the Internet, but rather are available through services such as the Federal Reporter and commercial Internet search engines, such as Westlaw and Lexis.

Appellate court opinions since the mid-1990s are available at Web sites for each circuit court of appeals. Links to those sites are available through FEDLAW.

Supreme Court opinions are available through many sources, such as FEDLAW. They are also available through law school Web sites such as Cornell University. http://www.supct.law.cornell.edu/supct/index.htm.

Agency Interpretations are prepared by agencies that administer and enforce laws and that also are charged with interpreting those laws. These interpretations may be published in pamphlet form, advising the public of their rights under these statutes. Agencies may also issue interpretations through letters to government officials and members of the public known as "opinion letters," which may address specific legal issues. A third method is through "letters of finding," which deal with the facts of a particular case and advise the recipient as to whether the law has been violated. For example, a letter of finding might advise whether a school's procedures violate the IDEA, the ADA, or the Rehabilitation Act (RA). These materials may be obtained through the agency Web sites. The two federal agencies relevant to our discussion are the U.S. Department of Justice (www.usdoj.gov) and the U.S. Department of Education (www.ed.gov).

Private organizations, such as the Learning Disabilities Association of America and the Council for Exceptional Children, also may be helpful.

G. Summary

The U.S. judicial system consists of state courts of general jurisdiction and federal courts of limited jurisdiction. State and federal courts generally operate independently of each other within the spheres assigned them by the U.S. Constitution. The U.S. Supreme Court has the final authority for interpreting the Constitution. Many cases, however, must be tried before state or federal administrative agencies before they may be presented to a court.

2 The Constitution

A. Basic Principles

The U.S. government is a limited government, which only has those powers expressly granted it by the U.S. Constitution. The Tenth Amendment to the Constitution provides: "The powers not delegated to the United States by the Constitution, nor prohibited by it to the states, are reserved to the states respectively, or to the people."

The federal government may exercise its power through legislation authorized by and enacted according to specific provisions of the Constitution. Thus, the federal legal rights of individuals with disabilities are found in or derived from the Constitution and statutes enacted by Congress in accordance with constitutional provisions.

For our purposes, the three relevant constitutional provisions are the Commerce Clause, the Spending Clause, and the Fourteenth Amendment (Figures 2.1–2.3).

COMMERCE CLAUSE

Congress has the authority

"To regulate Commerce . . . among the several States. . . ."
(Constitution, Art I, §8; Cl. 4)

FIGURE 2.1   Commerce Clause

SPENDING CLAUSE

"The Congress shall have Power To lay and collect Taxes . . . to . . . provide for the . . . general Welfare of the United States. . . ."

(Constitution, Art I, §8; Cl. 1)

FIGURE 2.2   Spending Clause

Fourteenth Amendment

Section 1. "No state shall make or enforce any law which shall abridge the privileges or immunities of citizens of the United States; nor shall any state deprive any person of life, liberty, or property, without due process of law; nor deny to any person within its jurisdiction the equal protection of the laws. . . ."

***

Section 5. "The Congress shall have power to enforce, by appropriate legislation, the provisions of this article."

FIGURE 2.3   Fourteenth Amendment

In order to be valid, disability legislation must be authorized by one or more of the constitutional provisions. In turn, regulations must conform to the statutes under which they are issued. Statutes exceeding constitutional authority and regulations exceeding statutory authority would be invalid.

B.   Statutory Measures

To protect individuals with disabilities, Congress has enacted three key federal statutes: the Rehabilitation Act of 1973 (RA), 29 U.S.C. §701 *et seq.;* the Education for All Handicapped Children Act, now called the Individuals with Disabilities Education Act (IDEA), 20 U.S.C. §1400 *et seq.;* and, the Americans with Disabilities Act of 1990 (ADA), 42 U.S.C. §12101 *et seq.*

The ADA and RA are statutes that prohibit discrimination but do not provide specific funds for the activities mandated by them. The IDEA provides funding for a civil rights–related objective, the provision of a free appropriate public education to students with disabilities who, in order to benefit from their educational experiences, require special education and related services.

The following section provides an overview of these laws, each of which is discussed in greater depth in subsequent chapters.

1.   The Rehabilitation Act of 1973

The Rehabilitation Act of 1973 (RA), 29 U.S.C. §701 *et seq.,* made discrimination against individuals with disabilities unlawful in three areas: employment by the executive branch of the federal government, employment by most federal government contractors, and activities that are funded by federal subsidies or grants. This last category includes all public elementary and secondary schools and most postsecondary institutions. The statutory section that prohibits discrimination in grants was numbered § 504 in the original legislation, and the RA is often referred to simply as "Section 504." Under Section 504, individuals with impairments that substantially limit a major life activity, such as learning, are entitled to academic adjustments and auxiliary aids and services, so that courses, examinations, and services will be accessible to them.

The RA is authorized by the "Spending Clause" of the U.S. Constitution that provides that "the Congress shall have Power To lay and collect Taxes . . . to . . . provide for the . . . general Welfare of the United States." Constitution, Art I, §8; Cl. 1.

Under this authority the federal government provides funding for services, such as education, through grants to states that operate much like contracts. Any contract, by definition, requires the agreement of the parties. Therefore, the question is: To what have the states agreed when they receive grants authorized under the Spending Clause? The Supreme Court has held that the states have *not* agreed to accept liability for punitive damages for violations of the RA. *Barnes v. Gorman, 536 U.S. 181 (2002)* In addition, the Supreme Court has suggested that states have not necessarily agreed to liability for violation of the myriad regulations issued pursuant to the RA in suits brought by private parties. See *Alexander v. Sandoval*, 532 U.S. 275 (2001)

2. The Individuals with Disabilities Education Act

In 1975, Congress enacted a statute titled the Education for All Handicapped Children Act. That statute, now called the Individuals with Disabilities Education Act (IDEA), 20 U.S.C.A. §1400 *et seq.*, which most recently was reauthorized in December 2004, provides funds to states for the education of children with disabilities, ages three through twenty-one. Funds used to provide a free appropriate public education (FAPE) to students with disabilities enable school districts to comply with the IDEA. Under the IDEA, the school district is responsible for identifying and evaluating students with disabilities who, due to their disabilities, need special education and related services and, subsequently, for providing these services under an Individualized Education Program (IEP). Services must be provided in the least restrictive environment (LRE), appropriate to the needs of the child. In other words, to the extent appropriate to their needs, the children should receive specialized services in integrated settings with other children with and without disabilities. This is sometimes referred to as inclusion. A child who is not eligible for services under the IDEA still may be eligible for services under Section 504 of the RA. The needs of some children who are not eligible under either IDEA or Section 504 may be addressed under the No Child Left Behind Act of 2001 (NCLB), discussed in Chapter 17.

There are differing views as to the constitutional authority for the IDEA. Congress viewed the IDEA as a statute implementing the Fourteenth Amendment.

> Parents of handicapped children all too frequently are not able to advocate the rights of their children because they have been erroneously led to believe that their children will not be able to lead meaningful lives. However, over the past few years, parents of handicapped children have begun to recognize that their children are being denied services which are guaranteed under the Constitution. It should not, however, be necessary for parents throughout the country to continue utilizing the courts to assure themselves a remedy. It is this Committee's belief that the Congress must take a more active role under its responsibility for equal protection of the laws to guarantee that handicapped children are provided equal educational opportunity.

(Senate Report [Labor and Public Welfare Committee] No. 94-168 June 2 , 1975 U.S. Code Cong. & Ad. News at 1433)

As recently as 2004, Senator Edward Kennedy, one of the cosponsors of the IDEA reauthorization, said:

> This has been a long and arduous march for our country as we fought to recognize the civil rights of children with disabilities. When Congress first passed IDEA, disabled children were shuttered away. They had no place in our society. We have all heard the horror stories. There is no need to revisit those dark days, but we should never, ever forget from where we have come. (Congressional Record: November 19, 2004 [Senate], Page S11543–S11553

And in the course of considering the bill that became the IDEA Amendments of 1997, Congressman George Miller observed

> We should never forget why we went through this process. Before the IDEA law was on the books over 20 years ago, more than a million children with disabilities were not being educated. Schools refused to take them, and States did not force them to. . . . IDEA is a civil rights law. For a parent with a disabled child, there is nothing more important than knowing your child will get as good an education as any other child. (Congressional Record, May 19, 1997, Page E952)

If the IDEA were, in fact, a statute to implement the Fourteenth Amendment, it would do so in a remarkable way. It is the only federal law under which funds are provided to enable recipients to comply with the Fourteenth Amendment! In contrast, funds were not supplied to assist in the racial desegregation of public schools. Rather, the United States, through law enforcement and civil litigation, simply required that segregation cease. The same approach held true for gender discrimination. So why are schools being paid to obey a basic constitutional provision?

While the IDEA has been perceived by some as a civil rights statute equalizing access to education for students with disabilities, the IDEA is not primarily a civil rights statute. The IDEA does not implement the Fourteenth Amendment, but rather goes far beyond it. Much of the special education and related services provided for under IDEA is not otherwise required by the Fourteenth Amendment or any other constitutional provision.

The Supreme Court has explained that the constitutional basis of the IDEA is the Spending Clause. In *Cedar Rapids Community School District v. Garret F., 526 U.S. 66 (1999)*, the Supreme Court held that a school district was financially obligated under the IDEA to provide the services of a personal attendant to Garret F., a student whose spinal column was severed in a motorcycle accident when he was four years old and who was, therefore, "ventilator dependent," a condition requiring a "responsible individual nearby to attend to certain physical needs while he is in school." The court held that the school district was obligated to provide the service, rejecting the argument that the cost was prohibitive and therefore an undue burden. In so ruling, the Court said, "This case is about whether meaningful access to the public schools will be assured, not the level of education that a school must finance once access is attained." A vigorous dissent was filed, arguing that the interpretation of the IDEA was incorrect. However, both majority and dissent agreed that the IDEA is "legislation enacted pursuant to Congress' spending power."

Earlier in *Board of Education v. Rowley, 458 U.S. 176 (1982)*, the Supreme Court found that, under the Spending Clause of the Constitution, the IDEA may easily require states to provide special education and related services far in excess of what is required by the U.S. Constitution. In *Pace v. Bogalusa City Sch. Bd. (5th Cir. 2002)*, the Fifth Circuit made clear that the IDEA is not a civil rights statute. Congress could not enact the IDEA as a civil rights statute because "Congress did not find that any disparate treatment of students with disabilities resulted from unconstitutional state action." Moreover, even if Congress had identified constitutional transgressions by the states that it sought to remedy through the IDEA, the IDEA requirements . . . exceed constitutional boundaries" (citations and footnotes omitted).

3. The Americans with Disabilities Act of 1990

In 1990, Congress enacted the Americans with Disabilities Act (ADA); 42 U.S.C. §12101 *et seq.* This act extended the concepts of "Section 504" to (1) employers with fifteen or more employees (Title I); (2) all activities of state and local governments, including but not limited to employment and education (Title II); and (3) virtually all places that offer goods and services to the public, known as "places of public accommodation" (Title III). In addition, ADA standards apply to employment by Congress.

Two constitutional provisions authorize the ADA. First, Titles I and III are authorized by the Commerce Clause, which provides that Congress has the authority "To regulate Commerce . . . among the several States." (Constitution, Art I, §8; Cl. 4) Title II is authorized by the Fourteenth Amendment which provides in pertinent part that:

> Section 1. No state shall make or enforce any law which shall abridge the privileges or immunities of citizens of the United States; nor shall any state deprive any person of life, liberty, or property, without due process of law; nor deny to any person within its jurisdiction the equal protection of the laws. . . .
>
> ***
>
> Section 5. The Congress shall have power to enforce, by appropriate legislation, the provisions of this article.

The Fourteenth Amendment applies to states and not to the federal government, whereas the Fifth Amendment applies to the federal government and contains the prohibition against deprivation "of life, liberty, or property, without due process of law." While the Fifth Amendment does not contain the equal protection guarantees, in practice, the Fifth Amendment has been interpreted to include it. The Fourteenth Amendment also provides for the enactment of implementing legislation.

4.   The Reconstruction Civil Rights Acts

The Reconstruction Civil Rights Acts have applicability in the disability law area. This Reconstruction era legislation was originally intended to impose personal liability on those who, acting under color of law, sought to deprive African Americans of statutory or constitutional rights. Section 1983, 42 U.S.C. §1983 provides:

> Every person who, under color of any statute, ordinance, regulation, custom, or usage, of any State or Territory or the District of Columbia, subjects, or causes to be subjected, any citizen of the United States or other person within the jurisdiction thereof to the deprivation of any rights, privileges, or immunities secured by the Constitution and laws, shall be liable to the party injured in an action.

Though originally drafted to protect African Americans, the language of the statute is broader. It is frequently used by litigants to seek to hold school officials personally liable for acts that allegedly have harmed their children with disabilities. The statute applies only to violations of statutory or constitutional rights so clear that the official knew or should have known that his or her conduct was unlawful. *Bradley v. Simon (8th Cir. 2002)* Officials are immune from suit for lesser violations. In legal language, the officials have *qualified immunity.* One court put the matter this way:

> The doctrine of qualified immunity shields government officials acting within their discretionary authority from liability when their conduct does not violate clearly established statutory or constitutional law of which a reasonable person would have known. (*Wallace v. County of Comal, State of Texas et al.,* Docket No. 04-50280 [5th Cir., 2005])

In a 2004 case the U.S. Supreme Court addressed the matter of the types of cases in which Section 1983 is available to litigants. Basically the court found that Section 1983 may be used to obtain relief when there are violations of constitutional rights and, in some instances, violations of federal law. However, Section 1983 does not provide relief every time a state official violates a federal law. The availability of such relief depends on the intent of Congress in the context of the particular federal statute. *City of Rancho Palos Verdes v. Abrams,* 544 U.S. 113 (2005)

C.   Due Process

The Fifth Amendment (which applies to the federal government) and the Fourteenth Amendment (which applies to the states) contain prohibitions against the deprivation "of life, liberty, or property, without due process of law." There are two types of due process: substantive due process and procedural due process.

1.   Substantive Due Process

A statute violates substantive due process when it seeks to deny individuals one or more of their fundamental rights. In general, fundamental rights have included the right to privacy, the right to associate, and the right to choose between private education and public education. All these rights are considered fundamental because they are thought to be similar to rights that are expressly provided for in the Constitution. For example, it would be a violation of substantive due process for a state to refuse to educate all children who are members of a particular religious group.

2. Procedural Due Process

Procedural due process is basically the requirement that the government may not take life, liberty, or property without using fair procedures that are applicable to all. For example, a hearing that did not allow for an adequate presentation of evidence by all parties would violate procedural due process.

3. Due Process Protection

Due process rights are rights that protect the individual from improper government action. In general they include most of the rights set forth in the Bill of Rights, the first ten amendments to the Constitution. One of the most basic is the right to have access to the courts. Legislation that is intended to facilitate court access for individuals with disabilities will generally be held to be constitutional. For example, in *Tennessee v. Lane, 541 U.S. 509 (2004)*, the U.S. Supreme Court considered Title II of the ADA in a case involving the issue of physical access by persons with paraplegia to the courts. The court ruled in a 5–4 decision that private parties could sue states for monetary damages under Title II of the ADA where fundamental due process rights, such as access to the courts, are at issue. Applied in this manner, the ADA "is congruent and proportional" to the congressional "object of enforcing the right of access to the courts." In contrast, a free appropriate public education is not considered a fundamental constitutional right.

In *Bradley ex rel. Bradley v. Arkansas Dep't of Educ.* (8th Cir. 1999), the court held that the IDEA is not an "appropriate exercise" of Congress's authority to protect the civil rights of people with disabilities, because the Constitution does not *require* that children with disabilities receive a "free appropriate education." The court held that the IDEA, though not required by the Constitution, is a valid law under the Spending Clause because, under the IDEA, the states accepted a clearly defined set of obligations beyond those required by the Constitution in exchange for federal funding.

D. Equal Protection: Rational Basis Review Required

1. Basic Principles

There is no fundamental constitutional right to either education or employment, though both are of immense practical importance. The Constitution becomes involved where education or employment is denied because of intentional and unjustified discrimination. The limits of the Constitution are important. Where statutes exceed constitutional requirements and the states have not agreed to be sued under those statutes, the states may be immune from suit by reason of sovereign immunity.

2. Sovereign Immunity

Except as limited by the U.S. Constitution, each state of the United States has the legal rights and powers of an independent government, including the right to immunity from suit. The Eleventh Amendment to the Constitution essentially provides for state sovereign immunity. As interpreted by the U.S. Supreme Court, the Eleventh Amendment provides that the "judicial power of the United States shall not be construed to extend to any suit in law or equity, commenced or prosecuted against one of the United States by citizens of another state," or by citizens of the state in question. See *Kimel v. Florida Bd. of Regents,* 528 U.S. 62 (2000); *College Sav. Bank v. Florida Prepaid Postsecondary Educ. Expense Bd.,* 527 U.S. 666 (1999); *Seminole Tribe v. Florida,* 517 U.S. 44 (1996). State sovereign immunity means that private parties cannot sue state governments unless a specific provision of the Constitution permits it or the state has agreed that it can be sued. *Lapides v. Bd. of Regents, 535 U.S. 613 (2002)*

What is the effect of state sovereign immunity on the RA and ADA? States may be sued by individuals for intentional discrimination that violates the Fourteenth Amendment. To the extent that the RA and Title II of the ADA prohibit states from action that does not constitute intentional discrimination against an individual with a disability, many courts have held that state sovereign immunity would protect the states from suits by private parties. Intentional discrimination in violation of the Fourteenth Amendment essentially would be discrimination without any rational basis.

3. Rational Basis

The Fourteenth Amendment provides that no state shall "deny to any person within its jurisdiction the equal protection of the laws" and is the major source of rights for people with disabilities. The Fourteenth Amendment, in addition to protecting specific categories of people, actually protects all people. For example, a state that refused to educate individuals with parapalegia (a disability), while providing education to all other people, would violate the Fourteenth Amendment. A state that refused education to left-handed people (not a disability) would also violate the Fourteenth Amendment, even though left-handed people are not disabled and are not protected by disability or other statutes.

Federal courts review state laws to determine whether these laws infringe the Fourteenth Amendment. In doing so the courts review closely the reasons for apparently discriminatory statutes. How closely depends on the classification of the persons that are the target of the alleged discrimination.

There are three standards of judicial review: strict scrutiny, intermediate scrutiny, and rational basis review. Justice Scalia of the U.S. Supreme Court described "strict scrutiny" in his concurring opinion in *Adarand Constructors v. Pena,* 515 U.S. 200 (1995): "It is unlikely, if not impossible, that the challenged program would survive under this understanding of strict scrutiny."

Strict scrutiny is used whenever a statute uses classifications based on race or gender. The reason why statutes that treat one race differently from another are strictly scrutinized is that there simply can be no rationale for such different treatment. See *South Carolina v. Katzenbach*, 383 U.S. 301 (1966) (race) together with *United States v. Virginia*, 518 U.S. 515 (1996), and *Nevada Department of Human Resources v. Hibbs*, 538 U.S. 721 (2003) (gender). Intermediate and rational basis reviews are progressively less searching and less intense. More statutes and programs will survive these reviews than is the case with strict scrutiny.

Rational basis review is the standard of review that applies in the disability area. Statutes that require that people with disabilities be treated differently from other people are valid under the Fourteenth Amendment if they have a rational basis. *City of Cleburne, Texas v. Cleburne Living Center, Inc.* 473 U.S. 432 (1985), and *Kimel v. Florida Board of Regents*, 528 U.S. 62 (2000). In *Board of Trustees of the University of Alabama v. Garrett*, 531 U.S. 356 (2001), the Supreme Court held that Title I of the ADA governing employment could not constitutionally be applied to permit employees to sue for damages against states that allegedly failed to accommodate disabled employees. Accommodation was not required because there can be rational reasons for declining to provide it. Any attempt to require of the states more than the Constitution provides is unconstitutional. The court said

> States are not required by the Fourteenth Amendment to make special accommodations for the disabled, so long as their actions towards such individuals are rational. They could quite hard headedly—and perhaps hardheartedly—hold to job-qualification requirements which do not make allowance for the disabled. If special accommodations for the disabled are to be required, they [cannot come from] the Equal Protection Clause [of the Fourteenth Amendment]. (Footnote omitted.)

However, in contrast to the *Garrett* equal protection holding on Title I of the ADA, the Supreme Court has held that, where a fundamental due process right, such as access to the courts, is involved, private parties may sue the state under Title II of the ADA. *Tennessee v. Lane*, 541 U.S. 509 (2004) The court's constitutional theory is essentially that Congress, in enacting the ADA, can abrogate state sovereign immunity under the Eleventh Amendment and can provide for private suits against states for monetary damages if fundamental due process rights are being addressed. See also *United States v. Georgia*, 546 U.S.—(2006) ["Insofar as Title II creates a private cause of action for damages against States for conduct that *actually* violates the Fourteenth Amendment, Title II validly abrogates state sovereign immunity"].

In summary, under *Garrett* there is no private right of action against states for monetary damages under Title I, which covers employment. However, under *Lane* and *Georgia*, there is a private right of action against states under Title II, if the conduct that violates Title II of the ADA also violates the Fourteenth Amendment.

E. Equal Protection: Intentional Discrimination Barred

1. Overview

Two factors must be established in order to show intentional discrimination on the basis of disability in violation of the Fourteenth Amendment: that the individual with a disability has a fundamental right, and that the discriminatory act is knowing and deliberate. The same approach may be used in interpreting or determining the constitutionality of statutes that impose obligations on the states. Therefore, as applied in certain situations, the RA and Title II of the ADA may be found either to be unconstitutional, if interpreted to exceed the requirements of the Fourteenth Amendment, or interpreted to bar only the intentional discrimination that is also prohibited by the Fourteenth Amendment.

2.   The RA and ADA Must Be Interpreted Similarly

Title II of the ADA and the Rehabilitation Act (29 U.S.C. §794 or §504) contain virtually identical language and are interpreted in the same way. *Bragdon v. Abbott,* 524 U.S. 624 (1998)
  Title II provides in pertinent part:

> 42 U.S.C. §12132. Discrimination
>   Subject to the provisions of this title, no qualified individual with a disability shall, by reason of such disability, be excluded from participation in or be denied the benefits of the services, programs, or activities of a public entity, or be subjected to discrimination by any such entity.

The term "public entity" means "any State or local government" as well as "any department, agency, special purpose district, or other instrumentality of a State or States or local government." 42 U.S.C. §§ 12131(1)(A)-(B)
  The RA provides

> No otherwise qualified individual with a disability . . . shall, solely by reason of her or his disability, be excluded from the participation in, be denied the benefits of, or be subjected to discrimination under any program or activity receiving Federal financial assistance or under any program or activity conducted by any Executive agency or by the United States Postal Service. (29 U.S.C. §794[a])

Note that the RA's language is similar to statutory language that prohibits race and gender discrimination in grants. For example, Title IX (20 U.S.C. §1681[a]) provides that "no person in the United States shall, on the basis of sex, be excluded from participation in, be denied the benefits of, or be subjected to discrimination under any education program or activity receiving Federal financial assistance."

3.   Fundamental Right

The individual with a disability must have a fundamental right in order to establish a violation of the Fourteenth Amendment.

The Right of Freedom

The case of *Olmstead v. L. C. by Zimring,* 527 U.S. 581 (1999) involved essentially the fundamental right of freedom. The Supreme Court held that the ADA's "proscription of discrimination may require placement of persons with mental disabilities in community settings rather than in institutions." The persons in question were two women ("L.C." and "E.W."), both of whom were mentally retarded. In addition, L.C. suffered from schizophrenia and E.W. from a personality disorder. The court summarily noted, "There is no dispute that L.C. and E.W. are disabled within the meaning of the ADA."

Community placement, the court found, is "in order when the State's treatment professionals have determined that community placement is appropriate, the transfer from institutional care to a less restrictive setting is not opposed by the affected individual, and the placement can be reasonably accommodated, taking into account the resources available to the State and the needs of others with mental disabilities." The court considered the applicability of these rules: "Unjustified isolation, we hold, is properly regarded as discrimination based on disability."

L.C. and E.W. were entitled to liberty, the maximum reasonable freedom, under the Fourteenth Amendment. Anything less was illegal segregation.

Freedom of speech is also a fundamental right that could be the basis of a suit against a state. In *Roberts v. Pennsylvania Department of Public Welfare* (E.D. Pa. 2001), the Pennsylvania Department of Public Welfare allegedly retaliated against Roberts, one of its employees, for filing a disability claim, by "arbitrarily terminating his disability benefits, denying him limited duty, and excluding him from the premises." Roberts sued. The court declined to dismiss Robert's suit, holding that Roberts had alleged facts, which if true, showed that the department had violated the Fourteenth Amendment, whose requirement of due process incorporates the free speech standards of the First Amendment. Sovereign immunity did not and could not bar a suit based on a state action that allegedly violates both the Fourteenth Amendment and (in this case) Title V of the ADA.

The Right to Be Free From Cruel and Unusual Punishment

In *United States v. Georgia*, 546 U.S. _____ (2006) the U.S. Supreme Court held that "insofar as Title II creates a private cause of action for damages against States for conduct that *actually* violates the Fourteenth Amendment, Title II validly abrogates state sovereign immunity." Conduct that potentially constituted cruel and unusual punishment and therefore a violation of the Fourteenth Amendment included refusing to provide medical treatment to a paraplegic while confining him "for 23-to-24 hours per day in a 12-by-3-foot cell in which he could not turn his wheelchair around"; "refusing to provide accessible facilities," which "rendered him unable to use the toilet and shower without assistance," and in turn caused him to injure "himself in attempting to transfer from his wheelchair to the shower or toilet on his own"; and, on several other occasions, forcing him "to sit in his own feces and urine."

The Right to Meaningful Access to Public Education

In the context of elementary and secondary public education, the fundamental right is often meaningful access to education. In *Padilla v. School District No. 1* (10th Cir. 2000), the court held that the parents had alleged facts which, if true, would constitute a valid claim of intentional discrimination. The parents alleged that the school district repeatedly "placed her in a windowless closet, restrained in a stroller without supervision," contrary to her IEP. During one of these incidents, "she tipped over and hit her head on the floor, suffering serious physical injuries, including a skull fracture and exacerbation of a seizure disorder, which kept her from attending school for the remainder of the term." Surely being locked in a closet and physically abused would be considered deprivation of access to education.

In *Davis v. Monroe County Board of Education*, 526 U.S. 629 (1999), the U.S. Supreme Court considered what types of deprivation of access might be actionable. The court noted that the "most obvious example" of deprivation "would thus involve the overt, physical deprivation of access to school resources." Conduct that prevented "students from using a particular school resource—an athletic field or a computer lab, for instance," would give rise to liability. It "is not necessary, however, to show physical exclusion to demonstrate that students have been deprived . . . of an educational opportunity." Conduct "that is so severe, pervasive, and objectively offensive, and that so undermines and detracts from the victims' educational experience, that the victim-students are effectively denied equal access to an institution's resources and opportunities" is actionable. Note that, while the case cited was on allegations of sexual harassment, the same principles apply in the area of disabilities. See *Gebser v. Lago Vista Independent School District*, 524 U.S. 274 (1998), and *Rees v. Jefferson School District* (9th Cir. 2000).

A key factor in determining whether a right is fundamental is the extent to which an individual's participation in the program or activity in question is voluntary. The court in *Davis v. Monroe County* noted that the severity of misconduct is to be judged in light of the school district's degree of control over the environment in which the misconduct occurs. In other words, the children were required to attend school and to be supervised by teachers.

The *Davis* court made it clear that not every wrong constitutes a deprivation of educational access: "It is thus understandable that, in the school setting, students often engage in insults, banter, teasing, shoving, pushing, and . . . conduct that is upsetting to the students subjected to it. Damages are not available for simple acts of teasing and name-calling among school children."

A postsecondary school's refusal to provide accommodations to an individual with a disability does not usually amount to a deprivation of access to education. Entry into postsecondary education, unlike participation in public elementary and secondary education, is voluntary and requires that the student be otherwise qualified for that education.

In *Garcia v. State University of N.Y. Health Sciences Center* (2d Cir. 2001), the court held that a medical student dismissed from a state university could not maintain a suit for monetary damages against the university under either the ADA or Section 504 of the RA, unless the university violated the Fourteenth Amendment by committing intentional discrimination (not simply failure to accommodate a disability), and, as to Section 504, unless the state knowingly waived its sovereign immunity from suit when it accepted federal funds. In *Garcia*, the court found that the state had not waived its sovereign immunity. See also *Shepard v. Irving*, 77 Fed. Appx. 615 (4th Cir. 2003).

4.   Denial of the Right Must be Deliberate and Knowing

In order to show intentional discrimination, generally the denial of a disabled person's right must be based on actual knowledge of the circumstances or at least "deliberate indifference." *Rees v. Jefferson School District* (9th Cir. 2000)

F. What Is the Status of Regulations Issued under the RA/ADA?

1. Overview

There are extensive regulations under the RA and ADA governing the activities of federal funding recipients with respect to individuals with disabilities. For example, 34 C.F.R. §§ 104.33(a)-(b), entitled "Free appropriate public education," provides in part:

> (a) General. A recipient that operates a public elementary or secondary education program or activity shall provide a free appropriate public education to each qualified handicapped person who is in the recipient's jurisdiction, regardless of the nature or severity of the person's handicap.
> (b) Appropriate education. (1) For the purpose of this subpart, the provision of an appropriate education is the provision of regular or special education and related aids and services that (i) are designed to meet individual educational needs of handicapped persons as adequately as the needs of nonhandicapped persons are met and (ii) are based upon adherence to procedures that satisfy the requirements of §§ 104.34, 104.35, and 104.36.
> (2) Implementation of an Individualized Education Program developed in accordance with the Education of the Handicapped Act is one means of meeting the standard established in paragraph (b)(1)(i) of this section.

The regulation, in effect, incorporates the IDEA requirement of a free appropriate public education for children with disabilities into the RA/ADA requirements. Supreme Court decisions have raised questions concerning these regulations, and what remedies are available to enforce them.

2. Regulations: Alexander v. Sandoval

In 2001, the U.S. Supreme Court decided the case of *Alexander v. Sandoval*, 532 U.S. 275 (2001). Sandoval brought a class action against Alexander, director of the Alabama Department of Public Safety, to enjoin the department's decision to administer state driver's license examinations only in English. Sandoval argued that the decision violated a Department of Justice disparate impact regulation because it had the effect of discriminating against non-English speakers based on their national origin.

The court held that private individuals may not sue federal aid recipients to enforce certain regulations promulgated under Title VI of the Civil Rights Act of 1964, even though they may sue for discrimination based on grounds of race, color, or national origin. Only the federal government may sue to enforce the regulations. The case is important because the principles announced in the court's decision may be applicable to regulations issued under Section 504.

In a related case, the Supreme Court has ruled that individuals may not sue to enforce the confidentiality provisions of the Family Educational Rights and Privacy Act of 1974 (20 U.S.C. §1232g; FERPA). *Gonzaga University v. Doe*, 536 U.S. 273 (2002); see also *Jackson v. Birmingham Board of Education*, 544 U.S. 167 (2005).

The Supreme Court's decisions have significant implications for students who receive services under "504 plans," instead of under IEPs. The 504 plans are authorized by regulations that implement the RA. The *Sandoval* and *Gonzaga University* cases suggest that there is an issue as to whether parents may sue a state school system or district for failure to issue or to comply with a 504 plan. However, there has been no definitive court ruling specifically invalidating the RA regulations. Accordingly school systems continue to comply with and parents continue to rely upon the RA regulations.

As they apply to education, the RA/ADA are administered by the Department of Education. In other circumstances, the ADA is administered by the Department of Justice. Both agencies have administrative procedures for reviewing allegations of violations of these laws. Information on enforcing these laws can be accessed at the Department of Education (<www.ed.gov>) and the Department of Justice (<www.usdoj.gov>) Web sites. In general, these departments do not conduct proceedings identical to court trials. Rather, they rely on evidence submitted by the parties and form an opinion through administrative proceedings as to whether a violation occurred.

3.   Title II Regulations

Recent case developments raise the question of whether and how the *Sandoval* reasoning applies to regulations issued under Title II of the ADA. See *Ability Center of Greater Toledo v. City of Sandusky (6th Cir. 2004).*

G.   Summary

The government of the United States is a limited one and has only that authority that is conveyed to it by specific provisions of the U.S. Constitution. The statutes with which we are concerned are authorized by the Commerce Clause, the Spending Clause, and the Fourteenth Amendment.

Figure 2.4 illustrates the statutes and the constitutional authority for them.

IDEA	Spending Clause
RA	Spending Clause
ADA Titles I & III	Commerce Clause
ADA Title II	Fourteenth Amendment
NCLB	Spending Clause
FERPA	Spending Clause
42 U.S.C. §1983	Fourteenth Amendment

FIGURE 2.4   Table of Constitutional Authority

The IDEA and RA are spending clause statutes. However, they contain provisions that are based on civil rights concepts and have accomplished civil rights objectives, such as providing meaningful access to public school education to many children with disabilities.

The states agree to comply with the IDEA provisions when they accept IDEA funds. If a state adopts a policy that is contrary to IDEA, funds could be withheld unless and until the state policy is amended to comply with the IDEA.

Under the RA, it is generally accepted that the states have not agreed to liability that exceeds the requirements of the Fourteenth Amendment, absent a finding that the states affirmatively have agreed to accept such liability. In practice, this means that recipients of federal funding under Spending Clause legislation and grants, such as the RA, clearly may be held liable for intentional discrimination against people with disabilities. In addition, if the states consent to accept greater liability, they may be held liable for actions prohibited by the RA but not prohibited by the Fourteenth Amendment. The Fourteenth Amendment covers due process rights and equal protection of the law. Federal statutes that implement due process rights are highly likely to be valid. Those that implement the requirements for equal protection of the laws are valid if the conduct they address has no rational basis and amounts to intentional discrimination. Some regulations issued under the RA and ADA may not be enforceable against states by private right of action in court.

Many cases hold that Title II of the ADA, which applies to states, is authorized by the Fourteenth Amendment to the Constitution and can have no greater scope than that amendment.

Where a state's conduct toward an individual with a disability is an intentional violation of one of these provisions, both the Fourteenth Amendment and Title II of the ADA have been violated. When Title II prohibits conduct that does not violate the Fourteenth Amendment, then Title II goes beyond the Fourteenth Amendment and issues are raised as to constitutionality.

3 Statutory Overview

A. Introduction

In order to promote access to employment, education and public accommodations for citizens with disabilities in both the private and public sectors, the Congress enacted three key federal statutes. This chapter provides an overview of these laws, and each statute is discussed in greater depth in subsequent chapters.

B. IDEA: Meeting the Need for Special Education

In 1975 Congress enacted a statute titled the Education for All Handicapped Children Act. That statute, now known as the Individuals with Disabilities Education Act (IDEA), 20 U.S.C. §1400 *et seq.*, operates as a federal grant program to state educational agencies (SEA), and through the SEA to the local educational agencies (LEA), providing funds for a free appropriate public education (FAPE) for eligible children with disabilities. States and LEAs must locate, identify, and evaluate all children suspected of having a disability who, because of the disability, require special education and related services. An Individualized Education Program (IEP) is developed for each eligible child, with services that address the individual child's educational and functional needs. The IEP team consists of school professionals and the child's parents. Services must be provided in the least restrictive environment (LRE), appropriate to the unique needs of the child. In other words, to the extent appropriate, a child is expected to receive services in the general education classroom and to be integrated with other children with and without disabilities. This is sometimes referred to as inclusion. A child who does not meet the eligibility requirements of the IDEA may still be eligible for services under Section 504 of the RA.

The IDEA first impacted the education of children with mental retardation and mental illness. The Department of Education has noted that, in 1967, "state institutions were homes for almost 200,000 persons with significant disabilities. Many of these restrictive settings provided only minimal food, clothing and shelter." Few children were assessed, educated, and rehabilitated. Many children's disabilities were mislabeled, and education, if any was provided, was ineffective. Some were improperly incarcerated. Few parents were able to be involved in the planning or placement decisions for their children.

In the 1950s and 1960s, disability associations such as the Association for Retarded Children (ARC) joined with the federal government to develop practices for children with disabilities and their families. These practices in turn formed the templates for programs designed for the early identification and appropriate education of children with disabilities.

Their efforts bore fruit. Improved programs were created by the federal government under the authority of the Spending Clause. These included such landmark legislation as the Training of Professional Personnel Act of 1959 (P.L. 86-158), which helped train leaders to educate children with mental retardation; the Captioned Films Act of 1958 (P.L. 85-905), which sought to make films accessible; and the Teachers of the Deaf Act of 1961 (P.L. 87-276), which provided teacher training for those individuals who worked with the hearing impaired.

Congress branched out to address other disabilities. The Elementary and Secondary Education Act (P.L. 89-10) and the State Schools Act (P.L. 89-313) provided further grant assistance. Finally, the Handicapped Children's Early Education Assistance Act of 1968 (P.L. 90-538) and the Economic Opportunities Amendments of 1972 (P.L. 92-424) authorized support for early childhood programs.

By 1968, the federal government had supported training for more than 30,000 special education teachers and related specialists, provided captioned films for viewing by approximately 3 million persons who were deaf, and established programs for children with disabilities in preschool, elementary, secondary, and state schools throughout the country.

The Department of Education has summarized the legal developments of the early 1970s thus:

> Landmark court decisions further advanced increased educational opportunities for children with disabilities. For example, the *Pennsylvania Association of Retarded Citizens v. Commonwealth* (1971) and *Mills v. Board of Education of the District of Columbia* (1972) established the responsibility of states and localities to educate children with disabilities. Thus the right of every child with a disability to be educated is grounded in the equal protection clause of the 14th Amendment to the United States Constitution.

Like Senator Kennedy and Congressman Miller (see Chapter 2), the Department of Education views the IDEA as a civil rights statute. Indeed, to the extent that the IDEA freed children with mental retardation and mental illness from unnecessary incarceration, it achieved much the same result that could have been achieved under the Fourteenth Amendment, even without the IDEA and its predecessors. See *Olmstead v. L.C., 527 U.S. 581 (1999)* and Chapter 2.

In 1975, the Congress enacted a statute entitled the Education for All Handicapped Children Act. Known for years as Public Law 94-142, now the IDEA, the law included four specific purposes as shown in Figure 3.1.

According to the Department of Education, the IDEA "guaranteed a free, appropriate public education to each child with a disability in every state and locality across the country" (*History: Twenty-Five Years of Progress in Educating Children with*

THE FOUR PURPOSES OF IDEA

"To assure that all children with disabilities have available to them
. . . a free appropriate public education which emphasized special
education and related services designed to meet their unique needs"

"To assure that the rights of children with disabilities
and their parents are protected"

"To assist States and localities to provide for the education
of all children with disabilities"

"To assess and assure the effectiveness of efforts to educate
all children with disabilities"

FIGURE 3.1   Four Purposes of IDEA

Disabilities through IDEA [U.S. Department of Education: OSEP]). In the Department's view, IDEA has accomplished three major objectives as illustrated in Figure 3.2.

The accuracy of some of these statements has been repeatedly challenged by critics of state and local education, in general, and of the IDEA, the RA, and ADA, in particular. Critics have alleged that the public education system relies heavily on social promotions, rather than accomplishment, and that the significant rise in the number of disabled college students has more to do with overdiagnosis to obtain an advantage over other students than it does with accommodating a true disability. One author, for example, has concluded that the "impetus for coining the technical term [learning disability] in 1963 and popularizing it soon thereafter was to lend scientific credibility to what was at its core a political movement." He points out that, in 1988, only 16.1 percent of disabled college freshmen identified themselves as learning disabled, but that by 2000, 40.1 percent did so. He attributes the increase to a number of potential factors, including a "change in medical definition" which broadened the learning disability category. Then "there are the legal advantages held out to those who secure an LD diagnosis," which can include "shortened homework assignments, additional and personalized assistance, exemptions from otherwise required classes, and accommodations on exams." These "preferences can outweigh any social stigma attached to an LD diagnosis." Lerner,

Three IDEA Accomplishments

The majority of children with disabilities are now being educated
in their neighborhood schools in regular classrooms with their
nondisabled peers.

High school graduation and employment rates are significantly
higher for students who had been serviced under IDEA than for
those who had not

Postsecondary enrollments of individuals with disabilities have increased dramatically. The percentage of college freshmen reporting
disabilities has more than tripled since 1978

FIGURE 3.2   Three IDEA Accomplishments

Craig S., *"Accommodations" for the Learning Disabled: A Level Playing Field or Affirmative Action for Elites?* 57 Vand. L. Rev. 1043 (Apr. 2004). Despite criticisms, significant anecdotal evidence shows that the IDEA has led to the inclusion in public education of students with significant disabilities and has improved educational opportunities available to those students.

C. The Rehabilitation Act of 1973

The Rehabilitation Act of 1973 (RA), 29 U.S.C. §701 *et seq.*, made discrimination against individuals with disabilities unlawful in three areas: employment by the executive branch of the federal government, employment by most federal government contractors, and activities that are funded by federal subsidies or grants. All public elementary and secondary schools and most postsecondary institutions receive federal subsidies or grants and therefore must comply with the RA. Section 504 of the RA is the statutory provision that prohibits discrimination in grants, and the RA is most often referred to simply as "Section 504." To qualify for services under Section 504, individuals must have impairments that substantially limit a major life activity, such as learning. Eligible individuals are entitled to academic adjustments and auxiliary aids and services, so that courses, examinations, and services will be accessible to them.

D. The Americans with Disabilities Act of 1990

In 1990, Congress enacted the Americans with Disabilities Act (ADA), 42 U.S.C. §12101 *et seq.* This act extended the concepts of "Section 504" to (1) employers with fifteen or more employees (Title I); (2) all activities of state and local governments, including but not limited to employment and education (Title II); and (3) virtually all places that offer goods and services to the public, known as "places of public accommodation" (Title III). In addition, ADA standards apply to employment by Congress.

Court cases and administrative rulings interpret these statutes and apply statutory provisions to individual situations. Cases discussed illustrate particular applications of these laws, and, while some of the cases discussed do not involve learning disabilities, they establish principles that are applicable to individuals with learning disabilities.

E. The Relationships among the RA/ADA and the IDEA

1. Two Approaches to One Goal

The ADA and RA are statutes that prohibit discrimination but do not provide specific funds for the activities mandated by them. The IDEA provides funding for an objective beyond civil rights requirements: the provision of a free appropriate public education to students with disabilities whose needs are such that they require special education and related services.

2. The RA/ADA Mandate Access for Individuals with Disabilities

The RA and ADA are traditional civil rights statutes. They prohibit discrimination on the basis of disability, just as other civil rights laws ban race and gender discrimination. Collectively the RA and ADA apply to virtually every educational institution; most state, local, and federal governmental entities (including professional licensing boards, but not the federal judiciary); and all sizable private employers.

In order to accomplish their purpose, the RA and ADA require that public and private schools provide access to education to qualified students with disabilities. This means two things. First, the school is required to review its academic and other requirements to ensure that they properly measure academic accomplishment and do not unnecessarily penalize students for the consequences of their disabilities. Second, these statutes require that students receive reasonable accommodations in the methods by which tests are administered and instruction and materials are delivered. The education provided under these laws must be tailored to the individual recipients, such that discriminatory aspects of the educational process are eliminated. However, educational institutions are not required to make fundamental changes in the nature of their programs.

While the coverage differs, the elements to be proven in any case brought under these statutes are the same. In order to obtain the protections of the ADA/RA, it must be established that (1) the person is an "individual with a disability"; (2) the person is "otherwise qualified"; (3) the person was denied a job, education, or other benefit by reason of the disability; and (4) the ADA or RA applies to the case.

Public Education Students Are Otherwise Qualified

Public education differs from private education under the RA/ADA standards. It is not necessary to prove that the individual in question is "otherwise qualified" to receive public elementary or secondary education. All states require that elementary and secondary education be provided to all children. Everyone, therefore, is qualified to receive public education at these levels. With respect to individuals with disabilities under the RA, the Office for Civil Rights (OCR) of the U.S. Department of Education notes that the Code of Federal Regulations (34 CFR §104.3[k]):

> provides that for elementary and secondary schools, such an individual is "qualified" when he or she is of an age during which it is mandatory under state law to provide such services, or an age during which it is mandatory under state law to provide such services to persons with disabilities, or to whom a state is required to provide a free and appropriate public education under the Individuals with Disabilities Education Act. *Letter of Findings issued to Susquehanna Community School District.* Docket No. 03931473, October 18, 1993

Private Education—The Need to Prove That Students Are Otherwise Qualified

The standard for determining who is "otherwise qualified" to receive private education is different. In *Bercovitch v. Baldwin School, Inc.* (1st Cir. 1998), for example, the United States Circuit Court of Appeals held that Jason, a student with ADHD, was not entitled to "be exempted from the normal operation of the school's disciplinary code" as a reasonable accommodation under either the ADA or the RA and that Jason was not otherwise qualified for the private school program! The proposed accommodation was that the student "only be suspended after at least three warnings, and then only for the remainder of the day." This modification would eliminate "the normal progressive discipline built into the school's code," and would have prevented the school "from suspending Jason, as it would any other student, for repeated disruptive behavior."

Comparing the RA/ADA to the IDEA, the Court found:

> That a private non-special needs school is covered by the ADA does not, as a matter of law, transform it into a special needs school. The Baldwin School is not equipped to handle special needs students with severe behavioral problems. Despite the district court's order that Baldwin create an individualized "accommodation plan" for Jason which creates special treatment for Jason, the ADA imposes no requirement on Baldwin to devise an individualized education plan such as the IDEA requires of public schools. The district court order comes perilously close to confusing the obligations Congress has chosen to impose on public schools with those obligations imposed on private schools.

Differences between IDEA and the RA/ADA—The Courts

In *Sellers v. School Board of Manassas* (4th Cir. 1998), the Fourth Circuit examined the difference between the IDEA and the RA/ADA. Kristopher Sellers was diagnosed as learning disabled and emotionally disturbed for the first time at the age of eighteen. The Sellers sued for compensatory and punitive damages under the IDEA and RA because of the school district's failure to test and evaluate Kristopher for disabilities. The district court granted the school district's motion to dismiss, and the Sellers appealed. The U.S. Court of Appeals for the Fourth Circuit held that the Sellers' claims were properly dismissed because the IDEA does not provide for compensatory or punitive damages, and the RA does not require outreach and identification of children with disabilities. The Court of Appeals noted that "IDEA and the Rehabilitation Act are different statutes. Whereas IDEA affirmatively requires participating States to assure disabled children a free appropriate public education . . . section 504 of the Rehabilitation Act instead prohibits discrimination against disabled individuals." The court then said:

> We have held that to establish a violation of section 504, plaintiffs must prove that they have been discriminated against—that they were "excluded from the employment or benefit due to discrimination solely on the basis of the disability.". . .
>
> To prove discrimination in the education context, "something more than a mere failure to provide the 'free appropriate education' required by [IDEA] must be shown. . . . We agree with those courts that hold "that either bad faith or gross misjudgment should be shown before a § 504 violation can be made out, at least in the context of education of handicapped children." (Citations omitted)

The Supreme Court declined to review the Fourth Circuit's decision. The Sixth Circuit agrees. *N.L. v. Knox County Schools* (6th Cir. 2003)

In order to establish a violation under section 504, a disabled individual must establish that he was subjected to prohibited discrimination, which means he was denied the opportunity to participate in or benefit from the aid, benefit, or service because of a disability. . . .To prove discrimination in the education context, courts have held that something more than a simple failure to provide a free appropriate public education must be shown. *See Monahan v. Nebraska,* 687 F.2d 1164, 1170 (8th Cir. 1982); *see also Lunceford v. D.C. Bd. of Educ.,* 745 F.2d 1577, 1580 (D.C. Cir. 1984).

The Federal Circuit Courts of Appeal, therefore, view the RA/ADA as imposing only a general duty of nondiscrimination on private and public schools subject to their requirements, duties which are vastly different from those created by the IDEA for public schools. Their language and reasoning tracks that of the U.S. Supreme Court in *Davis v. Monroe County Board of Education,* 526 U.S. 629 (1999), discussed in Chapter 2.

Differences between the IDEA and RA/ADA—The Department of Education

On the other hand, the Department of Education perceives a higher duty under the RA that is closer to the duty under the IDEA. The department has repeatedly held that the state and local educational agencies have a duty to identify children with disabilities who may be eligible to receive special education and related services under either the IDEA or the RA. On April 29, 1993, the Office for Civil Rights modified the September 16, 1991, Memorandum on Policy and issued a revised Questions and Answers Handout on ADD which established that point. ("OCR Facts: Section 504 Coverage of Children with ADD," Memorandum to Regional Civil Rights Directors Regions 1-X, From Jeanette J. Lim Acting Assistant Secretary for Civil Rights, dated April 29, 1993)

3. The IDEA: Access through Funded Special Education

The IDEA requires more than nondiscrimination. It requires access for those who need special education and related services and provides part of the funding to pay for those services. Under the IDEA, each school district is required to provide a "free appropriate public education" (FAPE), which means "special education and related services that . . . have been provided at public expense, under public supervision and direction, and without charge," that "meet the standards of the State educational agency," and that include an appropriate preschool, elementary, or secondary school education in the state involved and "are provided in conformity with the individualized education program required under" the IDEA.

The IDEA provides money for education of children with disabilities. It applies to each "child with a disability," which the law defines as follows:

(3) CHILD WITH A DISABILITY—
    (A) IN GENERAL—The term "child with a disability" means a child—
    (i) with mental retardation, hearing impairments (including deafness), speech or language impairments, visual impairments (including blindness), serious emotional disturbance (referred to in this title as "emotional disturbance"), orthopedic

impairments, autism, traumatic brain injury, other health impairments, or specific learning disabilities; and

> (ii) who, by reason thereof, needs special education and related services.
> 20 U.S.C. §1401(3)

To be eligible for services, a child both must have a listed disability *and* "by reason thereof need special education and related services."

The funding formula was described in the Senate Report which accompanied the bill that became the reauthorized IDEA, S. Rep. No. 17, 105th Cong., 1st Sess. 13 (1997), entitled the Individuals with Disabilities Education Act Amendments of 1997, dated May 9, 1997. The funding formula was described thus:

> Current law permanently authorizes such sums as may be necessary for this program and contains a formula for determining how much states would get if the program is fully funded—the number of children with a disability times 40 percent of the average per pupil expenditure.

Essentially the same formula is used in the 2004 IDEA Reauthorization. 20 U.S.C. §1411. Note that, for funding to occur there must be both *authorization,* which the amended and reauthorized IDEA provides, and *appropriation* of funds, which occurs annually through the congressional appropriations (funding) process.

The U.S. Supreme Court has made it clear that the IDEA's predominant concern is with providing funds to ensure that all children covered by its terms have *access* to the educational process. Of lesser importance for funding purposes is the *quality* of the education accessed. In *Board of Education v. Rowley,* 458 U.S. 176 (1982), for example, the Supreme Court said that the "intent" of the IDEA "was more to open the door of public education to handicapped children on appropriate terms than to guarantee any particular level of education once inside." More recently, in *Cedar Rapids Community School District v. Garret F.,* 526 U.S. 66 (1999), the Supreme Court held that a school district was financially obligated under the IDEA to provide the services of a personal attendant to Garret F., a student whose spinal column was severed in a motorcycle accident when he was four years old and who was, therefore, "ventilator dependent," a condition requiring a "responsible individual nearby to attend to certain physical needs while he is in school." The court held that the school district was obligated to provide the service, rejecting the argument that the cost was prohibitive and therefore an undue burden. In so ruling, the court said, "This case is about whether meaningful access to the public schools will be assured, not the level of education that a school must finance once access is attained."

The court noted that its ruling would "create some tension with the purposes of the IDEA." While recognizing that the IDEA "may not require public schools to maximize the potential of disabled students commensurate with the opportunities provided to other children," Congress did intend "to open the door of public education" to all qualified children and "require[d] participating States to educate handicapped children with nonhandicapped children whenever possible." [Citations omitted]

The IDEA provides a far broader reach than either the RA or ADA. First, the definition of disability is more comprehensive and specific. Second, special education and related services can include fundamental teaching and program alterations far beyond what would be required as accommodations under the RA/ADA. At the same time, certain accommodations may be obtained by students under the RA, even though those students are not covered by the IDEA. The relationship between the two statutes might be viewed this way:

> The fact that a school district has found a student to need special education and related services under IDEA because of a listed condition creates a strong, although rebuttable, presumption that the condition, with any mitigating measures used, is an impairment that substantially limits a major life activity such as learning or reading.
> [Internal Memorandum to OCR Staff, from Norma V. Cantu, Assistant Secretary for Civil Rights, Subject Internal Guidance Document Entitled "Sutton Investigative Guidance: Consideration of 'Mitigating Measures' in OCR Disability Cases" dated September 29, 2000.]

F. State Law

The focus of this text is federal law, because federal law has been most influential in assisting individuals with disabilities. However, state constitutional and statutory laws have evolved following federal leadership and, in some cases, have surpassed the federal models on which they were based. *See generally Roland M. v. Concord School Comm.*, 910 F.2d 983 (1st Cir. 1990), for an excellent discussion of this topic. The case contains a concise discussion of the IDEA, as does the Supreme Court's opinion in *School Committee of Burlington v. Department of Education*, 471 U.S. 359 (1985). In addition, state law may supplement or fill in the gaps where federal law is silent. The question of whether state law has been "preempted" by federal law is a complex question, which must be considered on a case-by-case basis and is beyond the scope of this book.

State law may contain a definition of disability which is more inclusive than the federal one. In *Kammueller v. Loomis, Fargo & Co.* (8th Cir. 2004), for example, the court held that, under the Minnesota Human Rights law, polycystic kidney disease is a condition that *materially limits* a major life activity and is therefore a covered disability. The Minnesota law only required proof that an impairment materially limits a major life condition. In contrast, the ADA/RA require proof of a substantial limitation, a more stringent test.

State law may provide remedies that are not available under federal law. In *Montoy v. Kansas* (Sup. Ct. Kan. 2005), the Supreme Court of Kansas held that the Kansas legislature had failed to provide adequate funds for the public school system. The court ruled that this failure violated the Kansas Constitution which requires that the legislature "make suitable provision for finance" of the public schools.

Kansas does not stand alone. To date twenty-five states have been sued successfully by plaintiffs seeking additional funds, eighteen have been sued unsuccessfully, and seven have not been sued at all. Farney, Davis, "States Resist Court-Ordered School Funds: Advocates for Poor Students Fare Well with Judges, Not with Kansas' Antitax Legislators," *Wall Street Journal*, March 9, 2005.

All states except South Carolina have constitutions that promise universal education in sweeping terms. The New York State Constitution, for example, requires that "the legislature shall provide for maintenance and support of a system of free common schools, wherein all the children of this state may be educated" (Art. XI, §1). Whether the legislature has met its obligations then becomes a question of state constitutional law.

The rationale for ordering increased spending is roughly the same. State constitutions and statutes require the provision of a first-class education, usually measured by a combination of student testing and accreditation reviews. Coupled with these elevated standards is a requirement that the legislature finance the public school system. It is, therefore, no large stretch to say that if the legislature is required to fund a superlative educational system, the funding must be adequate to the purpose. Whether this means increased taxes is unclear. Some states have responded by cutting other services in order to resist a tax increase.

G.   Summary

The RA and ADA are statutes that prohibit discrimination against qualified individuals with disabilities. These laws generally apply to elementary and secondary education, postsecondary education, and employment. The IDEA provides funds to state and local educational agencies in order to provide each child with a disability a free appropriate public education, which includes special education and related services.

4

The IDEA: Coverage

A. In General

1. The Special Education Population

In 1975, Congress enacted the Education for All Handicapped Children Act (now the Individuals with Disabilities Education Act), 20 U.S.C. §1400 *et seq.* The IDEA was reauthorized most recently on December 3, 2004, when President Bush signed Public Law 108-446. For federal funds to be provided to any recipient, Congress must both *authorize* and *appropriate* funds. The current IDEA authorizes the expenditure of specific funds through 2011. However, Congress will also have to *appropriate* funds annually to support the authorized funding. The RA is handled in a similar way because it is also a funding statute. The ADA is never "reauthorized" because it does not provide funds.

The final bill, which became the reauthorized IDEA, was accompanied by Conference Report No. 108-779 (November 17, 2004). Entitled Individuals with Disabilities Education Improvement Act of 2004, this report provides Congress's intent regarding the legislation. This report is an extremely useful companion to the text of the IDEA because it further explains federal policies in the educational area. Note that, while the formal reauthorization of the statute was entitled the "Individuals with Disabilities Education Improvement Act," this does not change the actual title of the statute which was amended by the 2004 legislation. Therefore, we will use the actual title of the statute, the Individuals with Disabilities Education Act, or IDEA.

The years between 1975 and 2004 were marked by an explosive growth in students served and in services provided. The U.S. Department of Education summarized the results:

> In 2000–01, states and outlying areas reported serving 5,775,722 students ages 6 through 21 under IDEA. This represents an increase of 28.4% since the 1991–92 school year. Students ages 6 through 17 with disabilities made up 11.5% of the estimated student enrollment for grades prekindergarten through 12th grade.

By 2000–2001 that number had reached 5,775,722, of whom nearly half had specific learning disabilities. One of the fastest growing categories is "other health impairments" (OHI) which has more than quadrupled since 1987. The latest IDEA regulations, issued in August 2006, add Tourette syndrome to the list of "chronic or acute health problems" covered under the OHI category. Therefore, it is likely that the number of children served under this category will continue to increase.

The Department of Education described it this way.

> It [OHI] comprised only slightly more than 1% of students with disabilities in this age range in 1987 but more than 5% in 2000. This change reflects, in part, the increase in the number of students diagnosed with attention deficit/hyperactivity disorder (ADHD) as a primary disability, who may be reported in the other health impairments category. A decline of similar size was evident for students with mental retardation (17% to 12%).

See the U.S. Department of Education Annual Report on the IDEA entitled "Twenty-Fourth Annual Report to Congress on the Implementation of the Individuals with Disabilities Education Act."

The department summarized the current data:

Disability	1991–92	2000–01	Percent change in number
Specific learning disabilities	2,247,004	2,887,217	28.5
Speech or language impairments	998,904	1,093,808	9.5
Mental retardation	553,262	612,978	10.8
Emotional disturbance	400,211	473,663	18.4
Multiple disabilities	98,408	122,559	24.5
Hearing impairments	60,727	70,767	16.5
Orthopedic impairments	51,389	73,057	42.2
Other health impairments	58,749	291,850	396.8
Visual impairments	24,083	25,975	7.9
Autism	5,415	78,749	1,354.3
Deaf-blindness	1,427	1,320	–7.5
Traumatic brain injury	245	14,844	5,958.8
Developmental delay	—	28,935	—
All disabilities	4,499,824	5,775,722	28.4

Note: Reporting in the autism and traumatic brain injury categories was optional in 1991–92 and required beginning in 1992–93.

Data from 1991–92 include children with disabilities served under the Chapter 1 Handicapped program.

Source: U.S. Department of Education, Office of Special Education Programs, Data Analysis System (DANS).

FIGURE 4.1   Number of Students Ages 6 through 21 Served under IDEA during 1991–92 and 2000–01

Note that four disability categories (specific learning disabilities, speech or language impairments, mental retardation, and emotional disturbance) account for 87.7 percent of all students aged 6 through 21. An additional 75,000 students in the age range 3 through 5 are covered.

Special education and related services may be delivered in a variety of settings, including the general education classroom, resource rooms, separate classes, separate schools, residential facilities, and homebound/hospital environments. *The 24th Annual Report to Congress on the Implementation of the IDEA* (U.S. Department of Education, 2002) notes that "the number of students placed in particular educational environments continues to vary by disability category." Students with low-incidence disabilities (e.g., visual or hearing impairments, autism, multiple disabilities) are more likely to be served outside of the regular classroom, while the majority of students with learning disabilities and speech-language impairments will be in general education classes.

The department summarizes the current distribution across education environment:

> Overall, students with disabilities continue to be served in less restrictive environments, although variation in placement by age, race/ethnicity, and disability continues to occur. Elementary students are more likely to be served in the regular classroom than are secondary students. Students served in separate public facilities are most likely to be those with emotional disturbance, mental retardation, or multiple disabilities. (24th Annual Report, p. III-47)

2. The Philosophy of the IDEA

The principal purposes of the IDEA are "to ensure that all children with disabilities have available to them a free appropriate public education that emphasizes special education and related services designed to meet their unique needs and prepare them for further education, employment, and independent living . . . [and] . . . to ensure that the rights of children with disabilities and parents of such children are protected." 20 U.S.C. §1400(d)(1)(A)-(B). Under the IDEA, funds are provided to local school systems for the education of children generally between the ages of three and twenty-one. Local schools are required to comply with the IDEA and its implementing regulations as a condition of receiving federal funds.

The ultimate goal of the IDEA is to ensure that children with disabilities receive the equal protection of the law. In *Corine R., B/N/F Rick & Stacey R. v. Marlin Independent School District* (SEA TX 1998), the special education hearing officer described the purpose of the IDEA, "The main thrust of IDEA is to provide equal access to education, and *no particular educational outcome is guaranteed.*" (Emphasis in original.)

The right to equal access does not mean the right to a quality education. In the *Corine* case, Corine, a student enrolled in a high school cosmetology program, was covered by the IDEA because of a specific learning disability. She completed the high school program but graduated with too few cosmetology hours to obtain a license for that profession. She and her parents then argued that the school district "failed to provide an appropriate education" for her, because her hours, though sufficient for graduation, were insufficient for licensure. However, the hearing officer found that no "senior cosmetology student," with or without a disability, "obtained that goal in 1997–98." Thus, Corine received education of the same quality as that given to a student with no disability.

The hearing officer made it clear that, while the IDEA mandates equality of access to education, it does not mandate access to an education of quality.

> It is outside the jurisdiction of an IDEA Hearing Officer to determine whether a high school cosmetology program must ensure that students have the opportunity to earn 1000 hours of cosmetology instruction during the regular school day, pursuant to general education law or cosmetology law, and such was not proven at hearing.

The U.S. Supreme Court has held access to be the principal goal of the IDEA. In *Cedar Rapids Community School District v. Garret F.*, 526 U.S. 66 (1999), discussed at greater length in both Chapters 2 and 3, the court, while recognizing that the IDEA "may not require public schools to maximize the potential of disabled students commensurate with the opportunities provided to other children," held that Congress did intend "to open the door of public education" to all qualified children and "require[d] participating States to educate handicapped children with non-handicapped children whenever possible." [Citations omitted]

3.   The 2004 Reauthorization of the IDEA

The 2004 IDEA legislation had its roots in President Bush's Commission on Excellence in Special Education. In July 2002, the commission released its report outlining principles for special education reform, including reduced paperwork for teachers, early intervention, parental choice, and academic results for students. The progress of the legislation was summarized in a November 17, 2004, press release from the Committee on Education and the Workforce:

> WASHINGTON, D.C.—A bipartisan House-Senate conference committee today approved a final special education reform bill that will reauthorize the Individuals with Disabilities Education Act (IDEA) and set in motion important reforms that will help teachers, parents, and schools ensure every student with disabilities receives a quality education. The bipartisan agreement is based on legislation authored by House Education Reform Subcommittee Chairman Mike Castle (R-DE) that passed the House in 2003 with bipartisan support. The measure includes reforms recommended in 2002 by President Bush's special education commission, as well as key elements of the IDEA reauthorization bill passed by the Senate in 2004.
>
> "This bipartisan agreement is an across-the-board win for teachers, parents, and students with special needs," said House Education and the Workforce Committee Chairman John Boehner (R-OH), who chaired the conference committee. "In No Child Left Behind, we put a system in place to ensure students with disabilities, and all students, are getting access to the education they deserve. In this bill, we're making sure the rules help special education teachers and parents get the most out of that system, instead of making it harder for them."

The congressional views were reflected in the congressional findings section of the IDEA. Congress stated that the "implementation" of the IDEA in the past "has been impeded by low expectations, and an insufficient focus on applying replicable research on proven methods of teaching and learning for children with disabilities." Additionally, over almost "30 years of research and experience has demonstrated that the education of children with disabilities can be made more effective by . . . having high expectations for such children and ensuring their access to the general education curriculum in the regular classroom, to the maximum extent possible in order to . . . meet developmental goals and, to the maximum extent possible, the challenging expectations that have been established for all children; and . . . be prepared to lead productive and independent adult lives, to the maximum extent possible." 20 U.S.C. §§1400(c)(4)-(5)

While the courts have continued to hold that access is the key goal of the IDEA, the 1997 and 2004 reauthorizations of the statute have moved the discussion more toward the outcomes of providing an appropriate education to children with disabilities. More specifically, expectations have been raised, and it is assumed that a large number of children with disabilities are more able and likely to attain higher levels of academic proficiency than previous acknowledged. Toward that end, the IDEA and the No Child Left Behind Act are more closely aligned toward challenging students with disabilities to meet the same set of state academic content standards, to the maximum extent possible, as children without disabilities. 20 U.S.C. §1400(c)(5)

4.   The IDEA Works through Funding

To accomplish its objectives, the IDEA provides federal money to state educational agencies that undertake to implement its substantive and procedural requirements. *Virginia Department of Education v. Riley* (4th Cir. 1997). A state may elect to participate in the federal grant-in-aid program established by the IDEA by meeting the eligibility requirements set forth at 20 U.S.C. §1411, including a demonstration that it has put into effect "policies and procedures to ensure" that a "free appropriate public education is available to all children with disabilities residing in the State between the ages of 3 and 21, inclusive, including children with disabilities who have been suspended or expelled from school." 20 U.S.C. §1412(a)(1)(A)

Receipt of federal funding generally operates as a waiver of sovereign immunity (referred to as "abrogation" in the IDEA). However, the waiver operates only as to claims under IDEA, not under other statutes. *Board of Education of the Pawling Central School District v. Schutz* (2nd Cir. 2002)

B.   Statutory Language and Coverage

1.   Child with a Disability

The IDEA (20 U.S.C. §1401[3]) provides this definition of a "child with a disability":

> (A) IN GENERAL.— The term "child with a disability" means a child—
>   (i) with mental retardation, hearing impairments (including deafness), speech or language impairments, visual impairments (including blindness), serious emotional disturbance (referred to in this title as "emotional disturbance"), orthopedic

impairments, autism, traumatic brain injury, other health impairments, or specific learning disabilities; and
(ii) who, by reason thereof, needs special education and related services.

The text makes it clear that the existence of a listed disability *and* the need for special education and related services must be shown in order to establish that a child is a "child with a disability" under the IDEA. (*Note:* Definitions of "special education" and "related services" are in Chapter 5.)

The case law supports this analysis. For example, in *Eric H. ex rel. Gary H. v. Judson Independent School District* (W.D. Tex. 2002), parents sought to have their child classified as suffering from Asperger's syndrome and to obtain special education and related services. They initiated a due process hearing but introduced no evidence to rebut the school's expert who testified that the child's adequate school performance and socialization levels precluded special education. The parents' opinion was based on the fear that present classification was needed to prevent future problems. The hearing was decided in the school district's favor and was affirmed by the court, which found that "that fear alone, with no supporting medical data, cannot form the basis for insisting that the district provide any sort of 'preventive' special education services." There must be a present need for special education and related services.

2. Specific Learning Disability

The IDEA, 20 U.S.C. §1401 (30), provides the following definition of a specific learning disability:
(30) SPECIFIC LEARNING DISABILITY.—

(A) IN GENERAL.— The term "specific learning disability" means a disorder in 1 or more of the basic psychological processes involved in understanding or in using language, spoken or written, which disorder may manifest itself in the imperfect ability to listen, think, speak, read, write, spell, or do mathematical calculations.
(B) DISORDERS INCLUDED.— Such term includes such conditions as perceptual disabilities, brain injury, minimal brain dysfunction, dyslexia, and developmental aphasia.
(C) DISORDERS NOT INCLUDED.— Such term does not include a learning problem that is primarily the result of visual, hearing, or motor disabilities, of mental retardation, of emotional disturbance, or of environmental, cultural, or economic disadvantage.

3. Severe Discrepancy

The IDEA was once routinely interpreted by local school districts to require the provision of special education and related services to children with specific learning disabilities only on a showing that the child with a disability has a "severe discrepancy" between intellectual potential and actual achievement. Frequently the school districts went further and required that a child be academically at least two years behind his or her peers in order to be eligible for services. Impact was measured primarily by grades and rate of progress when compared with other class members. A student often needed to continually show poor performance in order to obtain assistance.

The IDEA, as interpreted by the courts, provided that (1) the "severe discrepancy" standard once set forth in the regulations was intended only to assist school districts in identifying students requiring assistance and was never intended to limit the statutory definition of those entitled to special education and related services; and, (2) the consequent use of a rigid "severe discrepancy" standard was not intended. To prevent further misunderstandings, in the 2004 IDEA reauthorization Congress clarified that it had never intended the use of an ability-achievement discrepancy as the sole criterion for determining a specific learning disability. The law now provides:

> (6) SPECIFIC LEARNING DISABILITIES—
>
> (A) IN GENERAL.—Notwithstanding section 607(b) [dealing with the issuance of regulations], when determining whether a child has a specific learning disability as defined in section 602 [definitions], a local educational agency shall not be required to take into consideration whether a child has a severe discrepancy between achievement and intellectual ability in oral expression, listening comprehension, written expression, basic reading skill, reading comprehension, mathematical calculation, or mathematical reasoning.
>
> (B) ADDITIONAL AUTHORITY.— In determining whether a child has a specific learning disability, a local educational agency may use a process that determines if the child responds to scientific, research-based intervention as a part of the evaluation procedures described in paragraphs (2) and (3) [describing the requirements for evaluation]. (20 U.S.C. §1414[b][6])

Note that this section does not say that the local educational agency "shall not consider the existence of a severe discrepancy." It does say that the local educational agency (LEA) "shall not be required" to do so. However, the state educational agency (SEA) is charged with developing state criteria for eligibility under this disability category, which the LEAs within that state must follow. The IDEA regulations now state that an SEA "must not require the use of a severe discrepancy." 34 C.F.R. §300.307. Further, the Department of Education has interpreted this provision to mean that a state's eligibility criteria may, in fact, prohibit the use of a severe discrepancy.

The IDEA provides that to be eligible, a child must (1) have a "specific learning disability," for example, an "imperfect ability" in one or more of the listed processes, and (2) "by reason thereof need special education and related services." The terms "imperfect ability" and "need" constitute the only statutory language that addresses the question of how severe a learning disability must be in order to entitle one to the benefits of the IDEA.

Showing the existence of a "severe discrepancy" has been, of course, an *acceptable* way to show the existence of a specific learning disability. It may still be used if the state's eligibility criteria allow. The child's achievements may be documented in various ways. Often, standardized IQ tests are used to measure ability, but the IQ test is not the only means. In *Ford v. Long Beach Unified School District* (9th Cir. 2002), the court approved alternative testing methods which included: Developmental Test of Visual Motor Integration (VMI), the Visual Aural Digit Span Test

(VADS), the Test of Auditory Perceptual Skills (TAPS), the Wide Range Assessment of Memory and Learning (WRAML), the Matrix Analogies Test (MAT), and the Woodcock-Johnson, Revised (WJ-R). These tests, the court found, contained both "achievement" and "ability" components and were a proper means of measuring the severity of a discrepancy.

To summarize, first, there are various ways to determine whether a severe discrepancy exists. IQ tests are frequently used but, as the *Ford* case illustrates, may not necessarily be required. Second, if the parents wish a particular test included in the child's evaluation, the time to raise the issue is before, rather than after, the evaluation. Third, showing severe discrepancy should not be the sole means of establishing a learning disability.

4. Students with ADHD and Asperger's Syndrome

The question of whether the IDEA applies to individuals who have ADHD once was quite controversial. This question was initially resolved by the Department of Education's Office of Special Education and Rehabilitative Services in a memorandum issued on September 16, 1991. The department confirmed that ADHD can be considered within the scope of the IDEA—depending on the circumstances—in any of the following categories: "other health impairments," "serious emotional disturbance" (now shortened to "emotional disturbance"), or "specific learning disabilities." The implementing regulations now specifically address ADHD under the heading "other health impairment," discussed in the next section.

The IDEA (20 U.S.C. §1401[3]) includes in the definition of children with disabilities those with "other health impairments" (OHI). Leukemia is an OHI because it results in reduced vitality. *Elida Local School District Board of Education v. Erickson* (N.D. Ohio 2003). The Department of Education determined under the predecessor statute that ADHD fits most naturally into this category. The department's views were implemented in the 1999 regulations and were continued in the current regulations (2006):

> (9) Other health impairment means having limited strength, vitality or alertness, including a heightened alertness to environmental stimuli, that results in limited alertness with respect to the educational environment, that—
>> (i) Is due to chronic or acute health problems such as asthma, attention deficit disorder or attention deficit hyperactivity disorder, diabetes, epilepsy, a heart condition, hemophilia, lead poisoning, leukemia, nephritis, rheumatic fever, sickle cell anemia, and Tourette syndrome; and
>> (ii) Adversely affects a child's educational performance.

However, a child with ADHD will be eligible for special education and related services only if the ADHD involves "limited alertness with respect to the educational environment" and "adversely affects a child's educational performance." In the *Analysis of Comments and Changes* accompanying the 1999 regulations, the Department of Education explained that this language was adopted because "according to commenters, at least 25 percent of the children referred for evaluation, who had been diagnosed medically as ADD/ADHD, were experiencing few, if any, educational problems at the time of their referrals." (Page 12542) Other commenters expressed concern that the requirement of an adverse impact on educational performance would limit the services provided to "those children who are academically gifted but who still need transition services to postsecondary education." The Department of Education responded by pointing out "that a child who is academically gifted but who may not be progressing at the rate desired is not automatically eligible under Part B (IDEA grants to States). Neither is the child automatically ineligible. Rather, determinations as to a child's eligibility for services under Part B must be made on a case-by-case basis in accordance with applicable evaluation procedures." (Page 12543)

The listing of ADHD in the previous and current regulations represents a compromise between those who wanted no mention at all and those who wanted it listed as a separate category, like autism or traumatic brain injury. The need for some action was clear. The 1999 analysis noted that many "commenters, parents of children with ADD/ADHD, described the tremendous problems they have had, and are having, in obtaining appropriate services for their children." (Page 12542) The department further agreed that, while "some children with ADHD are receiving services under these regulations [prior to 1999], experience and the numerous comments received have demonstrated that the Department's policy is not being fully and effectively implemented." (Page 12542) Interestingly, the *Analysis of Comments* accompanying the 2006 regulations make no mention of ADHD, perhaps indicating that this is now settled law.

The 1999 regulations also made clear that many students who had been diagnosed with ADHD and who were experiencing few, if any, educational problems at the time of their referrals (25 percent of ADHD referrals according to the Department of Education) will not be covered by the IDEA and may seek to obtain their goals under the Rehabilitation Act of 1973 and/or the Americans with Disabilities Act of 1990.

However, again, as with all eligibility determinations, the disability must "adversely affect" the "child's educational performance." Perhaps for this reason, the Department of Education has given considerable thought to the proper method of diagnosing ADHD for purposes of obtaining IDEA coverage. Its Professional Group for Attention and Related Disorders recommended:

> A two-tier evaluation to properly identify children with the disorder. Tier 1 is a clinical evaluation to see if the child's symptoms meet the accepted standards for diagnosis of the disorder, and Tier 2 is an educational evaluation to determine if symptoms of the disorder have a negative impact on the child's classroom performance. (Executive Summary: United States Department of Education Annual Report on the IDEA entitled To Assure the Free Appropriate Public Education of All Children with Disabilities—1997)

The department's advice was sound. A parent who seeks special education and related services for a child with ADHD should be prepared to show that ADHD has produced a "negative impact on the child's classroom performance."

A potential problem was also identified in using the other health impairment category for some children with ADHD who did not appear to have "limited alertness" or an adverse effect on educational performance. *Lyons v. Smith* (D.D.C. 1993) spoke to these circumstances. The case involved an eight-year-old boy with ADHD who scored average to superior on all tests administered but whose social adjustment had been affected by ADHD. His parents objected to the proposed public school placement and sought a private placement instead. A hearing officer found that the boy was not other health impaired under the IDEA because he showed no diminished alertness. He then held that the boy was an otherwise qualified individual with a disability under the RA. The matter was appealed up to the U.S. District Court for the District of Columbia which concurred with the hearing officer's finding that the child did not qualify under the OHI category.

What about other disability categories under the IDEA? In its 1991 memorandum, the Department of Education stated that children with ADHD might be served under the specific learning disabilities and emotional disturbance categories as well as under OHI. That interpretation is still current under the recently issued regulations.

Several cases have lent support to the proposition that ADHD is a specific learning disability under the IDEA. See, for example, *Capistrano Unified School District v. Wartenberg by & Through Wartenberg* (9th Cir. 1995), *Susan N. v. Wilson School District* (3d Cir. 1995), and *Laughlin v. Central Bucks School District* (E.D. Pa. 1994).

Autism and Asperger's syndrome are now major conditions addressed under IDEA and litigated in the courts. At issue are the proper educational approaches to the problems posed by these conditions. In one case, the court found that the difference between an intense one-on-one method, such as the Lovaas method, was so much superior to the school's preferred method, that the refusal to employ the Lovaas method amounted to a denial of a free appropriate public education. The court said:

> The "difference in outcomes" between the Lovaas method and the school district's is so great that "provision of the lesser program could amount to denial of a FAPE." *Deal v. Hamilton County Board of Education*, Docket No. 03-5396 (6th Cir. 2004)

In *J.P. ex rel. Popson v. West Clark Community School* (S.D. Ind. 2002), the court rejected the arguments of parents that a refusal to fund an intense one-on-one method of dealing with autism—in this case, applied behavioral analysis (ABA)—was a denial of FAPE. The court said:

> The Popsons have argued strongly that J.P. began progressing much more rapidly once he started his ABA/DTT training. But while such an argument is highly relevant at a case conference meeting, it does not carry much weight in this legal action. The law does not require West Clark to provide J.P. with the better or best possible education. West Clark's duty is only to provide an education that is reasonably calculated to benefit J.P.

In summary, the critical issues in providing services for children with autism spectrum disorders are the same as for other disabilities: (1) is the child's educational performance adversely affected by the disability, and (2) does the child need special education and related services to address the lack of "educational benefit."

C. The Duty to Evaluate

1. Child Find

States are required, as a condition of receiving IDEA funds, to engage in "child find" procedures. "Child find" is defined as follows:

> (3) CHILD FIND.—
> (A) IN GENERAL.— All children with disabilities residing in the State, including children with disabilities who are homeless children or are wards of the State and children with disabilities attending private schools, regardless of the severity of their disabilities, and who are in need of special education and related services, are identified, located, and evaluated and a practical method is developed and implemented to determine which children with disabilities are currently receiving needed special education and related services.
> (B) CONSTRUCTION.— Nothing in this title requires that children be classified by their disability so long as each child who has a disability listed in section 602 and who, by reason of that disability, needs special education and related services is regarded as a child with a disability under this part.

In fact, the child find responsibility extends to locating, identifying, and evaluating *any* child in the state suspected of having a disability, including homeless and migrant children and children who have not failed and are advancing from grade to grade. 34 C.F.R. §300.111(c)

2. Evaluations

The IDEA requires that children with suspected disabilities be evaluated to determine whether they require special education and related services. The IDEA provides:

> (A) IN GENERAL.— A State educational agency, other State agency, or local educational agency shall conduct a full and individual initial evaluation in accordance with this paragraph and subsection (b), before the initial provision of special education and related services to a child with a disability under this part. (20 U.S.C. §1414[a][1][A])

The law states further that, after appropriate notice, "the local educational agency shall—

> (A) use a variety of assessment tools and strategies to gather relevant functional, developmental, and academic information, including information provided by the parent, that may assist in determining—
> (i) whether the child is a child with a disability;
> and

(ii) the content of the child's individualized education program, including information related to enabling the child to be involved in and progress in the general education curriculum, or, for preschool children, to participate in appropriate activities; (B) not use any single measure or assessment as the sole criterion for determining whether a child is a child with a disability or determining an appropriate educational program for the child; and (C) use technically sound instruments that may assess the relative contribution of cognitive and behavioral factors, in addition to physical or developmental factors. (20 U.S.C. §1414[b][2])

Additionally, each local agency "shall ensure that . . . assessments and other evaluation materials" are not racially or culturally biased and are proper in purpose and methods of administration. Finally, the child must be "assessed in all areas of suspected disability." 20 U.S.C. §1414 (b)(3)

3. Initial Evaluation

Either a parent of a child or a state or local agency may initiate a request for an initial evaluation to determine if the child is a child with a disability. The evaluation must be conducted within sixty days of receiving parental consent, or within an established state time line. 34 C.F.R. §300.301(c)(1). The evaluation consists of procedures designed to determine the child is a "child with a disability" and to determine the child's educational needs. If the parent refuses consent for an evaluation, "the local educational agency may pursue the initial evaluation of the child by utilizing the procedures described in section 615." (20 U.S.C. §1415, due process hearing provisions) If the parents refuse consent to the provision of special education and related services, the agency may not use the dispute process and may not provide services. 34 C.F.R. §300.300(b)(3), (4)

4. Content of Evaluations

The determination of whether a child is a child with a disability must be made by "a team of qualified professionals and the parent of the child." 20 U.S.C. §1414(b)(4)(A)

The team may find that the child does not have a disability under the meaning of the IDEA if the child's difficulties are caused by a "lack of appropriate instruction in reading," a "lack of instruction in math," or "limited English proficiency." As a practical matter, these factors must be ruled out before a finding of disability can occur. 20 U.S.C. §1414(b)(5)(A)-(C)

In making the assessment, the team may rely on "evaluations and information provided by the parents of the child," as well as "current classroom-based, local, or State assessments, and classroom-based observations," "observations by teachers and related services providers," and any other data that might be relevant. 20 U.S.C. §1414(c)(1)(A)(i)-(iii). Data from the child's response to "scientific research-based interventions" may also be considered for children suspected of having a specific learning disability. On the basis of these data, the team may determine if the child has a disability and needs special education and related services.

5. Failure or Refusal to Evaluate

In *Seattle School District, No. 1 v. B.S.* (9th Cir. 1996), the U.S. Court of Appeals for the Ninth Circuit considered the consequences of the school district's refusal to evaluate. The school district was required to reimburse the parents for a proper evaluation initially conducted at the parents' expense. Courts reached similar results in *Department of Education v. Cari Rae S.* (D. Haw. 2001), *Reid v. District of Columbia (D.D.C. 2004)*, and *New Paltz Central School District. v. St. Pierre* (N.D.N.Y. 2003). See also *Veronica P. v. Garland Independent School District* (SEA TX 2002).

The school district may not evade its responsibilities. In *Pasatiempo v. Aizawa* (9th Cir. 1996), a school district created a special class of assessments for students who it did not suspect of having a disability, but who exhibited "achievement delays or adjustment difficulties, which may require alternative teaching strategies." The scope of these evaluations was comparable to the evaluations conducted for students with "suspected" disabilities, with one critical difference: the district's due process procedures did not apply to disputes concerning these evaluations.

This method would have allowed the district to answer parents' requests for evaluations with a determination that the district did not "suspect" the existence of a disability. The district would follow up with its own assessment and placement, neither of which could be contested in a due process hearing or in court. The court prohibited the use of this procedure, stating that:

> The procedural safeguards, which allow parents the opportunity to be notified of and to contest school district decisions, were not intended merely to facilitate parental responses to a school district's suspicion of disability. Congress intended the procedural protections to counteract the tendency of school districts to make decisions regarding the education of disabled children without consulting their parents, and to require school districts to respond adequately to parental concerns about their children.
>
> ***
>
> We conclude that, when a teacher refers a student [for its own non-IDEA] evaluation, the parents must be notified and given the procedural protections connected with a[n] evaluation [under the IDEA]. When a parent suspects a disability and requests an evaluation, [the District] must notify the parents of its response and the means by which the parents can challenge it. If [the District] undertakes a non [IDEA] evaluation in response to such a parental initiative, the procedural protections . . . of the IDEA . . . must apply.

The Office for Civil Rights (OCR) also will enforce the evaluation requirement. *Letter of Findings issued to Marysville School District*

6. Comment on the Duty to Identify & Evaluate

The requirement that all children who potentially need special education and related services be "identified, located, and evaluated" could possibly conflict with the privacy requirements of the RA/ADA, particularly where private schools are concerned.

The §504 Regulations

The "504" regulations concerning the duty to serve students with disabilities (34 C.F.R. 104.33[a]) provide that:

> A recipient that operates a public elementary or secondary education program or activity shall provide a free appropriate public education to each qualified handicapped person who is in the recipient's jurisdiction, regardless of the nature or severity of the person's handicap.

An "appropriate education" is, essentially, "the provision of regular or special education and related aids and services" that "are designed to meet individual educational needs of handicapped persons as adequately as the needs of nonhandicapped persons are met." 34 C.F.R. 104.33(b)

The RA regulations also address "Evaluation and Placement." (34 C.F.R. 104.35) These regulations provide that a "recipient that operates a public elementary or secondary education program shall conduct an evaluation in accordance with the requirements of paragraph (b) of this section of any person who, because of handicap, needs or is believed to need special education or related services before taking any action with respect to the initial placement of the person in a regular or special education program and any subsequent significant change in placement." 34 C.F.R. 104.35(a)

RA regulations state further that a "recipient . . . shall establish standards and procedures for the evaluation and placement of persons who, because of handicap, need or are believed to need special education or related services." The evaluation and placement procedures must ensure that "tests and other evaluation materials have been validated for the specific purpose for which they are used and are administered by trained personnel in conformance with the instructions provided by their producer." Procedures must also ensure that "tests and other evaluation materials include those tailored to assess specific areas of educational need and not merely those which are designed to provide a single general intelligence quotient," and that "tests are selected and administered so as best to ensure that, when a test is administered to a student with impaired sensory, manual, or speaking skills, the test results accurately reflect the student's aptitude or achievement level or whatever other factor the test purports to measure, rather than reflecting the student's impaired sensory, manual, or speaking skills (except where those skills are the factors that the test purports to measure)." 34 C.F.R. 104.35(b)

Cases—No Duty to Identify under the RA/ADA

Searching inquiries generally are not allowed under the RA/ADA. In *Roe v. Cheyenne Mt. Conf. Resort* (10th Cir. 1997), the U.S. Court of Appeals prohibited an employer from asking employees about their prescription medications. In doing so, the court held that the ADA "prohibits a medical examination or inquiries as to whether an employee is an individual with a disability, unless shown to be job-related and consistent with business necessity."

In *Sellers by Sellers v. School Bd., 141 F.3d 524* (4th Cir. 1998), cert. denied, 525 U.S. 871 (1998), also discussed in Chapter 3, the Fourth Circuit Court of Appeals held that the RA, unlike the IDEA, does not require outreach and identification of children with disabilities.

These cases view the RA/ADA as imposing a general duty of nondiscrimination and privacy on private and public schools subject to their requirements, duties that are vastly different from those created by the IDEA.

7.   The Problem of Comorbidity (Co-occurring Disorders)

Often a child may have co-occurring disabilities and other factors that adversely affect the child's learning and behavior. In some cases, among the several impairments, only some may be recognized as potential disabilities under the IDEA definition. In *Capistrano Unified School District v. Wartenberg by & Through Wartenberg* (9th Cir. 1995), a sixteen-year-old boy had a specific learning disability, conduct disorder, and ADHD. A hearing officer found that the ADHD was the primary cause of his learning disability. The hearing officer then held that the child's IEP was insufficient under the IDEA and awarded the student's parents private school tuition. The court agreed with the hearing officer's finding and found that the student was assigned to too many teachers, was given insufficient structure, and was not provided critical feedback and clear directions. In sustaining the hearing officer's decision, the court addressed the question of multiple causation:

> The Secretary of Education has resolved the problem of mixed causation. That is where the child's learning problems are caused partly by covered learning disabilities, and partly by non-covered matters such as willful bad behavior or non-"serious" "emotional disturbance." The child falls into the "specific learning disability" category unless the learning problems are "primarily the result" of the non-covered causes. 34 C.F.R. §300.7(b)(10). Because of this administrative decision, commingled causes such as in Jeremy's case are covered, where the hearing officer and district court properly determine on a preponderance of the evidence that the learning disabilities are not "primarily" the result of a non-covered cause.

School districts sometimes take the position that behavioral disorders are nothing more than "bad behavior" and therefore not a disability at all. In *Springer v. The Fairfax County School Board* (4th Cir. 1998), the parents sought to recover the costs of placing their adolescent child, Edward, in a residential school, on the grounds that he had a serious emotional disturbance as defined in the IDEA. Edward had been determined to have a conduct disorder and a dysthymic disorder (moderate depression), and he had developed significant behavioral problems during the eleventh grade, resulting in criminal charges for which he was placed on probation until age eighteen. The Court of Appeals dismissed the parents' claims and ruled that conduct disorder is a form of social maladjustment, and is not a disability covered by the IDEA. The court said:

> Courts and special education authorities have routinely declined, however, to equate conduct disorders or social maladjustment with serious emotional disturbance. . . . Adolescence is, almost by definition, a time of social maladjustment for many people. Thus a "bad conduct" definition of serious emotional disturbance might include almost as many people in special education as it excluded. Any definition that

equated simple bad behavior with serious emotional disturbance would exponentially enlarge the burden IDEA places on state and local education authorities.

In *Muller v. The East Islip Union Free School District* (2d Cir. 1998), the Second Circuit reached the opposite result.

The courts have generally been unsympathetic to school district claims that a failure to learn is simply the result of bad behavior or bad parenting rather than a disability. In *Mrs. B. v. Milford Board of Education* (2d Cir. 1997), the court held that the parents of a seventeen-year-old girl, eligible for special education services under the IDEA due to a specific learning disability, were entitled to recover the costs of a residential placement. The residential placement was intended to address both the learning disability and the accompanying "serious social and emotional problems that greatly impair her ability to learn." The problems addressed by the residential placement "include hyperactivity, an inability to interact with others, and lack of self-confidence." The District Court ruled for the parents, holding that the girl's educational and noneducational problems "are sufficiently intertwined such that her educational problems cannot be separated" from the noneducational ones. The court ruled further that the residential placement was necessary for her educational progress. The Second Circuit affirmed the District Court's actions.

D. Summary

Under the IDEA, a student with a disability that requires special education and related services has the right to a free appropriate public education. The IDEA provides funds for the purpose of providing equal access to education, and focuses on improving educational results for children with disabilities. School districts are required to locate, identify, and evaluate all children suspected of having a disability. Either the parent or the school district may initiate a request for an initial evaluation.

5 IDEA: FAPE

A. In General

The purpose of the IDEA is "to ensure that all children with disabilities have available to them a free appropriate public education that emphasizes special education and related services designed to meet their unique needs and prepare them for further education, employment, and independent living." 20 U.S.C. §1400(d)(1)(A)

Special education is defined as "specially designed instruction, at no cost to the parents, to meet the unique needs of a child with a disability." 20 U.S.C. §1401(29) Related services in general are "transportation, and such developmental, corrective, and other supportive services . . . designed to enable a child with a disability to receive a free appropriate public education as described in the individualized education program of the child." 20 U.S.C. §1401(26). The central purpose of the related services is to "enable a child with a disability to receive a free appropriate public education as described in the individualized education program of the child," and "to assist a child with a disability to benefit from special education." 20 U.S.C. §1401(26)

The IDEA provides in further detail that the term "related services" includes "supportive services" such as "speech-language pathology and audiology services, interpreting services, psychological services, physical and occupational therapy, recreation, including therapeutic recreation, social work services, [and] school nurse services." "Counseling services, including rehabilitation counseling, orientation and mobility services, and medical services," are also included except that "such medical services shall be for diagnostic and evaluation purposes," and "early identification and assessment of disabling conditions in children." School nurse services and interpreting services were added in the 2004 reauthorization. The 2006 regulations include "school health services" and "school nurse services," the latter defined as health services that must be provided by a qualified school nurse and the former as services that can be provided either by a qualified school nurse or other qualified person. Surgically implanted medical devices or their replacements are not considered related services.

In regard to related services required by a child other than those listed in the definition, the Department of Education has always and continues to interpret the list of services as nonexhaustive. In other words, if the child's IEP team determines that another service, for example, music or art therapy, will be necessary for the child to benefit from special education, then that service must be provided. In short, the services listed are instructive examples, rather than a complete list of all services that may be required.

It is also important to note that a child who required only related services and not "special education," that is, specialized instruction, would not be eligible for services under the IDEA. The child must first qualify for special education before receiving related services. Children who are not eligible for related services under the IDEA may be eligible for those services under Section 504 of the RA.

The reauthorized IDEA, like prior case law, does not require school districts to provide medical services except for diagnostic and evaluation purposes. However, psychiatric and other counseling services have been, and are now considered, related services where they are necessary to enable the student to complete the program described in the IEP. *Mark R. v. Board of Education* (N.D. Ill. 1982), aff'd, 705 F.2d 462 (7th Cir. 1983). Where psychiatric and other counseling services are not necessary to the implementation of the IEP, they are not required. *Papacoda v. State* (D. Conn. 1981)

In *Irving Independent School District v. Tatro*, 468 U.S. 883 (1984), the Supreme Court held that the IDEA required the state to provide catheterization several times daily to a student suffering from spina bifida in order that the student could be placed in and benefit from a special education class in accordance with the IEP. The U.S. Supreme Court since has reaffirmed its holding in *Tatro*. In *Cedar Rapids Community School District v. Garret F.*, 526 U.S. 66 (1999), the court considered the case of Garret F., a student whose spinal column was severed in a motorcycle accident when he was four years old. The student is "ventilator dependent, and therefore requires a responsible individual nearby to attend to certain physical needs while he is in school," found the court. The services described in these cases are "related services" under the IDEA because they are necessary for the child to participate in and benefit from the educational program. The justices ruled that, under "our opinion" in *Tatro*, the courts must undertake "a two-step analysis of the 'related services' definition in §1401(a)(17) [now subparagraph (26)]—asking first, whether the requested services are included within the phrase 'supportive services'; and second, whether the services are excluded as 'medical services.'"

The Supreme Court ruled that excluded medical services are services provided by a licensed physician. The court embraced what it termed a "bright line" test in ruling that medical services are only "the services of a physician" and those which "can be provided in the school setting by a nurse or qualified layperson are not." The court observed that "whatever its imperfections, a rule that limits the medical services exemption to physician services is unquestionably a reasonable and generally workable interpretation of the statute."

Finally, the court made plain its view that the cost of a related service, even when high, is not a proper legal basis for refusing to provide it.

> The District may have legitimate financial concerns, but our role in this dispute is to interpret existing law . . . Given that §1401(a)(17) does not employ cost in its definition of "related services" or excluded "medical services," accepting the District's cost-based standard as the sole test for determining the scope of the provision would require us to engage in judicial lawmaking without any guidance from Congress.

The court noted that its "cost is no object" ruling would "create some tension with the purposes of the IDEA." While recognizing that the IDEA "may not require public schools to maximize the potential of disabled students commensurate with the opportunities provided to other children," Congress did intend "to open the door of public education" to all qualified children and "require[d] participating States to educate handicapped children with nonhandicapped children whenever possible." (Citations omitted.)

> This case is about whether meaningful access to the public schools will be assured, not the level of education that a school must finance once access is attained. It is undisputed that the services at issue must be provided if Garret is to remain in school. Under the statute, our precedent, and the purposes of the IDEA, the District must fund such "related services" in order to help guarantee that students like Garret are integrated into the public schools.

Congress, according to the court, intended that cost is no object when incurred to provide access to education, but is a key consideration when deciding the quality of education accessed.

The educational benefit must be meaningful. In *Greenbush School Committee v. Mr. and Mrs. K., Civ.* (D. Me. 1996), the court upheld a hearing officer's determination that James, a student covered by the IDEA, should be placed at a different school due to a lack of educational benefit at the original school. The court found that the student had been subjected to serious and ongoing harassment, including an incident in which "the principal and a teacher carried him out of a classroom, threw him around, and held him down on the floor." In another incident, "he was forced to clean off a urinal after another child had used it, a task which obviously was not normally assigned to students." The parents believed that the "administration, teachers, students, and even James' bus driver were harassing their son to an extent that the environment at [the school] could not provide James with an adequate education." These incidents produced "hostility" in the student's parents and instilled in James "a gripping fear that accompanies him throughout his day at Dunn." Similarly, in *Ridgewood Board of Education v. N.E. for M.E.* (3rd Cir. 1999), the court held that an IEP must provide "significant learning" and "meaningful benefit," not merely "more than a trivial educational benefit."

B. Definition of FAPE

1. Statutory Language

The IDEA defines a "free appropriate public education," as follows:

> (9) FREE APPROPRIATE PUBLIC EDUCATION.— The term "free appropriate public education" means special education and related services that—
>   (A) have been provided at public expense, under public supervision and direction, and without charge;
>   (B) meet the standards of the State educational agency;

(C) include an appropriate preschool, elementary school, or secondary school education in the State involved; and

(D) are provided in conformity with the individualized education program required under section 614(d). (20 U.S.C. §1401 (9)

The IDEA provides that, as a condition of funding, the state must submit "a plan that provides assurances . . . that the State has in effect policies and procedures to ensure that the State meets a series of conditions, including:

A free appropriate public education is available to all children with disabilities residing in the State between the ages of 3 and 21, inclusive, including children with disabilities who have been suspended or expelled from school. 20 U.S.C. §1412(a)(1)(A)

The relationship of FAPE to students who have violated school disciplinary codes is addressed in the next chapter.

The "Individualized Education Program" or IEP is the centerpiece of the IDEA. The IDEA is based on providing to eligible students with disabilities individualized services designed to meet their unique educational and functional needs. The IEP delineates the services and the means by which those services are delivered. The IEP is a detailed description of the exact steps that must be undertaken by the school district in order to provide a "free appropriate public education" to a child with a disability.

2. Board of Education v. Rowley

The U.S. Supreme Court issued an authoritative definition of a "free appropriate public education" in the landmark case, *Board of Educ. of Hendrick Hudson Sch. Dist. v. Rowley*, 458 U.S. 176 (1982). This definition has been and continues to be the legal standard upon which special education cases are most often decided. The court concluded that the IDEA does not require that a student receive educational and related services calculated to maximize his or her potential, but only those "reasonably calculated to enable the child to receive educational benefits." "Thus," said the Court, "the intent of the Act was more to open the door of public education to handicapped children on appropriate terms than to guarantee any particular level of education once inside." The Rowley standard was reaffirmed by the Supreme Court in *Cedar Rapids Community School District v. Garret F.*, 526 U.S. 66 (1999).

3. Failure to Furnish FAPE

Basic Rule

The IDEA's requirement that each eligible child must receive a "free appropriate public education" is mandatory. A failure or refusal to furnish the required education may render the school district liable for the costs of placing that child in a private school. *Florence County School District Four v. Carter*, 510 U.S. 7 (1993)

If the school district fails to provide a required service, the school district may be liable for the cost of obtaining that service. The case of *Bucks County Department of Mental Health/Retardation v. Pennsylvania* (3d Cir. 2004) posed a unique issue. Barbara de Mora's daughter, I.D., suffered from "pervasive developmental delay (PDD), cerebral palsy, and deafness" and was eligible for early intervention services under Part C of IDEA (services for infants and toddlers with disabilities, aged birth to three). The Office of Mental Retardation of the Pennsylvania Department of Welfare administered the Pennsylvania Part C Early Intervention Program, and Bucks County was the local agency responsible for coordinating services for I.D. An individualized family service plan (IFSP; Part C document equivalent to an IEP) was developed, but de Mora disagreed with the services listed because I.D. did not benefit sufficiently from them. She requested additional hours of therapy and requested specifically that the Lovaas method, used with children with PDD, be provided. She also asked Bucks County to hire Patricia Laudon, a Lovaas-trained therapist, to provide the service. Bucks County refused, and de Mora hired Ms. Laudon herself. When Ms. Laudon was unable to provide all the hours necessary, Ms. Laudon "trained de Mora so that de Mora would be able to provide the Lovaas therapy to I.D. Laudon held one-on-one workshops where de Mora would act as the Lovaas therapist as Laudon coached her. De Mora read and learned discrete trial training teaching guidelines and other books on the Lovaas methodology."

Barbara de Mora sought $3,520 for the eighty-eight hours Ms. Laudon spent training I.D., and $6,842 for the 311 hours de Mora spent training I.D. during the same time period.

The court held that Bucks County was liable to de Mora for the costs of retaining Ms. Laudon for eighty-eight hours and for the 311 hours she spent training I.D. Based on 20 U.S.C. §1439(a)(1), the decision stated that a court "shall grant such relief as the court determines is appropriate." The award of both sums was appropriate because the county's Individualized Family Service Plan was deficient and services delivered by the private therapist and I.D.'s mother were appropriate, even if de Mora technically lacked the credentials of a therapist and was therefore not a "qualified" provider. See *Florence County School District Four v. Carter* 510 U.S. 7 (1993).

Moreover, "equitable considerations" dictated that de Mora be compensated for both.

> There is, however, ample evidence in the record to support the conclusion that de Mora stepped into the shoes of a therapist, ultimately acting over and above what is expected of parents under IDEA.

The case is unusual in that the parent was awarded compensation for services she had delivered herself. Ordinarily parents are not compensated. In this case, the lack of a sufficient number of Lovaas-trained therapists was an important factor.

The topic of reimbursement for private placement is addressed at length in Section F of this chapter. However, just *which* state agency must pay the bills for a denial of FAPE has sometimes proved troublesome.

Compensatory Education
Ideally, the administrative process for creating an IEP, discussed later in this chapter, will result in the appropriate delivery of FAPE. However, if the IEP is not appropriate, there may be a gap between when the need for an IEP is determined and

the development and implementation of a proper IEP. In *School Committee of Burlington v. Department of Education,* 471 U.S. 359 (1985), the U.S. Supreme Court concluded that the IDEA authorizes "reimbursement" for the costs of providing an appropriate education when the school district violates the IDEA. The court said:

> As this case so vividly demonstrates, however, the review process is ponderous. A final judicial decision on the merits of an IEP will in most instances come a year or more after the school term covered by that IEP has passed. In the meantime, the parents who disagree with the proposed IEP are faced with a choice: go along with the IEP to the detriment of their child if it turns out to be inappropriate or pay for what they consider to be the appropriate placement.

Courts also have determined that compensatory education to correct past failures to provide FAPE is a remedy. *M. C. v. Central Regional School District* (3d Cir. 1996); *Reid v. District of Columbia* (D.D.C. 2004). In *Reid,* the court affirmed a hearing officer's decision to provide a student with learning disabilities with over 800 hours of compensatory education, because the student had been denied an appropriate education. The school district had failed to meet its child find responsibilities and, therefore, had failed to provide special education services to the student during a particular time period.

Personal Liability

In cases of willful noncompliance by school officials, the violation can even serve as the basis for personal liability. In *Doe v. Withers* (W.Va. Cir. Ct. 1993), the IEP of a ninth-grade student with a specific learning disability required that the student be given oral testing. All teachers except Withers, his American history teacher, complied with the IEP requirements. Withers repeatedly and deliberately refused to administer oral tests. Instead, the teacher required the student to take a written test on the first semester history materials, which the student failed. A second teacher administered a second semester oral American history test, which the student passed. The student and his family sued under federal civil rights laws for injunctive relief with respect to his first semester grade and for damages. The court issued an injunction requiring that the first semester American history test be administered orally, but declined to require that the school award the student a passing grade for the first semester simply because the test had initially been given in violation of the IEP. In addition, the jury awarded the student and his family $5,000 in compensatory damages and $10,000 in punitive damages against the history teacher personally.

The actions of school officials may deprive students of constitutional rights and give rise to liability under 42 U.S.C. §1983, one of the Reconstruction Civil Rights statutes discussed in Chapter 3. *Pamela McCormick ex rel. Eron McCormick v. Waukegan School District* (7th Cir. 2004) is a clear illustration.

Eron was an adolescent suffering from a rare form of muscular dystrophy known as McArdle's disease which severely constrained his physical capabilities. He was given an IEP, which provided that his participation in physical education class would be limited. His doctors "advised Eron to be cautious when exercising and to stop anytime he was winded or felt muscle pain. The doctors suggested non-strenuous activities like walking, throwing lightweight objects, and social games." His limitations were explained to Jan Neterer, the physical education instructor who appeared to understand them.

Nonetheless, during one class, Ms. Neterer "instructed Eron to run laps and perform push-ups." Thinking to motivate him, she chose to "threaten Eron with failure and berate him until he consented to the exercises." She said "that if he could not complete the tasks she assigned, he would receive a failing grade in physical education and would have to repeat the ninth grade." Eron protested, stating that his "muscles were cramping and hurting during the exercise," and told the teacher the he was allowed by his IEP to stop when he was in pain. The teacher persisted, however, "ignoring the IEP." Eron completed the exercises, but with great difficulty. The next day, he was taken to the emergency room; he continued to experience increased muscle weakness and pain and suffered permanent kidney damage. "This damage may well have hastened the need for a kidney dialysis regimen and has increased the possibility of other kidney complications."

Not surprisingly, Eron's parents sued under 42 U.S.C. §1983, alleging that the school district and the teacher, acting under color of state law, that is, in their official capacities, violated his equal protection rights, right to privacy, and right to be free of cruel and unusual punishment. The suit also alleged several state law counts, including the intentional infliction of emotional distress. The defendants moved to dismiss on the grounds that the parents had failed to exhaust the administrative remedies provided by IDEA. The court held that there was no duty to exhaust administrative remedies because Eron's suit sought recovery for "his alleged injuries, which are non-educational in nature." They resulted from the "arguably outrageous actions of Neterer." Eron was not seeking a change in his IEP, but only that the school district comply with its terms. See also *Armijo v. Wagon Mound Pub. Sch.* (10th Cir. 1998), and *Roe v. Nevada* (D. Nev. 2004). To prevail in a case like this one, the courts have determined that the alleged conduct must be intentional or reckless conduct that is "so outrageous in character, and so extreme in degree as to go beyond all possible bounds of decency, and to be regarded as atrocious, and utterly intolerable in a civilized society." *Brennan v. Mercedes Benz USA, Universal Technical Institute* (5th Cir. 2004)

C.   The Individualized Educational Program (IEP)

1.   The IEP Team

The IDEA does not require any particular method for delivering special education and related services. Rather, it provides a procedure for the development of an IEP, under which all factors relevant to the education of the child with a disability should be considered. Specifically, the law requires the participation of a team of individuals, including the parents, the child where appropriate, at least one regular education teacher of the child if inclusion is an option, at least one special educator, and a "representative of the local educational agency who . . . is qualified to provide, or supervise the provision of, specially designed instruction to meet the unique needs of children with disabilities," and is both "knowledgeable about the general education curriculum" as well as "the availability of resources of the local educational agency." Finally, and perhaps most important, the IEP team must include "an individual who can interpret the instructional implications of evaluation results."

In order to ensure that *all* educational issues are considered, the U.S. Department of Education expects that IEP teams will not resolve the issues before it by a simple vote but will attempt to reach *consensus*. The department has stated:

> The IEP team should work toward consensus, but the public agency has ultimate responsibility to ensure that the IEP includes the services that the child needs in order to receive FAPE. It is not appropriate to make IEP decisions based upon a majority "vote." If the team cannot reach consensus, the public agency must provide the parents with prior written notice of the agency's proposals or refusals, or both, regarding the child's educational program, and the parents have the right to seek resolution of any disagreements by initiating an impartial due process hearing. Analysis of Comments and Changes, IDEA Regulations (1999)

It should go without saying that the IEP meeting must provide a serious consideration of the child's educational needs and not a one-size-fits-all package. *Deal v. Hamilton County Board of Education* (6th Cir. 2004) involved Zachary, a young student with autism whose parents wanted the school to use an applied behavioral analysis (ABA) program, a technique that relies on extremely structured teaching coupled with extensive data collection and analysis. Unfortunately, the school already had invested considerable money in an alternative, and no doubt less expensive, program. The school decided in advance of the IEP meeting that it would offer only the alternative, and cheaper, TEACCH (Treatment and Education of Autistic and Related Communication-Handicapped Children) program and wrote that program into the IEP over the parents' objection. "The evidence revealed that the school system and its representatives had pre-decided not to offer Zachary intensive ABA services regardless of any evidence concerning Zachary's individual needs and the effectiveness of his private program. This predetermination amounted to a procedural violation of the IDEA. Because it effectively deprived Zachary's parents of a meaningful participation in the IEP process, the predetermination caused substantive harm and therefore deprived Zachary of a FAPE."

The court ruled for the parents, saying:

> The facts of this case strongly suggest that the School System had an unofficial policy of refusing to provide one-on-one ABA programs and that School System personnel thus did not have open minds and were not willing to consider the provision of such a program. This conclusion is bolstered by evidence that the School System steadfastly refused even to discuss the possibility of providing an ABA program, even in the face of impressive results.

See also *Spielberg v. Henrico County Public Schools* (4th Cir. 1988), cert. denied, and *Henrico County Public Schools v. Spielberg*, 489 U.S. 1016 (1989).

The IEP meeting does not have to be highly formal. In *Burilovich ex rel. Burilovich v. Board of Education* (6th Cir. 2000), the court found that the parents did not show they were prevented from participating in the development of their child's education program because they attended several meetings, expressed their views clearly and vocally there, participated in the original creation of the program, and remained in contact with the school district through letters and phone conversations. The court concluded, "Plaintiffs have cited no support for their implicit assertion that schools may never discuss a child's IEP, goals, objectives, or educational methodology out of the presence of the parents. For these reasons, plaintiffs have failed to demonstrate that they were denied participation in the [program development] process." The U.S. Supreme Court refused to review the Sixth Circuit's decision. *Burilovich v. Board of Educ.,* 531 U.S. 957 (2000)

Failure to include a general education teacher on the IEP team will not necessarily nullify the IEP if placement in the general education classroom is not being considered. Cf. *Deal v. Hamilton County Board of Education* (6th Cir. 2004), and *Johnson ex. rel. Johnson v. Olathe District School* (D. Kan. 2003). However, where mainstreaming is an option, a regular education teacher should most often be included. *Deal v. Hamilton County Board of Education* (6th Cir. 2004)

2. Planning for the IEP Meeting

The IEP must be developed and finalized during the IEP team meeting and agreed to by the parent before services are provided. Parents' written consent is required before provision of services. The SEA is ultimately responsible for the development of the IEP. However, the IEP may be developed initially by any agency responsible for the education of the child. In most instances, the local school district would be responsible.

The IEP meeting is the single most important event in the delivery of special education and related services. Many court cases are won or lost because of the record developed at the IEP meeting. It is essential that parents prepare for this meeting.

The following steps are recommended for parents:

- Prepare. Decide, with the help of professionals, which special education and related services are required.
- Document your case. Be prepared to educate the school on the particular disability.
- Share your documents with the staff. Obtain copies of all reports that may be used.
- Don't go alone. Bring an attorney, advocate, and/or independent evaluators.
- Parents cannot be required to use their insurance if there is any adverse impact on benefits or future insurability.
- Network in advance of the IEP meeting to ensure that you understand as fully as possible the school's concerns.

The IEP provisions include a number of "special factors" that the team must consider. For children whose behavior impedes their learning, the team must consider using positive behavioral interventions and supports. In the case of children with limited English proficiency, their language needs as related to their IEP goals must be discussed. Braille instruction must be provided, unless the team determines it is not necessary, for children who are visually impaired or blind. Communication needs of deaf and hearing impaired students must also be considered, and assistive technology services and devices must be considered for every child. 20 U.S.C. 1414 § (d)(3)(B). Regarding participation of attorneys at IEP meetings, while an attorney's presence may be helpful, attorneys' "fees may not be awarded relating to any meeting of the IEP Team unless such meeting is convened as a result of an administrative proceeding or judicial action." Many parents elect to use the services of a nonattorney lay advocate. School districts have no obligation to pay for these services. *Connors v. Mills* (N.D.N.Y. 1998); *Arons v. New Jersey State Board of Education* (3d Cir. 1988). In fact, in at least one state, lay advocacy has been ruled an unauthorized practice of law. See *In re Arons* (Del. 2000), cert. denied; *Arons v. Office of Disciplinary Counsel*, 532 U.S. 1065 (2001).

The IDEA makes it clear that, in general, team members are expected to attend the IEP meeting. Team members may be excused if the "member's area of the curriculum or related services is not being modified or discussed in the meeting." If the team member's curriculum area or related service will be discussed, that member may be excused if the parent and the LEA agree to the excusal and the parent gives written consent. The excused member must also submit, in writing to the parent and the IEP Team, "input into the development of the IEP prior to the meeting."

3.   The IEP Document

The IDEA requires that at "the beginning of each school year, each local educational agency, State educational agency, or other State agency, as the case may be, shall have in effect, for each child with a disability in the agency's jurisdiction, an individualized education program." The IEP document is many things. It is (1) a commitment of resources, (2) a management tool to ensure that a FAPE is being provided, (3) a compliance monitoring document, and (4) an evaluation tool. However, school officials may not be held accountable for failing to meet IEP goals. On the other hand, it is expected that every reasonable effort will be made to help the child meet the those goals.

An IEP must include:

- "A statement of the child's present levels of academic achievement and functional performance."
- "A statement of measurable annual goals, including academic and functional goals, designed" to meet the child's needs. The purpose is "to enable the child to be involved in and make progress in the general education curriculum."
- "A statement of the special education and related services and supplementary aids and services . . . to be provided to the child . . . and a statement of the program modifications or supports for school personnel that will be provided for the child . . . to advance appropriately toward attaining the annual goals," and "to be involved in and make progress in the general education curriculum," and "to be educated and participate with other children with disabilities and nondisabled children."

- "A statement of any individual appropriate accommodations that are necessary to measure the academic achievement and functional performance of the child on State and districtwide assessments."
- "If the IEP Team determines that the child shall take an alternate assessment on a particular State or districtwide assessment of student achievement, a statement of why . . . the child cannot participate in the regular assessment; and why the particular alternate assessment selected is appropriate for the child."
- "An explanation of the extent, if any, to which the child will not participate with nondisabled children in the regular class."
- "The projected date for the beginning of the services . . . and the anticipated frequency, location, and duration of those services."
- Appropriate measurable postsecondary goals based upon age appropriate transition assessments related to training, education, employment, and, where appropriate, independent living skills and the transition services (including courses of study) needed to assist the child in reaching those goals.
- A statement describing the appropriate measurement and evaluation procedures for determining, at least annually, whether the annual goals are being met.
- "A description of how the child's progress toward meeting the annual goals . . . will be measured and when periodic reports on the progress the child is making toward meeting the annual goals (such as through the use of quarterly or other periodic reports, concurrent with the issuance of report cards) will be provided."

The regulations make clear that no additional information needs to be included in a child's IEP beyond what is explicitly required in this section of the law. This provision addresses the fact that states may, and in many instances have, added requirements beyond what is included in the federal law. The 2006 regulations require that a state inform the U.S. secretary of education and the local school districts in that state of any state regulation or policy that exceeds the federal requirements. 34 C.F.R. §300.199(a)(2)

An IEP can be a blessing or a curse. It is a document that contains concrete requirements. Generally, if it's not in the IEP, it is not required! A cautionary tale is the case of *Sherman v. Mamaroneck Union Free School District* (2nd Cir. 2003). In that case an IEP for a high school junior allowed him the use of a scientific/graphing calculator with a cable link to a computer but did not specify the model number. The student sought to use a Texas Instrument Model 92 that allowed him to check his answers and in some cases actually provided them. The school insisted he use a model 82 which required various steps of analysis to get the right answer. The parents sued to compel the use of the answer-providing calculator. The record before the court showed that the student was capable of doing junior year math with the model 82 and that his math failures were the result of insufficient effort. While failing grades may be evidence of a lack of educational benefit, they are not necessarily the only or critical factor, ruled the court.

Nevertheless, failing grades are not dispositive. The IDEA does not require school districts to pass a student claiming a disability when the student is able, with less than the assistive aids requested, to succeed but nonetheless fails. If a school district simply provided the assistive devices required, even if unneeded, and awarded passing grades, it would in fact deny the appropriate educational benefits the IDEA requires.

4.   Some IEP Defects Deny a FAPE

An IEP may fail to offer FAPE when the school has not "complied with the procedures set forth in the Act," or has not prepared an "individualized educational program" which is "reasonably calculated to enable the child to receive educational benefits." *Board of Education v. Rowley*, 458 U.S. 176 (1982)

The courts have found that the following defects denied a student a FAPE:

- An IEP for a student with behavioral problems that was not based on a functional behavioral assessment and did not include a behavior intervention plan denied FAPE. *Larson v. Independent School District No. 361* (D. Minn. 2004)
- Education that violated a consent decree containing a plan for FAPE for special education students denied FAPE. *Emma C. v. Eastin* (N.D. Cal. 2001)
- A failure and refusal to take steps to curtail bullying denied FAPE. *Shore Regional High School Board of Education v. P.S.* (3d Cir. 2004)

5.   Some IEP Defects Do Not Deny a FAPE

However, not every defect in an IEP amounts to a denial of FAPE. Courts have found that the following circumstances do *not* deny FAPE:

- An IEP that contained "no statement of transition services in the IEP" did not deprive a student of FAPE where there was transition language and provision for transition services. *Urban v. Jefferson County School District R-1* (10th Cir. 1996)
- Where an IEP for ninth grade focused on socialization and organizational goals but omitted academic goals and benchmarks, the IEP did not deny FAPE. The student had received passing grades. *Kings Local School District v. Zelazny* (6th Cir. 2003)
- The exclusion of the parents from one IEP meeting was not a fatal procedural flaw because parents were involved in all other meaningful steps. *Kings Local School District v. Zelazny* (6th Cir. 2003)
- Procedural violations do not deny FAPE and do not justify a private school placement at public expense. *County School Board of Henrico County v. Palkovics* (E.D. Va. 2003); *DiBuo v. Board of Education* (4th Cir. 2002)
- An IEP that did not train and teach the student to remediate his written language disability was nonetheless proper because it was reasonably calculated to enable him to progress from grade to grade. *D.B. v. Craven County Board of Education* (4th. Cir. 2000)
- FAPE does not require that a school district place a child in his neighborhood school to assist in social development. *White v. Ascension Parish School Board* (5th Cir. 2003)
- A school district need not pay for out of district transportation, which is unrelated to the child's educational needs. *Fick v. Sioux Falls 49-5* (8th Cir. 2003)

- The use of reasonable restraints on a student with brain lesions and a long history of psychiatric illness who began kicking others, hitting the school staff with pencils, and banging his head against the wall did not deny the student FAPE. *CJN v. Minnesota. Minneapolis Public Schools, Special School District No. 1* (8th Cir. 2003)
- Post graduation services are generally not a part of a FAPE. Generally graduation from high school ends the school district's IDEA obligations. In *T.S. v. Independent School District No. 54, Stroud, Oklahoma* (10th Cir. 2001), the court outlined the rules. "If a student has graduated from high school and does not contest his graduation, the case is moot. . . . Once a student has graduated, he is no longer entitled to a FAPE; thus any claim that a FAPE was deficient becomes moot upon a valid graduation. . . . This rule applies, of course, only where a student does not contest his graduation, and where he is seeking only prospective rather than compensatory relief."

6. The 2004 IDEA

Prior to the 2004 IDEA amendments, there was little clear-cut statutory guidance for due process hearing officers on how to decide when a FAPE had been denied. In fact, a large number of special education cases were decided on procedural, rather than substantive, grounds. Current law and regulations clarify that, for the most part, due process complaints must be decided on substantive grounds. This provision essentially codifies the case law discussed earlier.

> (E) Decision of Hearing Officer.
> (i) In General.— Subject to clause (ii), a decision made by a hearing officer shall be made on substantive grounds based on a determination of whether the child received a free appropriate public education.
> (ii) Procedural Issues.— In matters alleging a procedural violation, a hearing officer may find that a child did not receive a free appropriate public education only if the procedural inadequacies—
> (I) impeded the child's right to a free appropriate public education;
> (II) significantly impeded the parents' opportunity to participate in the decisionmaking process regarding the provision of a free appropriate public education to the parents' child; or
> (III) caused a deprivation of educational benefits.
> (iii) Rule of Construction—Nothing in this subparagraph shall be construed to preclude a hearing officer from ordering a local educational agency to comply with procedural requirements under this section. 20 U.S.C. §1415(f)(3)(E)

D. Placement

A public school system is not required to support a private school placement, simply because the parents assert that the private school is superior to the public program offered. *Hessler v. State Board of Education* (4th Cir. 1983). A private program may be required, however, if there is no public school equivalent. *Yaris v. Special*

School District of St. Louis County (E.D. Mo. 1983, aff'd, 728 F.2d 1055 (8th Cir. 1984). The statute requires that the child remain in his or her current educational placement pending the outcome of any legal proceedings. This is commonly known as the "stay-put" provision. That is an excellent protection where the present placement is desirable. However, where the present placement is undesirable, the parents may want to change it immediately.

If parents move the child to a private school without first obtaining the school's agreement to pay for it or in advance of a hearing where private school placement is at issue, the school district may not be liable for these costs.

Sometimes a unilateral placement by the parents will be permitted at public expense. These cases generally turn on the fact that the private program provides educational benefit that cannot be afforded the child in the public school. In *Board of Education of Harford County v. Bauer* (D.MD 2000), the court held that the parents of a student with ADHD were entitled to reimbursement for private school tuition where the public school did not provide one-on-one instructional assistance and placement in smaller classes with fewer distractions. In contrast, the private school provided the individualized and intensive learning environment necessary for him to progress academically and socially. See also *Wolfe v. Taconic-Hills Central School District* (N.D.N.Y. 2001).

In *Spilsbury v. District of Columbia* (D.D.C. 2004), the court held that the District of Columbia had to reimburse five special education students for private school under the IDEA stay-put provision. The District had sought to cease funding during a school year and to seek the return of previous funding for that year. The court pointed out that the stay-put provision is designed to allow the parents the opportunity to challenge a proposed change in placement in advance of the change taking place.

E.   Related Services

"Related services" include all "supportive services" except "medical services." *Cedar Rapids Community School District v. Garret F.*, 526 U.S. 66 (1999)

The administration of medication has posed problems. School districts may not require that a child take certain medications to improve behavior. In fact, IDEA 2004 prohibits mandatory medication as a condition of school attendance. 20 U.S.C. §1412(a)(25) provides:

> (25) Prohibition on Mandatory Medication—
>
>   (A) In General.—The State educational agency shall prohibit State and local educational agency personnel from requiring a child to obtain a prescription for a substance covered by the Controlled Substances Act (21 U.S.C. 801 et seq.) as a condition of attending school, receiving an evaluation under subsection (a) or (c) of section 614, or receiving services under this title.
>
>   (B) Rule of Construction—Nothing in subparagraph (A) shall be construed to create a Federal prohibition against teachers and other school personnel consulting or sharing classroom-based observations with parents or guardians regarding a student's academic and functional performance, or behavior in the classroom or school, or regarding the need for evaluation for special education or related services.

This provision, which was quite controversial, was adopted because Congress received anecdotal reports of schools requiring that children, especially those with ADHD, take methylphenidate (Ritalin) in order to calm their behaviors. The prohibition applies only to "Controlled Substances," and not to other medicines a child might need during school hours, for example, for conditions such as asthma or diabetes. The IDEA makes it clear that there is no "Federal prohibition against teachers and other school personnel consulting or sharing classroom-based observations with parents or guardians regarding a student's academic and functional performance, or behavior in the classroom or school, or regarding the need for evaluation for special education or related services."

Transportation is also listed as a related service in the IDEA. However, as with all related services, if the service is not necessary to enable the student to benefit from special education, the school district is not required to provide it. See *Donald B. v. Board of School Commissioners of Mobile County, Alabama* (11th Cir. 1997).

F. Inclusion

1. The IDEA and Least Restrictive Environment

The IDEA requires that all children with disabilities be educated in the least restrictive environment (LRE) appropriate to meet their individual needs. The reauthorized IDEA defines the least restrictive environment as follows:

> To the maximum extent appropriate, children with disabilities, including children in public or private institutions or other care facilities, are educated with children who are not disabled, and special classes, separate schooling, or other removal of children with disabilities from the regular educational environment occurs only when the nature or severity of the disability of a child is such that education in regular classes with the use of supplementary aids and services cannot be achieved satisfactorily. 20 U.S.C. §1412(a)(5)(A)

The current language reflects a long held preference, both in the statutes and case law, for integration or inclusion of children with disabilities in the general education classroom.

2. Cases—Inclusion

The Supreme Court's ruling in *Board of Education v. Rowley*, 458 U.S. 176 (1982) has been cited to require the use of mainstreaming. (See Section B of this chapter.)

In deciding whether the LRE has been considered, the courts generally examine: (1) the academic benefits of mainstreaming with aids, (2) the nonacademic benefits of mainstreaming, (3) the negative effects on teachers and students of mainstreaming, and (4) the cost of mainstreaming.

In *James C. v. Corpus Christi Independent School District* (SEA TX 2002), the Texas Education Agency held that a placement in the school's self-contained Autism Unit (AU) was the least restrictive environment and did not deprive James C. of a FAPE.

James was a "student with Autism with Asperger's Disorder, Speech Impairment, and Other Health Impairment with Attention Deficit Hyperactivity Disorder." The parents requested that James be returned to the regular classroom, a solution which "even with the assistance of his one-on-one aide—would require a regular education teacher to devote most or all of the classroom time to meeting James' needs."

The agency found that "The party challenging the appropriateness of the school district's individualized education plan ('IEP') bears the burden to demonstrate the inappropriateness of the program offered by the school district." The elements to be proven were:

> To analyze whether a child is receiving a free appropriate public education ("FAPE"), the Fifth Circuit identified four factors as an indication of whether a child's IEP is reasonable calculated to provide a meaningful benefit under IDEA: 1) whether there is an individualized program based on the student's assessment and performance; 2) whether the individualized program is administered in the least restrictive environment; 3) whether the services are provided in a coordinated and collaborative manner by the key stakeholders; and, 4) whether positive benefits are demonstrated both academically and non-academically. *Cypress Fairbanks Indep. Sch. Dist. v. Michael F.,* 118 F.3d 245 (5th Cir. 1997).

The agency found that the facts justified assignment to the AU under these standards.

In *Clyde K. v. Puyallup School District No. 3* (9th Cir. 1994), the court, after weighing the factors mentioned earlier, found that a "self-contained" school was the LRE for a child with ADHD who violently attacked two students, assaulted a staff member, and disrupted class with profanity and sexually explicit comments to females. See also *Sacramento City Unified School District, Board of Education v. Rachel H. by & Through Holland* (9th Cir. 1994). In *Board of Education of the Baldwin Union Free School District v. Sobel,* 21 IDELR ¶ 106 (N.Y. Sup. Ct. 1994), the court found that a regular education with resource aids was appropriate for an other health impaired/ADHD student with emotional problems. The school district had wanted an out-of-state placement; the parents contended the student was entitled to a less restrictive environment. Together these cases show that the courts ordinarily are reluctant to authorize the use of separate placements for children with disabilities, absent special circumstances. Further, in *Taylor v. Corinth Public School District* (N.D. Miss. 1996), the court found that an interim forty-five-day placement of a student in a classroom located in the sheriff's office was the LRE. The student had a behavior disorder and emotional problems, and the school had determined that he was a risk to himself and others.

The major means of justifying a more restrictive environment is to show that the child is disruptive. In *Hartmann v. Loudoun County Board of Education* (4th Cir. 1997), the Fourth Circuit considered a parental claim that the IDEA required inclusion for Mark, a student with autism who "engaged in daily episodes of loud screeching and other disruptive conduct such as hitting, pinching, kicking, biting, and removing his clothing." These outbursts not only required teachers "to calm Mark and redirect him, but also consumed the additional time necessary to get the rest of the children back on task after the distraction." The school district sought, and state administrative proceedings authorized, a placement for Mark in a "regular elementary school which houses the autism class in order to facilitate interaction between the autistic children and students who are not handicapped."

Mark's parents sued, alleging that the school "failed to ensure that Mark was educated with non-disabled children 'to the maximum extent appropriate' as required by the IDEA's mainstreaming provision." The District Court reversed the board, finding that Mark did "receive significant educational benefit in a regular classroom" and that "the Board simply did not take enough appropriate steps to try to include Mark in a regular class." On appeal, the Fourth Circuit reversed, vacated the district court's judgment, and held that the "IDEA's mainstreaming provision establishes a presumption, not an inflexible federal mandate."

The court, citing Fourth Circuit precedents, ruled "that mainstreaming is not required where (1) the disabled child would not receive an educational benefit from mainstreaming into a regular class; (2) any marginal benefit from mainstreaming would be significantly outweighed by benefits which could feasibly be obtained only in a separate instructional setting; or, (3) the disabled child is a disruptive force in a regular classroom setting." The U.S. Supreme Court refused to review the case. *Hartmann v. Loudoun County Board of Education*, 522 U.S. 1046 (1998)

Nor is there an absolute requirement that all public educational services under the IDEA be furnished at the location closest to the child's home. In *Flour Bluff Independent School District v. Katherine M.* (5th Cir. 1996), the Fifth Circuit said:

> Flour Bluff School District was free to utilize the regional day school for its disabled students. Educating Katie "close to home" was only a factor for the school district to consider when determining her placement in the Least Restrictive Environment; and with the proximity of the regional day school to Katie's home, that factor was not controlling.

In *Brillon v. Klein Independent School District* (5th Cir. 2004), the court ruled that implementation of IEP goals for a child with Down syndrome in a regular classroom would "change the curriculum beyond recognition" and would force the teacher to operate a "classroom within a class." The school was not required to educate the student in regular social studies and science class. The IEP properly required mainstreaming only for nonacademic subjects such as music. See also *McLaughlin v. Holt Public School Board of Education.* (6th Cir. 2003).

In *Walter K. v. Goliad Independent School District* (SEA TX 2001), the court ruled that a highly restricted environment was the least restrictive environment possible. That case involved Walter, a "17 year old, six foot five, 360 pound student with a history of violence" who suffered from the following: "an attention deficit hyperactivity disorder combined type; major depression disorder, recurrence severe, without psychotic features; a possible personality disorder; and a cognitive disorder." These "disorders and resulting abnormal thought processes" caused "significant mood swings, including rages and suicidal and homicidal ideation." Walter had "a propensity to explosively lash out and attack peers and others." For him, the LRE was quite structured:

> The least restrictive environment for implementation of Walter's current IEP is a 24-hour highly structured educational and therapeutic environment with highly

trained personnel capable of adequately and appropriately addressing his emotional, behavioral, academic and vocational needs.

In *L.B. v. Nebo School District.* (10th Cir. 2004), the court ruled that the placement of a student with autism in a special education preschool class was not the least restrictive environment. The parents were entitled to receive the benefits of the Applied Behavioral Analysis (ABA) program and aide services to support a mainstream placement which the school did not provide. Accordingly, they were entitled to recover the costs of providing those services.

G. Private School

1. Private School Placement

A public school system is not required to send a child to a private school because the private school is alleged to be superior to the public school. *Hessler v. State Board of Education* (4th Cir. 1983). Under some circumstances, private resources may be required. Under the IDEA, a child with a disability may receive a private school education at public expense when either (1) "such children are placed in, or referred to, such schools or facilities by the State or appropriate local educational agency as the means of carrying out the requirements of [the IDEA]" [20 U.S.C. §1412(a)(10)(B)]; or (2) the educational agency failed to make a "free appropriate public education available to the child" [20 U.S.C. §1412(a)(10)(C)(ii)].

Where no public facilities are available, private schools may be used, with the costs borne by the public school district. Nonetheless, public funding for private education premised on the public school's failure to provide a FAPE has proven controversial in many instances.

Sometimes a unilateral placement by parents, that is, placement without the public school district's consent, will be reimbursed. The U.S. Supreme Court has ruled that three conditions must exist before private education at public expense would be authorized by the IDEA. The parents of a child with a disability are entitled to reimbursement for the costs of privately educating their child only if a federal court concludes that (1) the public school district's proposed IEP fails to provide a "free appropriate education" and therefore violates the IDEA, (2) the private institution selected by the parents provides an "appropriate education" under the IDEA, and (3) the cost of the private tuition is reasonable. See the Supreme Court's decision in *Florence County School District Four v. Carter,* 510 U.S. 7 (1993).

In *Gerstmyer v. Howard County Public School* (D.Md 1994), the court ordered the parents of a child with learning disabilities to be reimbursed for private school where the public school failed to develop any IEP at all, despite the fact that the school had been on notice of the student's need for evaluation.

In *Capistrano Unified School District v. Wartenberg* (9th Cir. 1995), discussed earlier, the court held that the school's IEP was insufficient under the IDEA because the IEP (1) moved the student around too much, (2) assigned him to too many teachers, (3) gave insufficient structure, and (4) did not provide constant feedback and clear commands. The case involved a sixteen-year-old who had a specific learning disability, conduct disorder, and attention deficit disorder. The student's parents recovered the private school tuition.

In *Cleveland Heights–University Heights City School District v. Boss*, *144 F.3d 391 (6th Cir. 1998)*, a school district attempted an unusual argument to avoid the consequences of the Supreme Court's decision in *Florence County School District Four v. Carter* 510 U.S. 7 (1993). The school district refused to reimburse parents for the costs of placing their child, Sommer Boss, in the Lawrence School, which "admits only learning disabled children." The district refused to pay for the placement on the grounds that it "was not proper under the IDEA because the Lawrence School cannot satisfy the IDEA's mainstreaming requirement" and that to "the maximum extent appropriate," children with disabilities must be "educated with children who are not disabled." The Sixth Circuit rejected the school district's argument and held that "the failure of the Lawrence School to satisfy the IDEA's mainstreaming requirement does not bar the Bosses from receiving reimbursement for expenses associated with sending Sommer to Lawrence" for the school year at issue.

Often unilateral placement by parents will not be reimbursed. See *Rairdan M. v. Solanco School District* (E.D. Pa. 1998); *Douglas W. v. Greenfield Public Schools* (D. Mass. 2001); *Mark R. v. Board of Education* (N.D. Ill. 1982), aff'd, 705 F. 2d 462 (7th Cir. 1983); *Alexis v. Board of Education for Baltimore County Public Schools* (D. Md. 2003); *Greenland School District v. Amy N.* (1st Cir. 2004); *Berger v. Medina City School District* (6th Cir. 2003); and *Greenland School District v. Amy N.* (1st Cir. 2004).

Private school tuition is frequently sought by parents who want a "free appropriate public education" for their children without understanding that, legally speaking, "appropriate" means only "appropriate when compared to the quality of education given children who do not have disabilities." In *E.S. v. Independent School District No. 196* (8th Cir. 1994), the parents requested, but the school district refused to provide, one-on-one instruction to a child with a learning disability, using the Orton-Gillingham method. The parents sued under the IDEA. The Eighth Circuit rejected the parents' claims and held that the IDEA requires only that E.S. be given an IEP "reasonably calculated to enable the child to receive educational benefits" under the Supreme Court's ruling in *Board of Education v. Rowley*, 458 U.S. 176 (1982), discussed earlier. This standard was met, the court held, notwithstanding the fact "that despite three years of special education by the District, E.S. still lagged behind grade-level achievement in many critical skills."

> However, the IDEA does not require the District to provide E.S. the best possible education or to achieve outstanding results. . . . As long as a student is benefiting from her education, it is up to the educators to determine the appropriate methodology.

In *Hammond v. Hartford School District* (2d Cir. 1997), the Second Circuit found that an IEP was "reasonably calculated to enable the child to receive educational benefits." The court held that a student with learning disabilities who "was able to participate in classes, have an active social life, and participate in several sports" at the public school and able to meet "most of the objectives of his IEP, especially those relating to organizational skills and writing" received such a benefit. Accordingly, the court did not award the parents reimbursement for tuition paid to a private school for students with learning disabilities, finding that, while the private school "may be an excellent educational setting for Walter, as evidenced by his grades there and his own testimony," it is also "a purely segregated environment."

Generally the requirement that FAPE be provided does not mandate any particular medical or academic solution to learning problems. Many parents have, for example, argued that FAPE requires that children with dyslexia be educated using the Orton-Gillingham Method. In *Banks ex rel. Banks v. Danbury Board of Education* (D. Conn. 2002), the court found that an IEP providing for a one to three teaching ratio was an appropriate method of educating a child with dyslexia/ADHD, reasonably calculated for the child to progress. The one on one Orton-Gillingham method was not required. *J.P. v. W. Clark Community Schools* (S.D. Ind. 2002). An exception to the general rule is reflected in *Bucks County Department of Mental Health/Retardation v. Pennsylvania* (3d Cir. 2004) discussed in Section B-3 of this chapter.

The reauthorized IDEA attempts to reach a fair balance between the school's and the parents' interests:

> (ii) REIMBURSEMENT FOR PRIVATE SCHOOL PLACEMENT—If the parents of a child with a disability, who previously received special education and related services under the authority of a public agency, enroll the child in a private elementary school or secondary school without the consent of or referral by the public agency, a court or a hearing officer may require the agency to reimburse the parents for the cost of that enrollment if the court or hearing officer finds that the agency had not made a free appropriate public education available to the child in a timely manner prior to that enrollment. 20 U.S.C. §1412(a)(10)(C)(ii)

Then, the IDEA places some limits on parental reimbursement where the parents' withdrawal of the child is considered unreasonable by Congress:

> (iii) LIMITATION ON REIMBURSEMENT—The cost of reimbursement described in clause (ii) may be reduced or denied—
> (aa) at the most recent IEP meeting that the parents attended prior to removal of the child from the public school, the parents did not inform the IEP Team that they were rejecting the placement proposed by the public agency to provide a free appropriate public education to their child, including stating their concerns and their intent to enroll their child in a private school at public expense; or
> (bb) 10 business days (including any holidays that occur on a business day) prior to the removal of the child from the public school, the parents did not give written notice to the public agency of the information described in item (aa). (20 U.S.C. §1412[a][10][C][iii])

Reimbursement may also be denied if, after notice that was "appropriate and reasonable," the parents did not make their child available for a required "evaluation," or a court issues "a judicial finding of unreasonableness with respect to actions taken by the parents." However, if an excusable or justified failure of the parents to comply with this requirement exists, or physical harm to the child is a possibility, the reimbursement "shall not be reduced or denied." A court or hearing officer has the discretion to refuse reimbursement reduction where parents are "illiterate and cannot write in English," or if a refusal to reimburse "would likely result in serious emotional harm to the child."

2. Public Services; Private Setting

Under the IDEA, a child with a disability is not necessarily limited only to a choice between a full public education and a full private one. The IDEA authorizes the public school to provide services in a private setting when appropriate. However, there has been considerable disagreement as to what is "appropriate." The 1997 IDEA amendments were adopted to simplify the law by making it clear that school districts could provide public services at parochial and other private schools. However, Congress chose language, which, in the words of one court, was "not clear." As a result, a law, which was intended to encourage school districts to provide special education and related services to a private school population with disabilities, has resulted in the denial of services in a number of significant cases.

The Zobrest Decision

The proper role of parochial and other sectarian schools under the IDEA posed issues of public concern which were addressed by the U.S. Supreme Court in *Zobrest v. Catalina Foothills School District*, 509 U.S. 1 (1993). In *Zobrest*, the Supreme Court held that a public school district may constitutionally use IDEA funds to provide a sign language interpreter for a deaf student at a Catholic high school. The Supreme Court ruled that the provision of governmental services to a religious school is lawful under the First Amendment if (1) the services are provided in a neutral manner to a broad class of citizens defined without reference to religion; (2) the services are provided at the parochial school not as a result of legislative choice but rather as a result of the private choice of the individual utilizing the services; and (3) the funds traceable to the government do not "find their way into the sectarian schools' coffers." Here the child is the primary beneficiary, and the school receives only an incidental benefit. In addition, an interpreter, unlike a teacher or guidance counselor, neither adds to nor subtracts from the sectarian school's environment, but merely interprets whatever material is presented to the class as a whole. There is no absolute bar to the placing of a public employee in a sectarian school. Similarly, in *Peck v. Lansing School*, 148 F.3d 619 (6th Cir. 1998), the Sixth Circuit held that the Lansing School District could provide physical and occupational therapy to Elizabeth Peck on the premises of a parochial school.

The 2004 Reauthorization of the IDEA

The IDEA, as amended in 1997 and reauthorized in 2004, sought to confirm school district authority to provide services to private school students, including those in parochial schools. Essentially, Congress provided that (1) school districts must set aside a "proportionate" amount of IDEA funds to be used for providing public services to private school students, (2) school districts need not use their own funds for the purpose, and (3) school districts *may, in their discretion,* deliver those services at private school facilities.

The 2004 IDEA amendments provide that a State is eligible for [federal] assistance . . . if the State submits a plan that provides assurances to the Secretary that the State has in effect policies and procedures to ensure that . . . to the extent consistent with the number and location of children with disabilities in the State who are enrolled by their parents in private elementary schools and secondary schools in the school district served by a local educational agency, provision is made for the participation of those children in the program assisted or carried out under this part by providing for such children special education and related services in accordance with the following requirements . . .

> (I) Amounts to be expended for the provision of those services (including direct services to parentally placed private school children) by the local educational agency shall be equal to a proportionate amount of Federal funds made available under this part.
>
> ***
>
> (III) Such services to parentally placed private school children with disabilities may be provided to the children on the premises of private, including religious, schools, to the extent consistent with law. 20 U.S.C. §1412(a)(10)(A)(i)(I) and (II)

In addition, the statute mandates that the local educational agency "after timely and meaningful consultation with representatives of private schools . . . shall conduct a thorough and complete child find process to determine the number of parentally placed children with disabilities attending private schools [in its jurisdiction]."

The Senate Report on the 1997 IDEA amendments (S. Rep. No. 17, 105th Cong., 1st Sess. 13 [1997]) discussed the language that was inserted in the bill then and has been largely repeated in the 2004 reauthorization:

> The bill makes a number of changes to clarify the responsibility of public school districts to children with disabilities who are placed by their parents in private schools. These changes should resolve a number of issues that have been the subject of an increasing amount of litigation in the last few years. First, the bill specifies that the total amount of money that must be spent to provide special education and related services to children in the state with disabilities who have been placed by their parents in private schools is limited to a proportional amount (that is, the amount consistent with the number and location of private school children with disabilities in the State) of the Federal funds available under part B. Second, the bill specifies that school districts may provide the special education and related services funded under part B on the premises of private, including parochial, schools. This provision is designed to implement the principle underlying the ruling of the Supreme Court in *Zobrest* v. *Catalina Foothills School Dist.* that it was not an "entanglement" violation of the First Amendment to provide a sign interpreter paid for with IDEA funds to a deaf student at his parochial school. Third, the bill clarifies that the child-find, identification, and evaluation provision of section 612(a)(3) applies to children placed by their parents in private schools.

The Analysis of Comments and Changes [IDEA Regulations, May 1999, provided:

Placement of Children by Parent if FAPE is at Issue (Sec. 300.403)

Discussion: The statute in section 612(a)(10)(C)(i) is clear that an LEA must provide for the participation of parentally-placed private school children with disabilities in the Part B program with expenditures proportionate to their number and location in the State, even though the LEA is not otherwise required to pay the costs of education, including special education and related services, for any individual child with a disability who is voluntarily placed in a private school under the terms of Sec. 300.403.

[NOTE: In 2006 Regulations, this provision is found at 34 CFR § 300.148.]

The purpose of the 1997 Amendments was to clarify the law. However, matters became more complex. The 2006 regulations provide additional clarification, including an example for school districts on calculating the "proportionate share" that must be spent on private school students. (See Appendix B to Part 300— "Proportionate Share Calculation," IDEA Regulations, 2006.)

H. Summary

Under the IDEA, a student with a disability has the right to a free appropriate public education, provided that he or she requires special education and related services. A free appropriate public education (FAPE) is an education "provided at public expense, under public supervision and direction, and without charge," which meets "the standards of the State educational agency," is "provided in conformity with the individualized education program and is delivered in the "least restrictive environment [LRE]."

CHAPTER

6   Discipline

A.   Overview

1.   Discipline Is a Fundamental Requirement

On January 26, 2005, two boys, aged nine and ten, were charged with making a written threat to kill or harm another person, which is a felony, and were taken away from their Ocala, Florida, public school in handcuffs. The boys allegedly had repeatedly bullied a third student and escalated their bullying by using a "pencil and red crayon to draw primitive stick figure scenes on scrap paper that showed a 10-year-old classmate being stabbed and hung." Both boys were in special education classes at the school. The victim told his teacher, who contacted the school dean, who in turn called the police. In addition to being charged with a felony, both boys were suspended from school.

This case illustrates the difficulties in school discipline. First, the victim was being bullied and finally threatened with death. The school has an obligation to protect its students from bullying that threatens to deprive the victim of access to education. *Davis v. Monroe County Board of Education*, 526 U.S. 629 (1999). Moreover, with horrific cases such as the Columbine shootings in mind, no school official can ignore threats of violence. Second, it is highly unlikely that the boys meant to act on the threat contained in the drawings. Third, no school hearing was held on either the misconduct or the possible relevance of the misconduct to the boys' disabilities. What might at one time have been handled solely as a matter of school discipline has become a criminal matter.

In *Bercovitch v. Baldwin School, Inc.*, 133 F. 3d 141 (1st Cir. 1998), the U.S. Circuit Court of Appeals for the First Circuit held that school discipline is a "fundamental requirement of the school's academic program." Congress has concurred with this view in the IDEA. At the same time, however, there is widespread recognition, under the IDEA, that disciplinary infractions may be the result of the very disabilities for which the school district is obligated to provide special education and related services. In addition, there is the concern that, to some extent, school districts might use their disciplinary codes as a means of removing students with the most challenging disabilities, either short term or permanently, from the regular classroom. The IDEA attempts to address all of these concerns.

2.   The IDEA Approach to Discipline

The IDEA's approach to discipline is simple and straightforward. Children with disabilities are subject to the same disciplinary requirements that govern children without disabilities. They are also entitled to the same free appropriate public education the school is obligated to provide students with no disability. Where serious disciplinary violations are concerned, such as those involving guns, drugs, and the potential for violence, school officials may act to protect the public. The only question is whether that free appropriate public education will be delivered in the public school setting or in some other setting.

In 20 U.S.C. §1412(a)(1)(A), the IDEA provides that a "State is eligible for assistance" if the "State has in effect policies and procedures to ensure" that a "free appropriate public education is available to all children with disabilities residing in the State between the ages of 3 and 21, inclusive, including children with disabilities *who have been suspended or expelled from school*" (emphasis added).

The IDEA makes a basic distinction between violations of the "code of student conduct" and the commission of serious crimes. The nature of the offense dictates how, where, and on what terms special education and related services will be provided to a child with a disability.

The Analysis of Comments and Changes, issued under the regulations, which preceded the current IDEA, made clear that school officials must exercise their disciplinary authority under the IDEA. However, that responsibility does not preclude reporting crimes to law enforcement authorities. This interpretation remains current under the 2006 regulations.

> Discussion: Paragraph (a) of Sec. 300.529 does not authorize school districts to circumvent any of their responsibilities under the Act. It merely clarifies that school districts do have the authority to report crimes by children with disabilities to appropriate authorities and that those State law enforcement and judicial authorities have the ability to exercise their responsibilities regarding the application of Federal and State law to crimes committed by children with disabilities. The procedural protections that apply to reports of a crime are established by criminal law, not the IDEA. Of course, it would be a violation of Section 504 of the Rehabilitation Act of 1973 if a school were discriminating against children with disabilities in how they were acting under this authority (e.g., if they were only reporting crimes committed by children with disabilities and not committed by nondisabled students).

How great a role may the school play in prosecuting children with disabilities whose in-school conduct is criminal?

> The Act does not address whether school officials may press charges against a child with a disability when they have reported a crime by that student. Again, school districts should take care not to exercise their responsibilities in a discriminatory manner. (Analysis of Comments and Changes)

The bottom line appears to be that the authors of the regulations believe that, in all but the most serious cases, the "appropriate response" to behavior that violates school disciplinary codes "almost always would be to use the behavioral strategies specified in the IEP rather than to implement a disciplinary suspension." School officials are reminded that enthusiastic support of prosecutions for criminal conduct on school property may violate the RA/ADA, if implemented in a discriminatory manner.

B. School Code Violations

1. School Codes

Codes of student conduct set the standard for good citizenship in the school environment, and may specify standards of dress, academic honesty, and deportment. In some cases, actions prohibited by the school code will also be unlawful. For example, if one student punches another, he or she may be in violation of the school conduct code. That punch may also constitute an assault and battery, which carries civil or criminal liability. In the past there was general agreement that actions such as a punch should be treated as conduct code violations, rather than criminal or civil offenses. That agreement has been eroded to some extent. Anecdotal evidence suggests that schools are resorting more often to the use of criminal and civil processes to address relatively minor disputes.

The IDEA makes it clear that school authorities may invoke criminal processes.

> Nothing . . . shall be construed to prohibit an agency from reporting a crime committed by a child with a disability to appropriate authorities or to prevent State law enforcement and judicial authorities from exercising their responsibilities with regard to the application of Federal and State law to crimes committed by a child with a disability. 20 U.S.C. §1415(k)(6)

The child's records must also be transmitted to the law enforcement authorities. The IDEA provides that an "agency reporting a crime committed by a child with a disability shall ensure that copies of the special education and disciplinary records of the child are transmitted for consideration by the appropriate authorities to whom the agency reports the crime."

2. Basic Rule

The IDEA specifies the following authority for school personnel:

> AUTHORITY—School personnel under this subsection may remove a child with a disability who violates a code of student conduct from their current placement to an appropriate interim alternative educational setting, another setting, or suspension, for not more than 10 school days (to the extent such alternatives are applied to children without disabilities). 20 U.S.C. §1415(k)(1)(B)

The law encourages a case-by-case consideration on its merits.

> CASE-BY-CASE DETERMINATION—School personnel may consider any unique circumstances on a case-by-case basis when determining whether to order a change

in placement for a child with a disability who violates a code of student conduct. 20 U.S.C. §1415(k)(1)(A)

The IDEA provides for the use of an "interim alternative educational setting" as a means of ensuring safety in the schools. In 1997 Congress created an entirely new section of the law, part of the "procedural safeguards" section (20 U.S.C. 1415[k]), to address student discipline. This language was retained with some changes in the 2004 reauthorization. The House Report explained the congressional purpose.

> The Committee recognizes that school safety is important to educators and parents. There has been considerable debate and concern about both if and how those few children with disabilities who affect the school safety of peers, teachers, and themselves may be disciplined when they engage in behaviors that jeopardize such safety. In addition, the Committee is aware of the perception of a lack of parity when making decisions about disciplining children with and without disabilities who violate the same school rule or code of conduct. By adding a new section 615(k) to IDEA, the Committee has attempted to strike a careful balance between the LEA's duty to ensure that school environments are safe and conducive to learning for all children, including children with disabilities, and the LEA's continuing obligation to ensure that children with disabilities receive a free appropriate public education (FAPE). Thus, drawing on testimony, experience, and common sense, the Committee has placed specific and comprehensive guidelines on the matter of disciplining children with disabilities in this section.

When the child's actions that violated the school's conduct code are not a result of the child's disability, the law states that the behavior is not a "manifestation of the child's disability." In that event, "the relevant disciplinary procedures applicable to children without disabilities may be applied to the child in the same manner and for the same duration in which the procedures would be applied to children without disabilities." If the school conduct code calls for expulsion for the particular offense, then the child with a disability may be expelled if nondisabled children would be. However, even in this event, special education and related services are to be provided "in an interim alternative educational setting." The IDEA extends the privilege of education regardless of personal misconduct to children with disabilities and to no other group. However, some state legislatures have passed laws requiring that *all* students who have been expelled receive educational services.

3. Manifestation Determinations

Expulsion or suspension of a child with a disability is considered a change of placement which triggers extensive procedural requirements. 20 U.S.C. §1415(k)(1(E)-(F). To begin, "within 10 school days of any decision to change the placement of a child with a disability because of a violation of a code of student conduct, the local educational agency, the parent, and relevant members of the IEP Team . . . shall review all relevant information in the student's file, including the child's IEP, any teacher observations, and any relevant information provided by the parents." The purpose of the review is "to determine" whether the conduct is "a manifestation of the child's disability."

When the discipline provisions were first added to the IDEA in 1997, the IEP team could only determine that the behavior was not a manifestation if first the team considered all information relevant to the behavior in question, including evaluation and diagnostic results, observations of the child, and the child's IEP and placement. After these considerations, the team had to determine that (1) in relationship to the behavior, the IEP and placement were appropriate and the IEP services and behavior intervention strategies were provided consistent with the IEP and placement; (2) the child's disability "did not impair the ability of the child to understand the impact and consequences of the behavior"; and (3) the disability "did not impair the ability of the child to control the behavior." 20 U.S.C. §1415(k)(4)(C) (IDEA 1997). If each of the three prongs of the analysis were not met, the IEP team had to conclude that the behavior under scrutiny was a manifestation of the child's disability.

For example, in *Aaron B. v. El Paso Independent School District* (SEA TX 2003), the Texas Education Agency held a manifestation determination improper where the team did not "make a finding as to whether [the student's] disability impaired his ability to control the behavior at issue." Rather, the team considered only the question of whether the student possessed the ability to control his behaviors.

This section of the law was changed significantly in 2004. School districts had expressed serious concerns that the complexity of the manifestation determination under the 1997 statute had resulted in almost universal findings of causal links between students' behavior and their disabilities. Therefore, the ability of school personnel to implement the discipline policies was seriously undermined in situations where, in fact, the behavior clearly was not caused by the disability.

The 2004 IDEA amendments require that the causal connection between the disability and the behavior be conclusively established, just as in the 1997 law. However, the new "test" for that causal link requires that the IEP team determines:

> (I) if the conduct in question was caused by, or had a direct and substantial relationship to, the child's disability; or
> (II) if the conduct in question was the direct result of the local educational agency's failure to implement the IEP. 20 U.S.C. §1415(k)(1(E)(i)(I)-(II)

Note that the cases cited in this section are based on the 1997 manifestation test, because very few cases have been reported thus far based on the 2004 discipline provisions.

4. Cases on School Code Violations and Disabilities

Misty S. v. Northside Independent School District, Docket No. 076-SE-1003 (SEA TX 2004) indicates how school code violations are often handled. Misty was an eighth-grade student who received special education and related services because of emotional disturbance. At the beginning of the eighth grade, she "began to demonstrate behavioral problems at school" that "resulted in numerous disciplinary referrals to detention, In School Suspension, suspension, and finally, a referral to an Alternative Educational Placement (AEP)." Generally, Misty was guilty of "being tardy or truant, chewing gum, being disruptive in the classroom, or demonstrating a defiant or disrespectful attitude." The school district proposed placing Misty in an alternative educational program based on a manifestation determination which concluded that Misty's misbehaviors were not "manifestations of Misty's emotional disability."

The special education hearing officer found in favor of the school district, saying:

> The evidence presented does not support the conclusion that any of the conditions exhibited by Misty have existed over a long period of time or to an obvious degree that adversely affects her educational performance. Rather, the evidence suggests that Misty began experiencing difficulties at the beginning of this school year, primarily as a result of conflicts with two of her teachers. Further, Misty's educational performance is good, with the exception of her grades in the classes taught by the teachers with whom she has a conflict.

T.N. v. Bridge City Independent School District (SEA TX 2002) considered the case of T.N., a ninth-grade boy who brought a less than 2.5-inch knife to school "in order to protect himself from a student that had previously threatened" him. T.N. kept the knife over a three-day period, threatening two other boys with it. The knife was not illegal under Texas law, but the school code prohibited bringing "any knife" to school. He was expelled for the remainder of the school year following a manifestation determination that concluded his conduct was not a result of the emotional disturbance for which he received special education and related services. The expulsion and manifestation determinations were held proper. The school "thoroughly reviewed all information regarding likelihood of repetition of the behavior, the student's lack of impulsivity, the student's cognizance of the consequences resulting from bringing the knife to school and breaking school rules, and his exhibition of control in the incident." It "correctly determined that the student's misbehavior was not a manifestation of his disability."

The case raises an interesting point. T.N.'s misbehavior was a result of an inappropriate response on his part to bullying. Acts of bullying and aggression that go unaddressed by school authorities may, in some circumstances, deny a student FAPE. *Loren H. v. Royal Independent School District* (SEA TX 2003). In *Davis v. Monroe County Board of Education*, 526 U.S. 629 (1999), the U.S. Supreme Court considered the question of whether and when bullying and harassment might give rise to legal liability. The court concluded that conduct "that is so severe, pervasive, and objectively offensive, and that so undermines and detracts from the victims' educational experience, that the victim-students are effectively denied equal access to an institution's resources and opportunities" is actionable. Note that while the court was discussing sexual harassment, the same principles apply in the area of disabilities. See *Gebser v. Lago Vista Independent School District*, 524 U.S. 274 (1998); *Rees v. Jefferson School District* (9th Cir. 2000).

5.   Consequences of Manifestation Determinations

The consequences of a positive manifestation determination are clearly specified.

> [If] the local educational agency, the parent, and relevant members of the IEP Team make the determination that the conduct was a manifestation of the child's disability, the IEP Team shall—

(i) conduct a functional behavioral assessment, and implement a behavioral intervention plan for such child [if not already done] . . . and

(ii) in the situation where a behavioral intervention plan has been developed, review the behavioral intervention plan if the child already has such a behavioral intervention plan, and modify it, as necessary, to address the behavior; and

(iii) [unless the child has engaged in specifically listed criminal acts] . . . return the child to the placement from which the child was removed, unless the parent and the local educational agency agree to a change of placement as part of the modification of the behavioral intervention plan. 20 U.S.C. §1415(k)(1(F)

This requirement has had real teeth. For example, in *J.C. v. Regional* 10 (2d Cir. 2002), the school was poised to expel a student for allegedly vandalizing a school bus. The child had a disability recognized under the IDEA. The parents retained a lawyer who invoked the manifestation provisions. The school terminated the expulsion proceedings for the child, determined that his actions were a manifestation of his educational disability, and drafted an IEP providing parents with all the relief they requested. Had J.C. not had a disability, he would have been expelled. However, it is still early to tell how the 2004 changes to the manifestation determination will affect the outcome of due process claims.

6. Children Who Might Have Disabilities

Under certain circumstances, the IDEA protects children who have not yet been determined eligible for IDEA services. For a student to receive the IDEA protections, the school must have had "knowledge" that the child might be a "child with a disability." The district is deemed to have "knowledge" generally if, before the behavior in question occurred, the child's parents expressed concern that the child needed special education and related services or requested the child be evaluated for services or the child's teacher or other school personnel expressed concerns about a pattern of behavior. The school district is not considered to have "knowledge" if the child had previously been evaluated and determined to be ineligible for IDEA services or if the parents had not allowed an evaluation or had refused services for the child. 20 U.S.C. §1415(k)(5)(B),(C). If the school district does not have prior "knowledge" that the child might be a child with a disability, then the student is disciplined in the same way as any student without a disability. However, the parents may request and receive an expedited evaluation to determine if, in fact, the child may qualify for future special education and related services. 20 U.S.C. §1415(k)(5)(D)

C. Selected Serious Criminal Misconduct

1. Crimes

Congress, bowing to popular pressure, selected certain crimes for different treatment under IDEA. 20 U.S.C. §1415(k)(1(G). If a student (1) "carries or possesses a weapon to or at school, on school premises, or to or at a school function under the jurisdiction of a State or local educational agency"; (2) "knowingly possesses or uses illegal drugs, or sells or solicits the sale of a controlled substance, while at school, on school premises, or at a school function"; or, (3) "has inflicted serious bodily injury upon another person while at school, on school premises, or at a school function," a different set of rules apply. Other serious crimes are not specifically mentioned in the statute.

2.   Consequences of Certain Criminal Conduct

When one of the listed crimes occurs, school personnel "may remove a student to an interim alternative educational setting for not more than 45 school days." The removal is "without regard to whether the behavior is determined to be a manifestation of the child's disability." The parents must be notified of the decision to discipline the child with a disability "and of all procedural safeguards accorded" under the IDEA. The "interim alternative setting" is determined by the IEP team, and the student continues to receive academic and behavioral services in the alternative setting that will allow the child to "progress toward meeting the goals" on the IEP. If a decision regarding the appropriate permanent placement for the child has not been reached by the end of the forty-five-day period and there is a danger in returning the student to the original placement, the district may ask a hearing officer to grant additional forty-five-day periods until a proper placement determination can be made.

Deliberate Conduct Not a Manifestation

In *Andrea G. v. Community Independent School District* (SEA TX 2004), the court found the misconduct to be deliberate and not a manifestation of a disability. Andrea was a fifteen-year-old ninth grader who was placed on in-school suspension for forty-five days (reduced to nineteen days) for the following behavior: "On January 20, 2004, Andrea was in a science class that was being taught by a substitute teacher. Andrea and several other students used a squirt bottle to place water on the floor in such a manner, and with the specific intent, that it would cause the teacher to slip and fall. The teacher did ultimately slip, falling completely to the floor and hurting her hip." The evidence showed that "Andrea and the other students involved in the incident had made a previous attempt to do it, but it had failed because they had not used enough water."

A manifestation hearing determined that Andrea exhibited "behaviors compatible with ADHD, inattentive type," but that these were not the cause of her actions. The special education hearing officer held the findings proper. First, the officer held, "The District had the burden of demonstrating that Andrea G's behavior in squirting the water on the floor to cause the teacher to slip and fall was not a manifestation of her disability, which in this case was ADHD, inattentive type." Second, the officer concluded that the misconduct was deliberate and planned.

> If Andrea could appreciate that she and the others did not use enough water on the floor in the first instance, and perhaps did not put it in the optimum place to precipitate a fall, and then eventually set out to do it the correct way, logic compels a decision that her ADHD did not impair her ability to understand the consequences of that behavior. It was a calculated, premeditated act by Andrea.

Eileen T. v. Northside Independent School District (SEA TX 2001) reached a similar result based on similar reasoning. Eileen T., a fourteen-year-old student with emotional disturbance, was expelled. Eileen had been discovered "with two bags of marijuana concealed in her bra. Eileen also had drug scales and drug paraphernalia concealed on her person." Eileen had prior discipline difficulties arising from misbehavior, including "profanity, walking out of class, and insubordination." She had "consistent problems of verbal aggression with her peers and teachers. Her instances of verbal aggression with her peers . . . consistently include[d] profanity and threats of physical violence." School officials concluded from the manifestation determination that Eileen's possession of the contraband did not constitute a manifestation of her emotional disturbance.

> Eileen's possession of the drugs and drug paraphernalia is indicative of a conscious choice because she had the marijuana hidden on her body, had drug paraphernalia in her purse, and attempted to conceal her illegal activity. Her actions were deliberate rather than impulsive, as what would be associated with a manifestation of an emotional disturbance.

In *John Doe v. Board of Education of Oak Park & River Forest High School District 200* (7th Cir. 1997), the Seventh Circuit considered the expulsion, for the remainder of the semester, of John, a student with learning disabilities and attention deficit disorder. John was accused of being in possession of a pipe and a small amount of marijuana at a freshman dance. The Court of Appeals upheld the District Court's ruling that John's misconduct was not a manifestation of a disability and that the school was not required to provide educational services to him when he had been properly expelled.

Impulsive Acts More Likely to be a Manifestation
Impulsive acts are likely to be considered to have resulted from a disability.

Jacob A. v. San Antonio Independent School District (SEA TX 2004) involved Jacob, a student who at various times was diagnosed with ADHD, oppositional defiant disorder, dysthymia, generalized anxiety disorder, bipolar disorder and "schizophrenia—disorganized type—severe."

During a basketball game in physical education class Jacob became angry when he thought it was his turn to enter the game and was told no. He attacked the first person he saw, another student, and kneed him in the stomach. Jacob also picked up a bench and tried to throw it at another student. After several punches that only made light contact with the student, Jacob stated that he was going to kill him. Jacob was completely uncooperative and had to be physically restrained and handcuffed by a police officer.

> The evidence in this case establishes . . . that Jacob's disability did in fact impair his ability to understand the impact and consequences of his behavior, and that he was unable to control the behavior that was subject to disciplinary action.

Note that Jacob committed the crimes of assault and battery, but the case was treated as a violation of school rules due to the determination that the behavior was directly related to Jacob's disability. Under the 2004 standard, that is, the behavior has a "direct and substantial relationship to the disability," it is most likely that the same result would have been reached in this case.

Impact of Procedural Failures on Manifestation Determinations

Procedural failures can some times result in a manifestation determination favorable to the student. *Veronica P. v. Evolution Academy Charter School* (SEA TX 2004) is such a case. "Veronica was suspended from school . . . for being in possession of marijuana at school." Though covered by IDEA, she did not have a current IEP.

> As a consequence, there was no current IEP from which to make a manifestation review. By law, if a determination cannot be made that the child's IEP and placement were appropriate as it relates to the behavior subject to the disciplinary action, then the behavior must be considered a manifestation of the child's disability.

George S. v. Webb Consolidated Independent School District (SEA TX 2003) also involved procedural failures. "A drug-sniffing dog alerted on several backpacks, including George's, during a routine investigation on the school bus." George permitted a search, and the dog handler said he found fragments of marijuana in George's backpack. The principal suspended George for three days and assigned George to thirty days in the Alternative Education Program ("AEP"). The district's administration decided to use in-school suspension instead. George was placed in relative isolation in the library, and no manifestation determination was conducted. The hearing officer ruled for George. The school "improperly removed George S. from his IEP placement for disciplinary reasons, and placed him in an inappropriate segregated setting, without convening an IEP Team meeting or conducting a manifestation determination review."

> The District's procedural violation was a serious one. It resulted in an extended removal of George from his IEP placement, and a drastic reduction in services and opportunities for contact with nondisabled peers, all without IEP Team review and parent input, and without any apparent recognition that IEP Team review was even necessary. George went from a full day mainstream placement with 45 minutes daily of special education math support, and many modifications in the regular education setting, to a situation of relative isolation in the library with assignments delivered weekly, no apparent modifications, and instruction provided for a few minutes daily on some but not all school days.

D. Continued Services

When a child with a disability is removed to an interim alternative educational placement, for either school code violations or serious criminal misconduct, the IDEA provides that the child must "continue to receive educational services . . . so as to enable the child to continue to participate in the general education curriculum, although in another setting, and to progress toward meeting the goals set out in the child's IEP." Moreover, the child must "receive, as appropriate, a functional behavioral assessment, behavioral intervention services and modifications, that are designed to address the behavior violation so that it does not recur." 20 U.S.C. §1415(k)(1(D)

Even where the placement of a student is prison, the school district may be obligated to deliver services.

In *Unified School District No. 1 v. Connecticut Department of Education* (Conn. Ct. App. 2001), the court held that a school district was obligated to provide one year compensatory education to a special education student who had been incarcerated for a short term. He had an IQ of 61, had been arrested for burglary, and had committed arson while in the correctional facility, which resulted in his being placed in punitive segregation where classes were not permitted.

In *Tunstall v. Bergeson* (Wash. Sup. Ct. 2000), cert. denied, *Tunstall v. Bergeson*, 532 U.S. 920 (2001), the Washington Supreme Court held that the IDEA does not require that states provide special education and related services to incarcerated persons with disabilities between the ages of eighteen and twenty-two. The court added that Section 504 of the RA does not require such education and services because compliance with IDEA equals compliance with Section 504.

E. Disputes

Disputes concerning the disciplining of a child with a disability are subject to the same due process procedures as other placement and IEP disputes. 20 U.S.C. §1415(k)(3)(A). Additionally, the school may seek a due process hearing to protect the public from a dangerous child.

> The parent of a child with a disability who disagrees with any decision regarding placement, or the manifestation determination under this subsection, or a local educational agency that believes that maintaining the current placement of the child is substantially likely to result in injury to the child or to others, may request a hearing.

The hearing officer has authority to:

> Order a change in placement of a child with a disability. In such situations, the hearing officer may—
>
> (I) return a child with a disability to the placement from which the child was removed; or
>
> (II) order a change in placement of a child with a disability to an appropriate interim alternative educational setting for not more than 45 school days if the hearing officer determines that maintaining the current placement of such child is substantially likely to result in injury to the child or to others. 20 U.S.C. §1415(k)(3)(B)

These procedures, like other placement procedures, are subject to the stay-put provision.

> PLACEMENT DURING APPEALS—When an appeal under paragraph (3) has been requested by either the parent or the local educational agency—

(A) the child shall remain in the interim alternative educational setting pending the decision of the hearing officer or until the expiration of the time period provided for in paragraph (1)(C), whichever occurs first, unless the parent and the State or local educational agency agree otherwise. (20 U.S.C. §1415[k][4])

An expedited hearing and decision are required in cases where students are considered dangers to themselves or to others or when parents or the school district are appealing a disciplinary action or the child's placement. "The State or local educational agency shall arrange for an expedited hearing, which shall occur within 20 school days of the date the hearing is requested and shall result in a determination within 10 school days after the hearing." Note again that school days are used, not calendar days or business days.

F.   Relationship to RA/ADA

The U.S. Department of Education treats the RA and IDEA as companion statutes. In issuing the regulations under the 1997 Amendments, the department made this statement:

> Under section 504 of the Rehabilitation Act of 1973, if the behavior is a manifestation of a child's disability, the child cannot be removed from his or her current educational placement if that removal constitutes a change of placement (other than a 45 day placement under Secs. 300.520(a)(2), 300.521, and 300.526(c)), unless the public agency and the parents otherwise agree to a change of placement. If the behavior is related to the child's disability, proper development of the child's IEP should include development of strategies, including positive behavioral interventions, strategies and supports to address that behavior, consistent with Secs. 300.346(a)(2)(i) and (c).

The Department of Education's comments were made as the courts were clarifying the meaning of the RA and the differences between the RA and IDEA. Accordingly the comments may not fully reflect court decisions issued during and after 1997.

G.   Summary

Every child with a disability is entitled to a FAPE. Children with disabilities may be disciplined for their misconduct at school. However, children with disabilities have certain procedural protections not available to other students. Possible expulsion or suspension of a child with a disability triggers procedural requirements, including a determination of whether the misconduct is a manifestation of the child's disability. Generally, if the misconduct is a manifestation of the disability, then, instead of punishment, such as expulsion, the misbehavior should be addressed through a behavioral intervention plan. However, if the misconduct falls within specified categories of serious misconduct, then the child may be moved to an interim alternative educational placement for no more than forty-five school days, even if the misconduct is a manifestation of the disability.

7 Mediation

A. In General

There was a time when Americans did not generally go to court to resolve their disputes. Beginning with the Industrial Revolution, court proceedings to resolve disputes began to increase. The number of cases decided doubled once between 1920 and 1960 and more than doubled again between 1960 and the present.

The cost of litigation has become legendary. Litigation may involve attorneys' fees, court filing fees, deposition costs, and expert witness fees. The personal costs of time lost from work and the personal stresses that result also must be considered. The price of civil litigation is staggering for parents, state and local educational agencies, and the taxpayer. As a result, many policy makers have sought alternatives to litigation, termed "alternative dispute resolution" or ADR.

There are two ways to resolve a dispute: litigation and agreement. This is as true of controversies concerning the provision of a "free appropriate public education" under the IDEA as it is of any other matter. Due process hearings and lawsuits in court are all forms of litigation. The two basic forms of ADR are arbitration and mediation. Arbitration is a form of streamlined and expedited hearing. Mediation is a form of negotiation that relies on a neutral facilitator to achieve a settlement. A third method of dispute resolution, relevant to educational disputes, is an informal complaint to the state educational agency. This procedure is similar to the complaints filed with the Office for Civil Rights in the U.S. Department of Education (discussed in Chapter 13).

1. Arbitration

Generally, arbitration is a private trial conducted by a "judge," called an arbitrator. The parties choose either a single arbitrator or a panel of three arbitrators who will conduct a hearing, receive evidence, and decide the dispute. The arbitrators have only those powers provided by the arbitration agreement. They receive a fee, agreed upon by the parties, which is based often upon a daily or hourly rate. Many arbitration agreements also provide for the recovery of attorneys' fees and costs of the winning party. Administrative services (such as finding a suitable hearing location, collecting arbitrators' fees, etc.) are often provided by an agency whose powers are spelled out in the arbitration agreement.

Arbitration proceedings are similar to court trials but are shorter, simpler, and less expensive. Evidence is presented through witness testimony and the introduction of documents, just as in court proceedings. However, technical rules of evidence are not strictly followed. Decisions of the arbitrators ordinarily are brief and state basically only the result reached, for example, the amount of money awarded to the prevailing party and a statement regarding who must pay the attorneys' fees, arbitration costs, and filing fees.

Arbitration awards are usually final and ordinarily may not be overturned by a court. As a result, arbitration is the fastest and least expensive method of presenting essentially the same evidence that would be presented in a court proceeding. Arbitration is used in hearing some claims under the ADA and other civil rights statutes.

2.   Mediation

Mediation is a form of negotiation in which the parties select an experienced neutral person who helps the parties explore means of resolving their differences. Mediation is, first and foremost, voluntary. The role of the mediator is to facilitate resolution of the dispute. Therefore, the mediator generally is permitted to discuss the disputed issues with the parties together and/or privately with each party. Statements and documents originating in the course of mediation may not be introduced as evidence in a later trial if mediation fails. Mediation is a simple and inexpensive method of resolving disputes. However, it is effective only if the parties genuinely desire to resolve their dispute.

3.   State Educational Agency Complaint

A third method of resolving disputes short of full scale litigation is a complaint to the state educational agency (SEA). The differences among various methods of resolving disputes was addressed in a report to the U.S. Senate Committee on Health, Education, Labor, and Pensions. The report stated:

> Disagreements can be formally resolved through state complaint procedures, through a due process hearing, or through mediation. A state complaint is initiated through a signed written complaint that includes a statement that a public agency has violated a requirement of IDEA and the facts on which the statement is based. If the complaint is against a school district, the SEA typically informs the school district of the complaint by formal notification, requests documentation from the local education officials, and, when necessary, conducts an on-site investigation. The SEA must issue a written decision to the complainant that addresses each allegation in the complaint and contains findings of fact and conclusions, and the reason for the SEA's final decision. If violations are found, the decision specifies the corrective actions to achieve compliance. A due process hearing is an administrative agency process initiated by a written request by one of the aggrieved parties to either the SEA or the LEA, depending on the state's process. An impartial hearing officer listens to witnesses, examines evidence, and issues a written decision. In the decision,

the hearing officer determines whether violations occurred and issues remedies. Mediation is a voluntary process whereby parents and school districts agree to meet with an impartial third party in an informal setting to reach a resolution that is mutually agreeable. Agreements are mutually designed, agreed to, and implemented by the parties. (*Report to the Ranking Minority Member, Committee on Health, Education, Labor and Pensions,* Government Accounting Office [September 9, 2003])

Generally the SEA complaint is used most frequently, the mediation process next, followed by due process hearings.

4. Agreements That Determine Civil and Statutory Rights

Alternative dispute resolution (ADR) methods often require the use of two different types of agreements. The first is an agreement to use ADR methods, such as arbitration or mediation. The second is a settlement agreement that results from the process and sets forth the resolution of the dispute. In both cases, it is essential that the agreements be clear and specific.

Agreement to Use ADR

The U.S. Supreme Court has ruled that arbitration of claims under the ADA is permissible, provided that the agreement to arbitrate such claims uses language that shows a "clear and unmistakable" intention to arbitrate. However, an arbitration agreement that is "very general," and provides only for arbitration of "matters under dispute" is not sufficiently clear. *Wright v. Universal Maritime Service Corp.,* 525 U.S. 70 (1998)

Settlement Agreement

In *E.J. v. Matula* (3d Cir. 1995), the court considered a settlement agreement where a mother, on behalf of her disabled child, sought damages under 42 U.S.C. §1983 (see Chapter 2, Section B.4). The mother claimed that the persistent refusal of school officials to evaluate, classify, and provide necessary educational services to her daughter deprived the child of the "rights, privileges, or immunities secured by the . . . laws" of the United States, specifically, the IDEA.

A due process hearing was held, and a settlement agreement worked out. In the agreement the court found there was "no specific mention of damages, and the language indicates that the agreement merely resolved all issues raised in the due process petitions in [the due process hearing] namely evaluation and classification of E.J." The court held that the settlement agreement did not bar claims for damages, such as "generalized pain and suffering," should a court decide them to be appropriate. The court then held that a settlement agreement compromising civil rights claims must be construed against a higher standard than the standard used in interpreting a simple contract. The court must consider:

Such factors as whether (1) the language of the agreement was clear and specific; (2) the consideration given in exchange for the waiver exceeded the relief to which the signer was already entitled by law; (3) the signer was represented by counsel;

(4) the signer received an adequate explanation of the document; (5) the signer had time to reflect upon it; and (6) the signer understood its nature and scope. We may also look to whether there is evidence of fraud or undue influence, or whether enforcement of the agreement would be against the public interest. (Citations omitted)

It is important that the settlement agreements be clear and specific and address all of the issues in the claim.

B. Mediation under IDEA

1. Congressional Preference

Congress sought to encourage mediation. Representative William F. Goodling, then chairman of the House Committee on Education and the Workforce, stated in his introduction of the 1997 Amendments to the IDEA:

> The bill ensures that States will offer mediation services to resolve disputes. Mediation has proved successful in the nearly three-quarters of the States that have adopted it. This change will encourage parents and schools to work out differences in a less adversarial manner. (Remarks on the *IDEA Amendments of 1997*, Cong. Rec., E61 [January 7, 1997])

The use of mediation is now established law and continues under the 2004 amendments with few substantive changes.

2. Proper Subjects of Mediation

Whenever "the local educational agency— (A) proposes to initiate or change; or (B) refuses to initiate or change, the identification, evaluation, or educational placement of the child, or the provision of a free appropriate public education to the child," the agency must notify the parents of the "availability of mediation." The IDEA states:

> (1) IN GENERAL.— Any State educational agency or local educational agency that receives assistance under this part shall ensure that procedures are established and implemented to allow parties to disputes involving any matter, including matters arising prior to the filing of a complaint pursuant to subsection (b)(6), to resolve such disputes through a mediation process. (20 U.S.C. §1415(e)(1))

However, mediation may be undertaken by parties to a dispute concerning "any matter."

3. Improper Use of Mediation Prohibited

Mediation may not be "used to deny or delay a parent's right to a due process hearing" or to "deny any other rights" afforded by the IDEA.

4.   Mediators Must Be Impartial and Expert

The mediation must be "conducted by a qualified and impartial mediator who is trained in effective mediation techniques." Each state is required to "maintain a list of individuals who are qualified mediators and knowledgeable in laws and regulations relating to the provision of special education and related services." Each state "shall bear the cost of the mediation process," part of which is the mediator's fee.

C.   The Mediation Process

Because mediation is an alternative to litigation, it must precede the due process hearing. Typically the parties take the following steps.

1.   Notice of Hearing

Mediation may be initiated at any time, but it is usually undertaken at or shortly before the time when the notice of a due process hearing is prepared.

2.   Parents Decide Whether to Mediate

Mediation is a voluntary process. The parents review the case, possibly in consultation with an attorney, and make a decision whether to enter mediation. If parents are unsure about using mediation, a " local educational agency or a State agency may establish procedures to offer to parents and schools that choose not to use the mediation process, an opportunity to meet, at a time and location convenient to the parents, with a disinterested party . . . who will explain the benefits of, and encourage the use of, the mediation process." Parents also may seek other forms of ADR, including arbitration. However, arbitration would require the agency's agreement.

3.   The Mediator Is Selected

The mediator usually is selected, through an impartial process, from "a [state educational agency] list of individuals who are qualified mediators and knowledgeable in laws and regulations relating to the provision of special education and related services." Parties may also agree to a mediator of their choosing.

Mediation Sessions Are Scheduled
The IDEA provides that each "session in the mediation process shall be scheduled in a timely manner and shall be held in a location that is convenient to the parties to the dispute."

Ending Mediation
Mediation may end with an agreement or with a decision to proceed to a due process hearing. If an agreement is reached, the regulations provide that it must be set forth in writing. The topic of agreements is discussed below.

How to Prepare for Mediation

Parties to the mediation should prepare by:

- Assembling the pertinent papers in order in a folder so they can be located easily. These will most likely include the child's "educational records."
- Reviewing pertinent papers and preparing an outline of the major points to be covered and the results desired.
- Reviewing the matter with the attorney who will be representing them at the mediation or advising them in connection with the mediation.

4.   Mediation Confidentiality

Mediation can be effective only when the parties to it are candid about their goals and their reasons for pursuing them. It is essential, therefore, that the parties agree to the confidentiality of the mediation process. The IDEA provides that discussions "that occur during the mediation process shall be confidential and may not be used as evidence in any subsequent due process hearing or civil proceedings." States may allow the parties to sign a confidentiality pledge, but the federal regulations do not require that they do so.

The House Report covering the 1997 Amendments explained Congress's views of the importance of confidentiality in mediation. The views remain those of the Congress in the 2004 Reauthorization.

> The legislation requires that agreements reached in mediation shall be put in writing. Furthermore, the amendments require that discussions held in mediation would be confidential and could not be used as evidence in any subsequent due process hearing or civil action. However, the Committee intends that nothing in this bill shall supersede any parental access rights under the Family Educational Rights and Privacy Act of 1974 or foreclose access to information otherwise available to the parties. Mediation parties may enter into a confidentiality pledge or agreement prior to the commencement of mediation.

5.   Mediation Confidentiality Agreement

The House recommended the following when the mediation procedures were first established:

> a. The mediator, the parties, and their attorneys agree that they are all strictly prohibited from revealing to anyone, including a judge, administrative hearing officer or arbitrator the content of any discussions which take place during the mediation process. This includes statements made, settlement proposals made or rejected, evaluations regarding the parties, their good faith, and the reasons a resolution was not achieved, if that be the case. This does not prohibit the parties from discussing information, on a need-to-know basis, with appropriate staff, professional advisors, and witnesses.

b. The parties and their attorneys agree that they will not at any time, before, during, or after mediation, call the mediator or anyone associated with the mediator as a witness in any judicial, administrative, or arbitration proceeding concerning this dispute.

c. The parties and their attorneys agree not to subpoena or demand the production of any records, notes, work product, or the like of mediator in any judicial, administrative, or arbitration proceeding concerning this dispute.

d. If, at a later time, either party decides to subpoena the mediator or the mediator's records, the mediator will move to quash the subpoena. The party making the demand agrees to reimburse the mediator for all expenses incurred, including attorney fees, plus mediator's then-current hourly rate for all time taken by the matter.

e. The exception to the above is that this agreement to mediate and any written agreement made and signed by the parties as a result of mediation may be used in any relevant proceeding, unless the parties agree in writing not to do so. Information which would otherwise be subject to discovery, shall not become exempt from discovery by virtue of it being disclosed during mediation. (House Rpt. No. 105-95, *Individuals with Disabilities Education Act of 1997,* Committee on Education and the Workforce [May 13, 1997])

6.   Settlement Agreements that Result from Mediation

Mediation agreements are set forth in a document known as a settlement agreement. In reviewing the proposed agreement, it is important to remember that, while the mediator is a skilled professional, the mediator is not the attorney for either party! If the parents are not represented by an attorney at the mediation, and they have concerns about the agreement, they may wish to consult with an attorney. The requirement that the agreement be legally binding inevitably requires that both parties consult counsel. The IDEA provides:

(F) WRITTEN AGREEMENT—In the case that a resolution is reached to resolve the complaint through the mediation process, the parties shall execute a legally binding agreement that sets forth such resolution and that—
(i) states that all discussions that occurred during the mediation process shall be confidential and may not be used as evidence in any subsequent due process hearing or civil proceeding;
(ii) is signed by both the parent and a representative of the agency who has the authority to bind such agency; and
(iii) is enforceable in any State court of competent jurisdiction or in a district court of the United States. (20 U.S.C. §1415[e][2][F])

7.   Attorneys' Fees in Mediation

The IDEA clearly defines when parents may recover attorneys' fees in connection with mediation. "Attorneys' fees may not be awarded relating to any meeting of the IEP Team unless such meeting is convened as a result of an administrative proceeding or judicial action, or, at the discretion of the State, for a mediation." So, parents may be able to recover attorneys' fees for mediation if the state provides for such recovery.

D.   Summary

Parties to a dispute may use ADR methods, rather than court litigation, to resolve their agreements. Arbitration and mediation are forms of ADR. Mediation is a voluntary process for reaching agreement that essentially is a form of negotiation where the parties select an experienced mediator to help the parties explore their differences and facilitate resolution of the dispute. Arbitration is a streamlined and expedited hearing, under which ADA and some other civil rights claims may be decided.

CHAPTER

8

The Due Process Hearing

A. In General

States must establish procedural safeguards to protect the rights of children with disabilities and their parents in the special education process. The IDEA provides:

> (a) ESTABLISHMENT OF PROCEDURES—Any State educational agency, State agency, or local educational agency that receives assistance under this part shall establish and maintain procedures in accordance with this section to ensure that children with disabilities and their parents are guaranteed procedural safeguards with respect to the provision of a free appropriate public education by such agencies. 20 U.S.C. §1415(a)

The procedures generally provide for (1) access to information, (2) mediation, and (3) an administrative ["due process"] hearing. Federal law also provides that a party may challenge the state's due process hearing decision in state or federal court. These mechanisms are described below.

1. Notice and Prehearing Matters

The IDEA requires that parents are provided with a "procedural safeguards notice" which must be "written in an easily understandable manner" and must address all major rights under the IDEA. 20 U.S.C. §1415(d). Congress incorporated a set of "procedural safeguards" to ensure the full participation of the parents and proper resolution of substantive disagreements. The IDEA entitles the parents "to examine all records relating to such child and to participate in meetings with respect to the identification, evaluation, and educational placement of the child, and the provision of a free appropriate public education to such child, and to obtain an independent educational evaluation of the child." 20 U.S.C.§ 1415(b)(1)

2. Due Process Hearing Requirement

In General
Most state education agencies have a simple complaint form that asks for essential information about the complaint, including the complainant's name, address, relationship to the child, and a basic statement of the nature of the case. However, the

relatively simple form is only the first step in a more complex process. It is essential that, before initiating a due process proceeding, there is a plan for litigation strategy.

A study by the General Accounting Office (now the Government Accountability Office [GAO]) addressed the frequency of due process hearings. The GAO said:

> On occasion, parents and schools disagree about what kinds of special services, if any, are needed for children and how they should be provided. Disagreements between school officials and families that cannot be resolved quickly sometimes become formal disputes that can be costly, both financially and in terms of the harm done to relationships. In May 2003, the Special Education Expenditure Project (SEEP) reported that school districts spent at least $90 million on resolving such disputes in the 1999–2000 school year. (*Special Education: Numbers of Formal Disputes Are Generally Low and States Are Using Mediation and Other Strategies to Resolve Conflicts,* Report to the Ranking Minority Member, Senate Committee on Health, Education, Labor, and Pensions [September 9, 2003])

The GAO found that the number of due process hearings is declining over time, while the number of requests for due process proceedings has nearly doubled. The GAO "calculated that nationwide, in 2000, about 5 due process hearings were held per 10,000 students with disabilities," a slight increase from the earlier years studied by the GAO.

Significantly, the use of due process hearings was concentrated in a few states. According to the GAO's data "over three-quarters of the due process hearings had been held in five states—California, Maryland, New Jersey, New York, and Pennsylvania—and the District of Columbia." In general, four due process hearings are held for every 10,000 students and seven mediations for that same number. In contrast, ten state education department complaints were filed for every 10,000 students. These are the "three formal dispute resolution mechanisms" considered by GAO.

> The GAO concluded that while data are limited and inexact, four national studies indicate that the use of the three formal dispute resolution mechanisms has been generally low relative to the number of children with disabilities. Due process hearings, the most resource-intense dispute mechanism, were the least used nationwide.

This report might also support the conclusion that the increased number of due process requests and the decreased number of actual hearings reflects the impact of a significant increase in the use of mediation and other alternative dispute resolution techniques. This topic is discussed in Chapter 7.

3. The Complaint and Response

Either party—parents or the school district—may initiate a due process hearing. Generally the parents of the child are the initiators, but the school system may also initiate. The 2004 statute requires filing of a due process complaint notice, so that all parties have the essential information of the complaint.

Complaints must include the name, address, and school of the child in question together with:

A description of the nature of the problem of the child relating to such proposed initiation or change, including facts relating to such problem; and a proposed resolution of the problem to the extent known and available to the party at the time.

When the agency responds to a parental complaint, the response must include:

An explanation of why the agency proposed or refused to take the action raised in the complaint

A description of other options that the IEP Team considered and the reasons why those options were rejected

A description of each evaluation procedure, assessment, record, or report the agency used as the basis for the proposed or refused action; and

A description of the factors that are relevant to the agency's proposal or refusal.

The following chart illustrates the relationship among the mechanisms for dispute resolution:

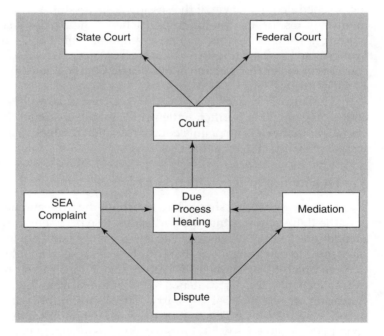

FIGURE 8.1   Special Education Dispute Forum Matrix

On receipt of the complaint notice, the hearing officer will make a determination of its legal sufficiency. This ruling is critical because the "party requesting the due process hearing shall not be allowed to raise issues at the due process hearing that were not raised in the notice" described earlier "unless the other party agrees otherwise." 20 U.S.C. §1415(f)(3)(B)

The law authorizes further that:

Whenever a complaint has been received . . . the parents or the local educational agency involved in such complaint shall have an opportunity for an impartial due process hearing, which shall be conducted by the State educational agency or by the local educational agency, as determined by State law or by the State educational agency. (20 U.S.C. §1415[f][1][A])

4.   The Resolution Conference

Before a due process hearing may proceed, the school district must convene a meeting known as a resolution session to determine whether the complaint can be resolved amicably. The resolution session offers an opportunity for the parents to discuss the issues in the complaint and or the district to resolve the issues presented. Parents and the district may agree in writing to waive the meeting or to use the mediation process instead. Participants in the meeting include the parents, a representative of the school district with decision-making authority, and members of the IEP team with knowledge of the issues in dispute.

On completion of the session, if the dispute has not been resolved, the hearing is scheduled. However, if the session is successful, a written settlement agreement may result. If a resolution is reached," the parties shall execute a legally binding agreement" that is "signed by both the parent and a representative of the agency who has the authority to bind such agency; and . . . enforceable in any State court of competent jurisdiction or in a district court of the United States." 20 U.S.C.§ 1415(f)(1)(B)(iii)

This provision does not provide for award of attorneys' fees or costs. Some courts may treat this "written settlement" as if it were a court judgment, while others will hold that it is not a final court action that renders an individual a "prevailing party" within the meaning of IDEA.

5.   Disclosure of Key Documents

The due process hearing should be a search for the truth and not an ambush. To that end, the IDEA requires that the parties disclose pertinent evaluations and recommendations before the hearing. The law provides that "not less" than "5 business days prior to a hearing . . . each party shall disclose to all other parties all evaluations completed by that date, and recommendations based on the offering party's evaluations, that the party intends to use at the hearing." 20 U.S.C. §1415(f)(2)(A). A hearing officer "may bar any party that fails to comply with this provision from introducing the relevant evaluation or recommendation at the hearing without the consent of the other party." There is a general requirement that *all* documents be disclosed to the other side reasonably in advance of the hearing date, and failure to comply may result in the rejection of evidence.

6.   Right to a Hearing

(A) If the parents are dissatisfied with the IEP or the child's placement, the state or local school district must convene "an impartial due process hearing." See 20 U.S.C. §1415(f)(1)(A).

The right to a hearing includes the right to be represented by a lawyer, the right to subpoena witnesses, the right to present evidence, the right to confront and cross-examine witnesses, the right to obtain a transcript of the proceedings, and the right to challenge an adverse decision in court. Finally there is the right to retain the child's placement until a decision is reached. See generally *Roland M. v. Concord School Committee, cert. denied,* 499 U.S. 912 (1991) and *School Committee of Burlington v. Department of Education,* 471 U.S. 359 (1985) for excellent discussions of these topics.

B. Preparing for a Hearing

The due process hearing is the heart of the disputes process. It is the most effective opportunity for the parties to present their positions in a reasoned and persuasive manner. However informal the complaint requirements may be, an effective presentation demands rigorous preparation and practice to ensure each party's case is presented in the best possible light. The following checklist should be helpful:

- Obtain copies of all relevant documents concerning the child, including:
    1. Teacher notes
    2. Progress reports
    3. Grades or report cards
    4. Achievement tests
    5. Discipline reports
    6. Parent contact notes
    7. Assessments and reports (which may include tests of intelligence, achievement, motor skills, self-help skills, language development, social skills, and functional behavioral analysis)
    8. Reports from medical doctors (such as eye tests, hearing tests, and physical examinations)
    9. Individualized education programs (IEPs) and any behavioral intervention plan (BIP)
    10. Eligibility and IEP team reports and Individual Transition Plans (ITPs) for students by at least age sixteen
- Study the documents and identify the key issues. Make sure that the documents support the position, and, if they do not, prepare to rebut them.
- Review and organize the exhibits.
- Select credible witnesses. Prepare an outline of the elements of the case and the proposed testimony that addresses each. Determine how to handle the weaker points of the case.
- If an expert is required, determine what the expert proposes to say in general terms before the individual writes a more specific report. Remember a harmful report may find its way into evidence and adversely affect the outcome of the case.
- Prepare witnesses for the hearing.

C.   The Hearing

The rules of procedure governing hearings vary from state to state. Whatever the rules, their purpose is to promote the orderly presentation of evidence in a dignified environment. The rules of the Texas Education Agency are used as an example of state procedures in the following explanation of the hearing process.

1.   Time and Location

Texas rules require "reasonable notice" of at least ten days unless otherwise agreed, and the time and location must be "reasonably convenient to the parents and child involved."

2.   Statute of Limitations

Under the IDEA, the due process complaint must be filed within a two-year period of the alleged violation, or within the state's time limitation. However, if the LEA has engaged in certain specified misconduct, the statute of limitations may be extended. The law provides that:

> TIMELINE FOR REQUESTING HEARING—A parent or agency shall request an impartial due process hearing within 2 years of the date the parent or agency knew or should have known about the alleged action that forms the basis of the complaint, or, if the State has an explicit time limitation for requesting such a hearing under this part, in such time as the State law allows. (20 U.S.C. §1415(f)(3)(C))

3.   Representation

Parents may attend the hearing on their child's behalf. Parents also have "the right to be accompanied and advised by counsel." Additionally parents are permitted to utilize "individuals with special knowledge or training with respect to the problems of children with disabilities" in the presentation of their cases. 20 U.S.C. §1415(h)(1). Historically some courts have interpreted this provision to permit the use of "lay advocates," nonlawyers with practical experience concerning due process hearings. Many parents elect to utilize the services of a lay advocate, but school districts have no obligation to pay for these services. *Connors v. Mills* (N.D.N.Y. 1998); *Arons v. New Jersey State Board of Education* (3d Cir. 1988). In at least one state, lay advocacy constitutes the unauthorized practice of law, unless they simply are providing advice or consultation to the parents. See *In re Arons* (Del. 2000), *cert. denied, Arons v. Office of Disciplinary Counsel,* 532 U.S. 1065 (2001)

4.   Behavior

Parties and witnesses are required to "comport themselves with the same dignity, courtesy, and respect" that is required in court proceedings. All arguments "shall be made to the hearing officer alone."

5. Rules Governing the Conduct of the Hearing

As an example, the Texas "Rules of Civil Procedure shall govern the proceedings at the hearing," and the Texas "Rules of Evidence shall govern evidentiary issues." The hearing officer "may set reasonable time limits for presenting evidence at the hearing," may permit testimony to be received by telephone, and may "exclude witnesses from the hearing room" so that the testimony of one witness will not affect another's. In general, the hearings "shall be closed to the public," and will be "transcribed by a reporter." The parties are permitted to present evidence, compel the attendance of witnesses, and cross-examine witnesses, both under state law and under the IDEA.

6. Burden of Proof

Who has the burden of proof? Must the parents prove that the school district's proposed IEP denies their child a FAPE? In *Schaffer v. Weast,* 126 S.Ct. 528 (2005), the U.S. Supreme Court ruled that the party attacking the proposed IEP has the burden of proof. The court said:

> The burden of proof in an administrative hearing challenging an IEP is properly placed upon the party seeking relief. In this case, that party is Brian, as represented by his parents. But the rule applies with equal effect to school districts: If they seek to challenge an IEP, they will in turn bear the burden of persuasion before an ALJ. (Administrative Law Judge—the presiding officer in a due process hearing)

In most cases the parents will have the burden of proof. Occasionally it will be the school district.

7. Opening Statement

After calling the proceedings to order, the parties usually make opening statements that advise the hearing officer of the parties' positions and the evidence to be offered.

8. Introduction of Documents

Before documents may be offered or admitted into evidence, they must be identified as exhibits. All personally identifiable information must be removed from the exhibit.

9. Evidence of Facts

The Rules of Evidence vary from state to state and between states and the federal government. Their purpose is to ensure that all evidence is *"relevant, authentic,* and *probative."* In general, witnesses, other than expert witnesses, may testify only to facts about which they have personal knowledge. Testimony concerning privileged communications, such as between attorney and client, is generally not permitted. Documents must be authenticated through testimony concerning their preparation, agreement of the parties, or, in the case of certain records, because of their public nature. Witnesses called by one party will be examined to elicit relevant facts and are subject to cross-examination by the opposing party.

10. Opinion Evidence

State rules of evidence also have provisions regarding expert testimony. State rules generally follow Federal Rule of Evidence 702:

> Rule 702. Testimony by Experts
>
> If scientific, technical, or other specialized knowledge will assist the trier of fact to understand the evidence or to determine a fact in issue, a witness qualified as an expert by knowledge, skill, experience, training, or education, may testify thereto in the form of an opinion or otherwise, if (1) the testimony is based upon sufficient facts or data, (2) the testimony is the product of reliable principles and methods, and (3) the witness has applied the principles and methods reliably to the facts of the case.

This rule reflects the limits on expert testimony imposed by the U.S. Supreme Court in *Kumho Tire Co. v. Carmichael*, 526 U.S. 137 (1999), and *Daubert v. Merrell Dow Pharms.*, 509 U.S. 579 (1993). Those cases held that courts have an obligation, under the Federal Rules of Evidence, to assess the reliability of expert testimony before admitting it. The purpose is to prevent the use of "junk science" in deciding disputes. To the extent that a state follows the Federal Rules, these cases may be applied to limit testimony in a due process hearing.

11. Decision

In general, posthearing briefs are discouraged. The hearing officer "shall issue a final decision, signed and dated, no later than 45 days after a request for hearing is received by the Texas Education Agency," A "final decision must be in writing and must include findings of fact and conclusions of law separately stated. Findings of fact must be based exclusively on the evidence presented at the hearing." These findings and the evidence on which they are based will serve as a road map in the event that further legal proceedings to review the decision are undertaken. Many attorneys prepare proposed findings of fact to guide the hearing officer. Parents appearing *pro se* (on their own behalf without an attorney) should at least make the hearing officer aware of their views on the key evidence and those conclusions that it supports.

Under the Texas rule, a decision provides the name of the case, docket number, and the identities of counsel; a "Statement of the Case and Procedural History," which is simply a recitation of the administrative steps leading to the hearing; and the findings of fact. The opinion itself contains a description of the applicable legal rules, including those setting the burden of proof; a discussion of the key evidentiary issues— "Change of Placement and Least Restrictive Environment" and "Meaningful Academic and Non-Academic Benefit"; and the Conclusions of Law and the Order. Finally there is a synopsis of the opinion.

The IDEA also contains requirements the decision must meet.

D.   Administrative Review

Texas has a one-step administrative hearing procedure. If one of the parties (usually, but not necessarily, the parents) objects to the decision, the party may proceed directly to court. Many states, however, provide for a two-step procedure, which includes an initial hearing before a local educational agency and a review of the local hearing decision by the SEA. Regarding the SEA review, the 2004 IDEA amendments provide that, if the hearing is "conducted by a local educational agency, any party aggrieved by the findings and decision rendered in such a hearing may appeal such findings and decision to the State educational agency." When this occurs, the "State educational agency shall conduct an impartial review of the findings and decision appealed," and the "officer conducting such review shall make an independent decision upon completion of such review." 20 U.S.C. §1415(g)(1)

E.   Judicial Review

Regardless of the levels of administrative review, the administrative process must be completed before going to court. Unless a state rule exists, the IDEA statute of limitations for filing civil actions is ninety days from the date of the final administrative decision. This is discussed in the next chapter.

F.   Summary

A due process hearing is an administrative proceeding to decide disputes that cannot be resolved by agreement. The hearing is conducted according to state laws governing procedure and evidence and by the IDEA. The proceedings consist of a complaint and response, a resolution hearing, and a due process evidentiary hearing. Both parties have the right to compel witness testimony and introduce both fact and opinion evidence. The hearing officer ensures that the proceedings are run fairly. In some states, the hearing officer's decision is subject to administrative appeal. However, in all cases, judicial review of the hearing officer's decision is allowed, after exhaustion of administrative remedies.

9

Court Proceedings

A. In General

Administrative decisions under the IDEA may be reviewed by either federal courts (the vast majority) or state courts (the minority).

B. Contesting Administrative Decisions in Federal Court

1. What May Be Litigated

The federal and state courts are given jurisdiction by the IDEA to review administrative decisions:

(A) IN GENERAL—Any party aggrieved by the findings and decision made under subsection (f) or (k) who does not have the right to an appeal under subsection (g) [State administrative review], and any party aggrieved by the findings and decision made under this subsection, shall have the right to bring a civil action with respect to the complaint presented pursuant to this section, which action may be brought in any State court of competent jurisdiction or in a district court of the United States, without regard to the amount in controversy. (20 U.S.C.§ 1415[i][2][A])

2. Are States Immune from Suit?

The IDEA provides:

(a) IN GENERAL—A State shall not be immune under the 11th amendment to the Constitution of the United States from suit in Federal court for a violation of this title.

(b) REMEDIES—In a suit against a State for a violation of this title, remedies (including remedies both at law and in equity) are available for such a violation to the same extent as those remedies are available for such a violation in the suit against any public entity other than a State. (20 U.S.C. §1403)

The law uses the term "abrogation" (annulment) of state sovereign immunity by Congress, rather than "waiver" of state sovereign immunity by the state upon accepting federal funds. The difference between "waiver" and "abrogation" is not merely semantic. In *Pace v. Bogalusa City School Board*, 325 F.3d 609 (5th Cir. 2002), the court found that the state of Louisiana had not waived its Eleventh Amendment immunity for particular school years, because at that time, judicial opinions had not yet recognized the existence of sovereign immunity. Louisiana could not, in a word, waive a right it did not know it had. The court then addressed the question of whether the IDEA abrogated or could validly abrogate state sovereignty in the absence of a waiver. Citing the abrogation language quoted earlier, the court said:

> The IDEA does not validly abrogate the State defendants' state sovereign immunity. Like the ADA and § 504 of the Rehabilitation Act, the IDEA contains an express statement of intent to abrogate state sovereign immunity, but in enacting the IDEA, Congress did not find that any disparate treatment of students with disabilities resulted from unconstitutional state action. . . . And even if Congress had identified constitutional transgressions by the states that it sought to remedy through the IDEA, the IDEA requirements, like the ADA and § 504 requirements, exceed constitutional boundaries." (Citations and footnotes omitted)

Upon review of the Louisiana decision, the entire Fifth Circuit (sitting en banc) disagreed with the prior decision and ruled that Louisiana had waived its sovereign immunity when it received IDEA and RA funding. It did not disturb the prior ruling that Louisiana's sovereign immunity was not abrogated by the IDEA. *Pace v. Bogalusa City School Board*, 2005 U.S. App. LEXIS 3926 (5th Cir., 2005)

The court noted:

> The term "abrogation" is not synonymous with "consent" or "waiver." When a state consents to suit or waives its Eleventh Amendment immunity, it knowingly and voluntarily forfeits the immunity's protections. In contrast, when Congress acts under its Fourteenth Amendment power to abrogate, the state has no choice.

So Congress has sought to abrogate stated sovereign immunity under IDEA. However, the view of at least one federal court of appeals is that the state can waive, but Congress cannot abrogate, state sovereign immunity.

3. A Suit That Cannot Be Brought

The IDEA expressly bars private suits for failure of an educational agency employee to be highly qualified:

> (E) RULE OF CONSTRUCTION—Notwithstanding any other individual right of action that a parent or student may maintain under this part, nothing in this section or part shall be construed to create a right of action on behalf of an individual student or class of students for the failure of a particular State educational agency or local educational agency employee to be highly qualified. (20 U.S.C. §1401[10][E])

4. Exhaustion of Administrative Remedies

The IDEA has created an administrative hearing process that must generally be completed before filing suit in court will be allowed. In legal language, this is known as exhaustion of administrative remedies.

In *Murphy v. Arlington Central School District Board of Education* (2d Cir. 2002), The court summarized the law thus:

> Before an aggrieved individual may bring an action in state or federal court for a violation of the IDEA, he or she must seek recourse from the administrative procedures established by the statute. . . . The plaintiff's failure to exhaust administrative remedies ordinarily deprives this court of subject matter jurisdiction over any IDEA claims.
>
> *Hope v. Cortines* (E.D.N.Y. 1995), *aff'd, Fennell v. Cortines* (2d Cir. 1995)

The IDEA expressly prohibits using the ADA and RA, which do not normally require exhaustion of administrative remedies in education cases, as a means of avoiding a due process hearing in favor of a full court trial. The IDEA provides that it shall not:

> Be construed to restrict or limit the rights, procedures, and remedies available under the Constitution, the Americans with Disabilities Act of 1990, title V of the Rehabilitation Act of 1973, or other Federal laws protecting the rights of children with disabilities, except that before the filing of a civil action under such laws seeking relief that is also available under this part, the procedures under subsections (f) and (g) shall be exhausted to the same extent as would be required had the action been brought under this part. (20 U.S.C.§ 1415[1])

The IDEA states the rule employed by the courts. The courts have barred suit under the RA and ADA where the claims under those statutes are essentially the same as a claim covered by IDEA. *Weber v. Cranston School Committee* (D.R.I. 2003); *Jeremy H. v. Mount Lebanon School District* (3d Cir. 1996)

The court in *Murphy v. Arlington Central School District Board of Education* (2d Cir. 2002) described the exceptions to the exhaustion doctrine.

> The exhaustion requirement is "not an inflexible rule." *Mrs. W. v. Tirozzi*, 832 F.2d 748, 755 (2d Cir. 1987). Rather, Congress specified that exhaustion is not necessary if (1) it would be futile to resort to the IDEA's due process procedures; (2) an agency has adopted a policy or pursued a practice of general applicability that is contrary to the law; or (3) it is improbable that adequate relief can be obtained by pursuing administrative remedies. Id. at 756 (quoting H.R. Rep. No. 296, 99th Cong., 1st Sess. 7 (1985)). The burden of proving the applicability of one of these exceptions falls on the party seeking to avoid exhaustion. (*Polera v. Board of Education*, 288 F.3d 478, 488 n.8 [2d Cir. 2002])

5. Futile to Resort to Due Process

If the remedy sought is one that the IDEA cannot provide, there is no duty to use the administrative hearing process. Thus a court held that the exhaustion doctrine did not bar an action by a high school graduate against a school district and school administrators for failing to assess his learning disabilities, because he sought monetary damages not available in a due process hearing. *Hicks v. Purchase Line School District* (W.D.Pa. 2003)

6. General Policy That Violates the Law

Sometimes the school systems are charged with violations of the IDEA that affect entire groups of students and not just a particular student. In those cases, compliance with due process procedures is not required. For example, in *Beth V. v. Carroll, Jr.,* (3d Cir. 1996), a group of parents brought suit against the Pennsylvania Department of Education and the state secretary of Education (PDE), to establish that the Commonwealth failed to comply with regulations promulgated by the U.S. Department of Education (DOE) governing procedures for resolution of complaints. The Third Circuit held that the parents were not required to follow Pennsylvania's due process dispute procedures because of the nature of the parents' broad and systemic claims.

> Consistent with the palpable nexus between the provision of a free appropriate public education mandated by IDEA and the DOE regulations requiring procedures for bringing complaints of violations of IDEA and related regulations to the attention of the state agency, we hold that the plaintiffs, who allege that the PDE has consistently failed to investigate and timely resolve such complaints, enjoy an express right of action under § 1415 of IDEA.

The PDE had argued that the exhaustion doctrine barred the parents because they had not sought a due process hearing.

> In the IDEA § 1415 context, plaintiffs may thus be excused from the pursuit of administrative remedies where they allege systemic legal deficiencies and, correspondingly, request system-wide relief that cannot be provided (or even addressed) through the administrative process.

See also *S. v. Attica Central Schools* (2d Cir. 2004); and *Christopher S. v. Stanislaus County Office of Education* (9th Cir. 2004).

But the alleged violations must be "systemic" in order to bypass due process procedures. In *Doe v. Arizona Department of Education* (9th Cir. 1997), the Ninth Circuit ruled that the alleged violations were not systemic in a case involving juveniles held in the county jail whose special education needs were not being addressed. The court held that the juveniles had "failed to exhaust their administrative remedies." The court said, "The Department simply didn't know that these juveniles were there, and that does not amount to a systemic failure which exhaustion would not cure or for which structural remedies are required." The case was then dismissed.

Other cases that are exceptions to the exhaustion doctrine are class action cases involving high-stakes testing challenges. A California case is an example. Under California law, members of the class of 2004 were required to pass the California High School Exit Examination (CAHSEE). Students with learning disabilities did not go through the IDEA administrative process, but sued under the IDEA and the RA to obtain an injunction requiring that reasonable accommodations be provided on the test. The District Court issued a preliminary injunction providing that:

1] Students may take the CAHSEE with all accommodations, modifications, and alternative testing provided for that test in their IEPs/504 plans.

2] Students whose IEP/504 plans did not specifically address CAHSEE may use all accommodations, modifications, and alternative testing their plans provide for standardized testing.

3] Students whose IEP/504 plans did not specifically address CAHSEE or standardized testing may use all accommodations, modifications, and alternative testing their plans provide for general classroom testing.

The court ruled that "an 'appropriate accommodation' is any accommodation necessary to render a student's score on the CAHSEE a meaningful measure of that student's academic achievement." *Chapman v. California Department of Education,* 229 F.Supp. 2d 981 (N.D. Cal. 2002). However, after protracted litigation, the court became convinced that portions of the relief requested were premature.

First, the court noted that some portions of the injunction were already being implemented:

With respect to paragraphs 1 and 2 of the district court's preliminary injunction order dated February 21, 2002, the State Defendants assure us that those provisions, which permit all members of the plaintiff class to take the California High School Exit Examination ("CAHSEE") with the necessary accommodations and modifications, are already in effect. To avoid any ambiguity on this point, we therefore decline to modify paragraphs 1 and 2 of the district court's order.

Second, the court ruled that some portions of the injunction requested relief that was premature, or, as the court put it, the issues were not ripe for adjudication.

The remainder of the plaintiffs' challenge to the administration of the CAHSEE is not currently ripe for adjudication. The development of the CAHSEE is, as the district court observed, a "highly dynamic process." The State Defendants argue with some justification that they need experience with administration of CAHSEE to further develop and refine the test, to decide whether there should be a delay in the date for imposing it as a requirement for a high school diploma, and for working out the waiver process by which students with disabilities may obtain diplomas even if they are unable to satisfy the normal CAHSEE requirement. The awarding of diplomas is what CAHSEE is fundamentally about. Thus, to the extent that the claims allege potential future harms caused by the possible denial of a waiver of CAHSEE requirements or of a diploma, the accommodations claims are not yet ripe.

On appeal, the case was titled *Smiley v. California Department of Education,* 53 Fed. Appx. 474 (9th Cir. 2002).

In *D.D. v. New York City Board of Education* (E.D.N.Y. 2004), the court ruled that, in an IDEA suit, all present and future children with IEPs who had not received or will not receive all the services required by the IEPs are a class. The court found these children to constitute a class because of (1) sufficient numbers, (2) a common complaint—failure to implement IEPs, (3) claims that were typical of the class as a whole, (4) individual plaintiffs representative of the class, and (5) defendants that "acted or refused to act on grounds generally applicable to the class, thereby making appropriate final injunctive relief or corresponding declaratory relief with respect to the class as a whole." Federal Rules of Civil Procedures (FRCP) 23(b)(2) However, in the end, the court ruled that the class was unable to make the case that the IEP inadequacies were to blame and refused to issue a preliminary injunction. See also *Virginia Department of Education v. Riley* (4th Cir. 1997).

7. Administrative Remedies Do Not Provide Adequate Relief

In *Pamela McCormick ex rel. Eron McCormick v. Waukegan School District* (7th Cir. 2004) (discussed in detail in Chapter 5, Section B.3.), the Seventh Circuit concluded that parents of a student with a rare form of muscular dystrophy, who suffered permanent kidney damage because his physical education teacher failed to properly implement his IEP, were not required to exhaust administrative remedies before bringing suit against the school district and the teacher under Section 1983 and several state laws.

The court stated that the parents sought remedies for physical, rather than educational, injuries to the child, whereas the IDEA does not offer remedies in situations like this one. Therefore, the court said that the parents did not have to meet the exhaustion requirements, since the IDEA administrative processes could not provide the damages they were seeking. The court determined that the outcome of the case hinged on the child's physical injury and not the compensation the parents were seeking.

8. Statute of Limitations

A party suing under IDEA to contest the result of a hearing is subject to a statute of limitations that can be quite restrictive:

> (B) LIMITATION—The party bringing the action shall have 90 days from the date of the decision of the hearing officer to bring such an action, or, if the State has an explicit time limitation for bringing such action under this part, in such time as the State law allows. (20 U.S.C. §1415[i][2][B])

The ninety-day rule applies, unless the "State has an explicit time limitation for bringing such action under this part." Must the state statute specifically reference the IDEA to trigger a period different from the ninety-day period? At present, state laws vary widely. The federal courts have enforced a thirty-day period prescribed by Indiana law for seeking judicial review of administrative decisions in special education matters. *Powers v. Indiana Department of Education* (7th Cir. 1995) The federal courts also have enforced a 120-day limitation period prescribed by Illinois law for suits seeking review of actions by school authorities. See *Reed v. Mokena School District No. 159* (7th Cir. 1994). One court declined to use a thirty-day limitations period prescribed by Kentucky law for appeals of administrative orders and instead applied the state's five-year statute of limitations for actions "upon a liability created by statute, when no other time is fixed by the statute creating the liability." *King v. Floyd County Board of Education* (6th Cir. 2000)

All parties must be especially careful to inquire into the applicable statute of limitations, because the IDEA does not require that parents be notified of the statute of limitations applicable to due process hearings, even though notice of other procedural rights is required. *R.R. v. Fairfax County School Board* (4th Cir. 2003). It is also important to note that there are two statutes of limitation, one for initiating a due process hearing (two years) and one for contesting the results of a due process hearing in a civil action (ninety days).

9. Injunctions

Every U.S. district court has the authority to issue (1) temporary restraining orders, (2) preliminary injunctions, and (3) permanent injunctions. These are orders by the court requiring or preventing some specific conduct. They are enforceable through contempt proceedings. The three differ primarily in the length of time during which they operate. The temporary restraining order and preliminary injunction are justified primarily on the grounds that the party seeking them is likely to obtain a permanent injunction after trial and will be harmed seriously if temporary relief is not given until trial occurs. The permanent injunction is granted or not granted based on the merits of the case following trial.

Injunctions are specifically authorized by the IDEA. The court, having reviewed and supplemented the administrative record (described later in this chapter), "shall grant such relief as the court determines is appropriate." 20 U.S.C§ 1415(i)(2)(C)(iii). This injunctive relief may be available where the stay-put provisions, discussed below, are not. For example, the stay-put remedy is not available where the prior placement is no longer available to the student, due to no fault of the school system. A preliminary injunction under 20 U.S.C. §1415(i)(2)(B)(iii) may be available, but the standards for a preliminary injunction must be met. The preliminary injunction is authorized by the provision that the court shall "grant such relief as the court determines is appropriate." *Wagner v. Board of Education of Montgomery County* (4th Cir. 2003)

10. Stay-Put Provisions

The IDEA provides for a unique type of relief, similar in many ways to a preliminary injunction, called the "stay-put" provision. It provides that:

> During the pendency of any proceedings conducted [to review administrative proceedings] . . . unless the State or local educational agency and the parents otherwise agree, the child shall remain in the then-current educational placement of the child, or, if applying for initial admission to a public school, shall, with the consent of the parents, be placed in the public school program until all such proceedings have been completed. (20 U.S.C.§ 1415[j])

The stay-put provisions also apply to certain aspects of the disciplinary procedures, such as interim educational placements.

The stay-put provision of the IDEA is similar to a preliminary injunction because courts use the stay-put provision to preserve the status quo pending resolution of the case. However, unlike a preliminary injunction, the parents do not need to show that there is a likelihood of success on the merits or that their child may be harmed if an injunction is not issued. What must be established is the "then-current educational placement of the child" or the "public school program" that must be continued.

For example, in *Drinker v. Colonial School District* (3d Cir. 1996), the court held that "Section 1415(e)(3) of the IDEA functions, in essence, as an automatic preliminary injunction." See also *Zvi D. v. Ambach* (2d Cir. 1982); and *Susquenita School District v. Raelee S.* (3d Cir. 1996).

The stay-put provision applies to a currently disputed placement. In one case, the parents argued that the stay-put provisions required the school district to pay for private school during certain years because litigation concerning other years was then ongoing. The court held that the stay-put provisions did not require reimbursement for the uncontested and unlitigated school years. *MM v. School District* (4th Cir. 2002)

11. Rules of Procedure

The Federal Rules of Civil Procedure and of Evidence govern all IDEA suits in federal court. State rules of procedure and evidence govern in state court.

12. District Court Evidentiary Proceedings.

The IDEA confers on the reviewing federal district court broad discretion to grant appropriate relief. See also *School Committee of Burlington v. Department of Education,* 471 U.S. 359 (1985).

Specifically, the IDEA provides that:

> (C) ADDITIONAL REQUIREMENTS.—In any action brought under this paragraph, the court—
> (i) shall receive the records of the administrative proceedings;
> (ii) shall hear additional evidence at the request of a party; and
> (iii) basing its decision on the preponderance of the evidence, shall grant such relief as the court determines is appropriate. (20 U.S.C.§ 1415[i][2][C])

In providing that the court shall hear additional evidence at the request of a party, the IDEA is different from other federal laws. Generally federal statutes require that administrative decisions be honored, unless they are not supported by substantial evidence or are erroneous as a matter of law. Usually administrative decisions are affirmed; however, when the decisions are vacated, they are remanded to the administrative agency for further proceedings. The IDEA allows a review where supplementary evidence may be provided. This has given rise to the question of what deference a district court must give to a due process hearing.

There are two approaches to the extent to which the federal district court will allow additional evidence to be presented: the limited approach and the broad approach.

13.   The Limited Approach

This approach provides that the district court's job is to supplement an inadequate administrative record by admitting evidence that would correct minor defects which would enable the court to complete a traditional review of the record. The IDEA provisions that allow supplementing the record apply only to claims under that statute and not to related claims under other statutes such as the RA and ADA. *Monticello School District No. 25 v. George L.* (7th Cir. 1994)

Under the limited approach, the reviewing court must review the administrative record but is permitted to add to that record where appropriate. Its decision must be independent of the administrative decision but must give "due weight" to the state agency's decision because that decision presumably reflects educational expertise. This is called, a "bounded, independent decision," that is, bounded by the administrative record and additional evidence, because it is based on a preponderance of the evidence before the court. *Roland M. v. Concord Sch. Comm.*, 910 F.2d 983 (1st Cir. 1990), *cert. denied*, 499 U.S. 912 (1991)

14.   The Broad Approach

Under the broad approach, the court uses a modified standard of review and may admit additional evidence to supplement the record for broader purposes than simply to correct minor defects.

The broad approach was adopted in *Deal v. Hamilton County Board of Education* (6th Cir. 2004). In that case the Sixth Circuit Court of Appeals adopted a "modified standard of review." The case involved Zachary, a boy with autism, whose parents and the school differed over the appropriate means of educating Zachary. A lengthy due process hearing took place, involving many witnesses and a transcript of thousands of pages. The hearing officer issued an exhaustive opinion, finding, among other things, that the failure to offer a Lovaas-type program denied Zachary FAPE. Attorneys' fees were denied. Both parties sued to overturn portions of the hearing officer's decision.

The District Court permitted discovery and the introduction of substantial additional evidence, including fact witnesses, expert witnesses, and exhibits. The District Court ruled that the hearing officer had "erred in exalting the Deals' preferred educational methodology above other appropriate methods," and ruled that no denial of FAPE had occurred. The Sixth Circuit Court of Appeals permitted the additional evidentiary proceedings, holding that the District Court may receive additional evidence to supplement its duties under the "modified standard of review." Under that standard, the "district court is required to make findings of fact based on a preponderance of the evidence contained in the complete record, while giving some deference to the fact findings of the administrative proceedings." See *Knable ex rel. Knable v. Bexley City School District* (6th Cir. 2001) *cert. denied, Bexley City School District v. Knable*, 533 U.S. 950 (2001); see also *Metro. Government v. Cook*, 915 F.2d 232 (6th Cir. 1990).

The Sixth Circuit has adopted the broad approach, allowing additional substantial evidence to supplement the record and giving some deference to the hearing officer's decision. Other circuits use the limited approach to the effect that "additional evidence is admissible only in limited circumstances, such as to supplement or fill in the gaps in the evidence previously introduced." In these circuits the federal district courts are to give "due weight" to the decision of the hearing officer.

A separate issue concerns the appropriate standard of review for a federal court of appeals in reviewing a decision of a federal district court. Absent a showing that the wrong legal rule was employed, the court of appeals may review a district court's ruling only for clear error on the record as a whole.

C.   Contesting Administrative Decisions in State Court

State court proceedings are conducted under state rules of civil procedure and evidence and are subject to the state statutes of limitation. In general, state court cases proceed in the same way as federal court cases.

D.   Summary

A party aggrieved by a due process or manifestation decision may sue in state or federal court to have the hearing officer's decision reviewed. Suit must be filed within ninety days, unless state law otherwise provides, and all cases are subject to the requirement that administrative remedies must be exhausted. Some IDEA suits do not seek review of administrative decisions and are not subject to the exhaustion requirement. Federal proceedings are conducted under the Federal Rules of Civil Procedure and the Federal Rules of Evidence. Under the IDEA, unlike other federal laws, the administrative record may be supplemented by additional evidence in a federal district court proceeding.

CHAPTER

10

Attorneys' Fees and Costs

A. In General

The IDEA contains more complex attorneys' fee provisions than are found in other statutes. The basic IDEA rule is:

> (3) JURISDICTION OF DISTRICT COURTS; ATTORNEYS' FEES—
> (B) AWARD OF ATTORNEYS' FEES—
> (i) IN GENERAL—In any action or proceeding brought under this section, the court, in its discretion, may award reasonable attorneys' fees as part of the costs—
> (I) to a prevailing party who is the parent of a child with a disability;
> (II) to a prevailing party who is a State educational agency or local educational agency against the attorney of a parent who files a complaint or subsequent cause of action that is frivolous, unreasonable, or without foundation, or against the attorney of a parent who continued to litigate after the litigation clearly became frivolous, unreasonable, or without foundation; or
> (III) to a prevailing State educational agency or local educational agency against the attorney of a parent, or against the parent, if the parent's complaint or subsequent cause of action was presented for any improper purpose, such as to harass, to cause unnecessary delay, or to needlessly increase the cost of litigation. (20 U.S.C. §1415[i][3][B])

Parents who prevail may recover their attorney's fees from the state or local educational agency (SEA, LEA). Sometimes, a prevailing SEA or LEA may recover its attorney's fees from parents. However, there is a much higher standard for an agency to recover attorneys' fees than for parents. The standard for parents is simply that they are a "prevailing party." However, for the SEA or LEA to recover attorneys' fees, the agency must prevail in a case where the parents or parents' counsel acted improperly.

B. Defining Prevailing Party

The U.S. Supreme Court defined the term "prevailing party" in *Buckhannon Board & Care Home, Inc. v. West Virginia Department of Health & Human Resource*, 532 U.S. 598 (2001). The court said:

Numerous federal statutes allow courts to award attorney's fees and costs to the "prevailing party." The question presented here is whether this term includes a party that has failed to secure a judgment on the merits or a court-ordered consent decree, but has nonetheless achieved the desired result because the lawsuit brought about a voluntary change in the defendant's conduct. We hold that it does not.

Strictly speaking, the court's ruling applied only to the Fair Housing Amendments Act of 1988 (FHAA), 42 U.S.C. §3601 *et seq.*, and the Americans with Disabilities Act of 1990 (ADA), 42 U.S.C. §12101. However, subsequent courts have held that *Buckhannon* also applies to the IDEA. *J.C. v. Regional School District* 10 (2d Cir. 2002)

The courts have explored the concept of how big a win is necessary to be a "prevailing party." To prevail, a party "must succeed on some significant claim within the litigation," resulting in "achieving at least some of the relief envisioned." A "prevailing party" under the IDEA must have prevailed on the IDEA claims. In *Warner v. Independent School District No. 625* (8th Cir. 1998), the plaintiff went to a due process hearing which considered both IDEA claims and claims under the state education laws of Minnesota. The state hearing review officer, "despite concluding that the School District had complied with IDEA," then made rulings against the school under Minnesota law which does not provide for attorneys' fees. Warner sued for attorneys' fees in federal court. The Eighth Circuit held that "prevailing party" under the IDEA means prevailing on IDEA claims. Warner was not the "prevailing party" because "the Hearing Review Officer expressly rejected Warner's IDEA claims before granting relief under state law."

C.   Conduct that Limits Recovery of Attorneys' Fees by Parents

The IDEA does not allow recovery by prevailing parents of attorneys' fees and costs generated by the parents' or their attorney's misconduct. This law provides that "whenever the court finds that . . . the parent, or the parent's attorney, during the course of the action or proceeding, unreasonably protracted the final resolution of the controversy or . . . the attorney representing the parent did not provide to the local educational agency the appropriate information in the notice of the [due process hearing] complaint . . . the court shall reduce, accordingly, the amount of the attorneys' fees awarded under this section." However, fees to parents will not be reduced or disallowed "if the court finds that the State or local educational agency unreasonably protracted the final resolution of the action or proceeding or there was a violation of this section." 20 U.S.C.§ 1415(i)(3)(F)(i)-(iv)

D.   The Educational Agency as Prevailing Party-Special Considerations

Sometimes the prevailing party is an educational agency, rather than the plaintiff. As discussed earlier, in order to recover attorneys' fees under the IDEA, the educational agency must prevail in a case involving some essentially improper conduct on the part of the parent's attorney or the parents.

The IDEA provides that state or local educational agencies that are prevailing parties may recover attorneys' fees. 20 U.S.C.§ 1415 (i)(3)(B). The IDEA provides more specific guidance than ordinarily appears in federal statutes.

1. Parents

An SEA or LEA may recover attorneys' fees from the parents "if the parent's complaint or subsequent cause of action was presented for any improper purpose, such as to harass, to cause unnecessary delay, or to needlessly increase the cost of litigation." 20 U.S.C.1415(i)(3)(B)(i)(III)

2. Parents' Attorneys

When is an award of costs and attorneys' fees against the parents' attorneys proper? An award of fees and costs against the attorneys would be proper whenever an award against the parents would be proper, or when the attorney "files a complaint or subsequent cause of action that is frivolous, unreasonable, or without foundation." Fees and costs may also be awarded against the parents' attorney if the attorney has "continued to litigate after the litigation clearly became frivolous, unreasonable, or without foundation." 20 U.S.C.§ 1415(i)(3)(B)(i)(II)-(III)

Cases under the ADA/RA are helpful in understanding the types of conduct that generally might lead to recovery by a prevailing defendant of attorneys' fees and costs from a plaintiff.

In *Seawright v. Charter Furniture Rental, Inc.* (N.D. Tex. 1999), for example, the defendant was awarded $29,800 in attorneys' fees where the plaintiff brought a suit that was frivolous, unreasonable, groundless, and in bad faith. The attorney was also sanctioned for filing and prosecuting the case without proper investigation.

In *Bercovitch v. Baldwin School, Inc.*, 133 F.3d 141 (1st Cir. 1998), the First Circuit reversed a finding by the District Court that the parents were entitled to injunctive relief under the ADA/RA. The District Court then considered the Baldwin School's demand for attorneys' fees and costs. The court denied the claim for attorneys' fees because the parents' claims were successful in the District Court and were not "frivolous, unfounded or unreasonable." However, the parents were ordered to pay "the school's litigation costs of slightly more than $14,000." The ruling was affirmed on appeal.

E.   Other Provisions Regarding Recovery of Attorney's Fees

1.   Sanctions and Misconduct under Federal Rule of Civil Procedure (FRCP) 11

School districts, parents, and their counsel alike may be liable for costs and attorneys' fees as sanctions for misconduct under FRCP 11 and 28 U.S.C. §1927 (counsel's liability for excessive costs).

2. Unproductive Litigation—IDEA and Federal Rule of Civil Procedure (FRCP) 68

The IDEA prohibits recovery of attorneys' fees and costs incurred in certain kinds of unproductive litigation.

> (D) *Prohibition of Attorneys' Fees and Related Costs for Certain Services—*
>   (i) IN GENERAL—Attorneys' fees may not be awarded and related costs may not be reimbursed in any action or proceeding under this section for services performed subsequent to the time of a written offer of settlement to a parent if—
>   (I) the offer is made within the time prescribed by Rule 68 of the Federal Rules of Civil Procedure or, in the case of an administrative proceeding, at any time more than 10 days before the proceeding begins;
>   (II) the offer is not accepted within 10 days; and
>   (III) the court or administrative hearing officer finds that the relief finally obtained by the parents is not more favorable to the parents than the offer of settlement. (20 U.S.C.§ 1415[i][3][D])

Federal Rule of Civil Procedure 68 is similar to the IDEA provision. However, the IDEA provision protects parents more than in the ordinary application of FRCP Rule 68. The IDEA provides that Rule 68 and the IDEA section based on it shall not be applied to "a parent who is the prevailing party and who was substantially justified in rejecting the settlement offer."

In the case of *Jason D.W. v. Houston Independent School District* (5th Cir. 1998), the court found that Jason's family, in rejecting a settlement offer, had unreasonably protracted the litigation and could not recover attorney's fees for the court litigation. Jason was a student "diagnosed with attention deficit disorder and a speech impairment that cause[d] him significant academic and social difficulty." His parents became dissatisfied with the school's efforts to educate him and initiated a due process hearing. The hearing officer found for the parents on three of the nineteen issues in the complaint: "that (1) Jason's parents were entitled to reimbursement for the fees of two psychologists whom they had retained to help the District develop a behavior management plan for Jason, (2) that the behavior management plan ultimately adopted by the District was not appropriate, and (3) that Jason's placement in a resource class from January 10, 1995 to February 2, 1995 was not appropriate and denied him a free appropriate public education (FAPE)."

The parents' attorney then filed a claim for "$32,943.97, a sum representing the total amount of attorneys' fees and costs." Settlement discussion ensued. The school district made, and the family rejected, two settlement offers of lower monetary amounts. Jason's parents then sued in court, under the IDEA, seeking recovery of all attorneys' fees and costs incurred in connection with the due process hearing. The school district then made an official offer of judgment under FRCP Rule 68 for $24,429. Jason's family rejected the offer. Under Rule 68, Jason's family had to obtain, at trial, a greater amount for the due process attorney's fees and costs than the settlement offer of $24,429, in order to recover the attorney's fees and costs the parents incurred in relation to the trial. After a trial, the District Court found that Jason's family was entitled only to total fees, costs, and expenses for the due process hearing in an amount well below the amount of settlement offer, and that Jason's family had unreasonably protracted the controversy by refusing to settle. Therefore, Jason's family did not recover any attorneys' fees or costs for the federal court trial. In addition, the court ruled that Jason's family had to reimburse the school district over $2,000 of the school district's costs incurred in relation to the trial after the family rejected its settlement offer. The Court of Appeals for the Fifth Circuit affirmed the district court's decision, stating that the policy behind Rule 68 is to encourage settlement and that no conflict exists between encouraging settlement and protecting the welfare of children with disabilities and their parents.

3. Specific Activities That Are Nonreimbursable

Generally speaking, attorneys' fees and costs "may not be awarded relating to any meeting of the IEP Team unless such meeting is convened as a result of an administrative proceeding or judicial action, or, at the discretion of the State, for a mediation." 20 U.S.C.§ 1415(i)(3)(D)(ii)

The complaint resolution process is not considered "an administrative hearing or judicial action," and therefore fees may not be collected.

4. Unreasonable Rates and Hours

The court may "award reasonable attorneys' fees as part of the costs," for which the IDEA provides specific guidance:

> (C) DETERMINATION OF AMOUNT OF ATTORNEYS' FEES.—Fees awarded under this paragraph shall be based on rates prevailing in the community in which the action or proceeding arose for the kind and quality of services furnished. No bonus or multiplier may be used in calculating the fees awarded under this subsection. (20 U.S.C.§ 1415[i][3][C])

For further clarity, the IDEA provides that "the court shall reduce, accordingly, the amount of the attorneys' fees awarded under this section, when

> The amount of the attorneys' fees otherwise authorized to be awarded unreasonably exceeds the hourly rate prevailing in the community for similar services by attorneys of reasonably comparable skill, reputation, and experience . . . [or]
> the time spent and legal services furnished were excessive considering the nature of the action or proceeding. 20 U.S.C.§ 1415[i][3][F])

This provision does not apply, notwithstanding excessive rates and hours, "if the court finds that the State or local educational agency unreasonably protracted the final resolution of the action or proceeding or there was a violation of this section."

What about contingent fee arrangements? In *Johnson v. Clearfield Area School District* (W.D. Pa. 2004), the court considered the settlement of the case of a child with mental retardation whose family sued the school district for violation of the child's civil rights and rights under the IDEA, RA, and ADA. The amount of the settlement was $67,500, of which 40 percent would go to the attorney as payment of a contingent fee. Counsel attempted to justify the bill with the unsupported statement that more than one hundred hours of attorney time were expended and that, in any event, the parties had agreed to a 40 percent contingent fee. The court disapproved the settlement.

F. Summary

Under the IDEA, parents are "prevailing parties" if they have obtained a significantly favorable court judgment or consent decree, or their equivalents. As prevailing parties, parents may recover reasonable attorneys' fees and costs. Local or state educational agencies may recover these fees and costs when they are prevailing parties and the court has found parents or their attorneys to have engaged in certain improper conduct. The IDEA also bars recovery of attorneys' fees and costs under other circumstances, such as for IEP meetings and resolution conferences. Attorneys' fees must be based on a reasonable hourly rate and number of hours expended. The IDEA and Federal Rule of Civil Procedure 68, as applied in IDEA cases, prohibit the recovery of attorneys' fees and costs incurred in litigation that essentially does not produce a better result than a prior rejected settlement offer, unless parents were justified in rejecting the offer. Either a party or counsel or both may be liable for costs and attorneys' fees as sanctions under FRCP 11 and 28 U.S.C. §1927. Sanctions under these provisions may be imposed regardless of prevailing party status.

CHAPTER

11 RA/ADA: Individual with a Disability

A. Introduction: Coverage

1. The Rehabilitation Act of 1973

In the mid-1970s, Congress adopted legislation to end discrimination against individuals with disabilities generally and to improve educational and other services available to them. The first of these was the Rehabilitation Act of 1973 (RA), 29 U.S.C. §701, *et seq.*, which prohibits discrimination against individuals with disabilities in federal employment, as well as in government contracts and programs receiving federal financial assistance.

The RA bans discrimination by (1) the U.S. Government (29 U.S.C. §791), (2) contractors with the U.S. Government (29 U.S.C. §793), and (3) recipients of federal funds (29 U.S.C. §794). The last provision, popularly known as Section 504, covers all federal grant and aid recipients, including most elementary, secondary, and postsecondary educational institutions. Section 504 also served as the model for the Americans with Disabilities Act of 1990.

2. The Americans with Disabilities Act of 1990

The Americans with Disabilities Act (ADA) (42 U.S.C. §12101 *et seq.)* was passed in July 1990 to end discrimination against individuals with disabilities in the areas of employment, state and local government activities, public accommodations, and other public activities.

The ADA was intended to extend to virtually all segments of society the basic disability-based civil rights set forth in the RA. The rights and obligations created by the ADA overlap, to some extent, with those of the RA. The simplest way to distinguish the two laws is to remember that the RA applies only to entities receiving *federal* funds, whereas the ADA applies more broadly.

The ADA prohibits discrimination in three major areas: private employment (Title I); the activities of state and local governments (public schools, employment, licensing, public programs, etc.) (Title II); and access to privately owned places of public accommodation (private schools, hotels, theaters, etc.) (Title III).

3.   A Common Language

The ADA was based on the RA and contains identical definitions, including the definition of an "individual with a disability." For this reason, court decisions regarding definitions under the ADA also would be instructive regarding definitions of the same terms under the RA. Together the ADA and RA were intended to create the same civil rights, including the protection of the civil rights of qualified individuals with disabilities. The relationship between the two laws is best understood through the Supreme Court's decision in *Bragdon v. Abbott*, 524 U.S. 624 (1998). Speaking for the court, Mr. Justice Kennedy explained the relationship:

> The ADA's definition of disability is drawn almost verbatim from the definition of "handicapped individual" included in the Rehabilitation Act of 1973, 29 U.S.C. §706(8)(B) (1988 ed.), and the definition of "handicap" contained in the Fair Housing Amendments Act of 1988, 42 U.S.C. §3602(h)(1) (1988 ed.). Congress' repetition of a well-established term carries the implication that Congress intended the term to be construed in accordance with pre-existing regulatory interpretations.

B.   Statutory Language

The ADA contains the following definition of a disability:

> The term "disability" means, with respect to an individual—
> (A) a physical or mental impairment that substantially limits one or more of the major life activities of such individual;
> (B) a record of such an impairment; or
> (C) being regarded as having such an impairment. (42 U.S.C. §12102[2])

The ADA defines an individual with a disability in precisely the same way as the RA. See 29 U.S.C. §706(8)(B).

For our purposes, the significant definition is "Test A," an impairment that substantially limits a major life activity. "Test B" was intended to prevent discrimination on the basis of past impairments, and "Test C" was intended to prevent discrimination on the basis of conditions such as disfiguring burns which, while not disabling in themselves, might lead to discrimination based on an erroneous perception that an individual has a particular disability.

The RA/ADA defines "disability" conceptually. Any impairment that substantially limits a major life activity can qualify. While the statutes and their implementing regulations identify specific impairments, the list is by no means exhaustive. Other impairments may qualify as "disabilities" if they substantially limit a major life activity.

The RA/ADA approach stands in direct and dramatic contrast to the IDEA, in that the RA/ADA are far more flexible in how those laws define disability. Under the IDEA, a "child with a disability" is a child with one or more of a specific list of impairments "who, by reason thereof, needs special education and related services." 20 U.S.C. §1401(3). See Chapter 4, Section B.1. for the IDEA listing of disabilities. If the child has a disability that is not included in the specific disability categories, the child would not be covered by the IDEA, even if he or she "needs special education and related services" because of it. Coverage of additional conditions would require congressional amendment of the IDEA.

C. Impairments Covered

The RA/ADA applies to *any* "individual with a disability," which includes one who has a "physical or mental impairment" that "substantially limits" one or more of such person's "major life activities." Under RA/ADA,

> (h) Physical or mental impairment means:
> (1) Any physiological disorder, or condition, cosmetic disfigurement, or anatomical loss affecting one or more of the following body systems: neurological, musculoskeletal, special sense organs, respiratory (including speech organs), cardiovascular, reproductive, digestive, genito-urinary, hemic and lymphatic, skin, and endocrine; or
> (2) Any mental or psychological disorder, such as mental retardation, organic brain syndrome, emotional or mental illness, and specific learning disabilities. (29 C.F.R. §1630.2)

Note that the RA and ADA expressly apply to individuals with "specific learning disabilities." That term has been held to have the same meaning as the IDEA definition. See *Lyons v. Smith* (D.D.C. 1993).

D. Substantially Limits

The concept of substantial limitation has been developed by regulations and court decisions. The impact of the impairment must be severe enough to result in an actual limitation of performance. The regulations provide that the impairment "substantially limits" a major life activity when the person is:

> (i) Unable to perform a major life activity that the *average* person in the *general population* can perform; or
> (ii) Significantly restricted as to the condition, manner or duration under which an individual can perform a particular major life activity as compared to the condition, manner, or duration under which the *average* person in the *general population* can perform that same major life activity. 29 (C.F.R. §§ 1630. 2[j][1][i]-[ii]) (Emphasis added)

Who is the "average person" and what is "the general population"? The answers to these questions are much easier for persons with physical impairments, such as mobility, vision impairments, and hearing impairments. On the other hand, the answers can be considerably more complex for individuals with learning, attentional, and psychiatric impairments.

The courts have made it clear that the average person is not "perfect." In *Wong v. Regents of the University of California* (9th Cir. 2004), the court provided an in-depth analysis of substantial limitation in considering the claim of a medical student who was discharged from medical school. The court ruled that he was not an individual with a disability because his learning impairment, which limited his ability to process and communicate information, did not limit him substantially in learning, reading, or working compared with the average member of the population. Though Wong's impairments caused him difficulty in coping with the last two years of medical school, the average person would also have had trouble completing those years. Wong did not demonstrate that he was substantially limited in learning compared with the average member of the population.

When a substantially limiting impairment has been shown, a disability within the meaning of the RA/ADA has been established. However, the individual also must show that he or she is capable of meeting the essential requirements of the educational program or employment with or without a reasonable accommodation and is thus a "qualified individual with a disability."

1.   Measuring the Severity of the Disability

When do you measure a disability's severity? Do you measure the severity with or without considering the effects of a person's coping strategies or the effects of medication?

The U.S. Supreme Court considered these questions in *Sutton v. United Air Lines, Inc.*, 527 U.S. 471 (1999). The Supreme Court ruled that "when judging whether that person is 'substantially limited' in a major life activity and thus 'disabled' under the Act," the court must consider "that if a person is taking measures to correct for, or mitigate, a physical or mental impairment, the effects of those measures—both positive and negative—must be taken into account."

Sutton concerned the question of whether the beneficial effects of prosthetic devices should be considered in evaluating the extent of an impairment. The court held they should. Companion cases ruled that the beneficial effects of medication (*Murphy v. United Parcel Service, Inc.*, 527 U.S. 516 [1999]) and coping or compensatory strategies (*Albertsons, Inc. v. Kirkingburg*, 527 U.S. 555 [1999]), should also be considered. Any negative consequences of the prosthetic devices, medications, or coping strategies also would have to be considered.

2.   *Scope of Impact:* Toyota v. Williams

Toyota Motor Manufacturing, Kentucky, Inc. v. Williams, 534 U.S. 184 (2002), involved a suit by an automobile assembly worker. The worker was assigned quality assurance duties, including a "shell body audit" job, which required her to apply a highlight oil to the body of a newly manufactured car at a rate of approximately one car per minute. She began to experience pain in her neck and shoulders and was eventually diagnosed with carpal tunnel syndrome and other disorders. She requested that her condition be accommodated by relieving her of her shell body audit duties. She was not relieved of those duties and was placed on "a no-work-of-any-kind restriction" by her treating physicians. Toyota then terminated her employment.

She sued under the ADA, claiming that she was disabled because she was substantially limited, among other things, in the major life activities of performing manual tasks and working. The trial court ruled that she was not substantially limited in any major life activity and was therefore not disabled under the law. The Court of Appeals reversed, ruling that she was disabled because she lacked the "ability to perform the range of manual tasks associated with an assembly line job," and was therefore substantially limited in her ability to perform manual tasks. The court noted that her ability to perform isolated, nonrepetitive manual tasks over a short period of time, such as tending to her personal hygiene or carrying out personal or household chores, did not preclude her from being covered by the ADA.

The U.S. Supreme Court reversed. The court applied the "demanding standard for qualifying as disabled" created by the ADA. It ruled that to be "substantially limited" in a "major life activity,"

> an individual must have an impairment that prevents or severely restricts the individual from doing activities that are of central importance to most people's daily lives. The impairment's impact must also be permanent or long-term.

Applying this reasoning to the case at hand, the Supreme Court noted that repetitive work with hands and arms extended at or above shoulder levels for long periods of time "is not an important part of most people's daily lives," and that the Court of Appeals therefore should not have considered Williams's "inability to do such manual work in her specialized assembly line job as sufficient proof that she was substantially limited in performing manual tasks." Rather the Court of Appeals should have also considered her ability to perform household chores, bathe, and brush her teeth, because these "are among the types of manual tasks of central importance to people's daily lives, and should have been part of the assessment of whether [Williams] was substantially limited in performing manual tasks." The case was then returned to the Court of Appeals for further proceedings.

3. Impact of the Supreme Court's Rulings

Together, the four key Supreme Court cases hold that the effects (both beneficial and negative) of prosthetic devices (*Sutton*), medicines (*Murphy*), and compensatory strategies (*Kirkingburg*) must be considered when determining whether an individual has an impairment that substantially limits a major life activity and is therefore covered by the ADA. The nature of the impact must be such that it "prevents or severely restricts the individual from doing activities that are of central importance to most people's daily lives. The impairment's impact must also be permanent or long-term." (*Toyota*)

Considering the total effects of the impairment—together with those of the prosthetic devices, medications, and strategies—makes the ADA/RA approach much closer to the test used under the Social Security Act (SSA). In *Andersen v. Apfel* (E.D. La. 1999), for example, the Court held that ADHD, which is "remedied" by medication, is not an SSI disability, because under the SSA any medical condition that is remedied by surgery, treatment, or medication is not considered disabling.

E.   Major Life Activities

To constitute a "disability," an impairment must substantially limit one or more of the person's major life activities, which are typically defined as functions such as caring for oneself, performing manual tasks, walking, seeing, hearing, speaking, breathing, learning, and working. 29 CFR § 1630.2(i)

Life activities that relate to individuals with learning disorders have received considerable analysis by the courts.

1.   Learning

Learning is a major life activity in which many individuals with learning, attentional, or other cognitive impairments may be substantially limited. However, in order to show the existence of a disability for this reason, it is necessary to show that *learning* truly is substantially limited. See *Price. v. The National Board of Medical Examiners* (S.D. W.Va. 1997).

When learning is substantially impaired, the effects of the impairment must be felt throughout the range of the individual's day to day life. Here are some examples of impairments whose impact affected, but did not substantially limit, learning: *McGuinness v. University of New Mexico School of Medicine*, 170 F.3d 974 (10th Cir. 1998), *cert. denied*, 526 U.S. 1051 (1999) (test anxiety); *Stephen N. Roth, M.D. v. Lutheran General Hospital* (7th Cir. 1995) (visual impairment); and *Leisen v. City of Shelbyville* (7th Cir. 1998) (emotional disability).

Thus, proof that learning is substantially limited requires a showing that learning is substantially limited in a broad sense and not just in one course or program.

2.   Reading

The Second and Ninth Circuits have recognized reading as a major life activity. *Bartlett v. New York State Board of Law Examiners*, 156 F.3d 321 (2d Cir. 1998), *vacated and remanded, N.Y. State Board of Law Examiners v. Bartlett* (U.S. June 24, 1999) (No. 98-1285) (plaintiff was substantially limited in reading and learning; the fact that she had self-accommodated didn't foreclose finding that she was "individual with a disability"); *Matthew Head v. Glacier Northwest*, Docket No. 03-35567 (9th Cir. 2005) (reading is a major life activity because of its central importance to most people's lives); *Wong v. Regents of the University of California* (9th Cir. 2004) (standard is substantial limitation in ability to read for purposes of daily living).

3.   Working

Working is treated differently from all other major life activities for purposes of considering whether an individual with an impairment is substantially limited. In order to determine whether a substantial limitation on working exists, the impairment must bar the individual from significant classes of jobs, and not just a particular job. Only disabilities with this or an even broader impact are considered substantially to limit working. See, generally, *Schultz v. Spraylat Corp.* (C.D. Cal.

1994); *Dutcher v. Ingalls Shipbuilding* (5th Cir. 1995); *Burke v. Virginia*, 938 F. Supp. 320 (E.D. Va. 1996), 20 MDLR 829; aff'd, 1997 U.S. App. LEXIS 13388 (4th Cir. 1997); *Davidson v. Midelfort Clinic* (7th Cir. 1998), *Coen v. Riverside Hospital* (N.D. Ohio 1999); and *EEOC v. J. B. Hunt Transport, Inc.* (2d Cir. 2003).

4. Concentration and Thinking

Both the Equal Employment Opportunity Commission (EEOC) and the Department of Education view concentration, thinking, and interacting with others as major life activities. However, many courts disagree. The Tenth Circuit, for example, has ruled that concentration is not a major life activity. In *Pack v Kmart Corp.* 166 F.3d 1300 (10th Cir. 1999), *cert. denied* (1999), 528 U.S. 811 (1999), the Ninth Circuit agreed with the EEOC that thinking and interacting with others are major life activities. *Matthew Head v. Glacier Northwest*, Docket No. 03-35567 (9th Cir. 2005)

F. Otherwise Qualified

The RA and ADA do not protect all individuals with disabilities, only those who are "otherwise qualified" for the educational program, job, or license at issue. The central problem with both the RA and ADA, when applied to individuals with learning disorders, is the very proof that establishes that an individual is substantially limited in learning—that is, that the impairment "prevents or severely restricts the individual from doing activities that are of central importance to most people's daily lives." See *Toyota*, Section E.2 this chapter. This also shows that the individual is not qualified for the job or program at issue.

The RA and ADA contain similar language. Like the RA, the ADA does not protect all disabled individuals. It applies only to a "qualified individual with a disability."

> (8) Qualified individual with a disability
> The term "qualified individual with a disability" means an individual with a disability who, with or without reasonable accommodation, can perform the essential functions of the employment position that such individual holds or desires. (42 U.S.C. §12111)

So under both the ADA and RA, an "individual with a disability" must also be "otherwise qualified." An "otherwise qualified" individual who, though having a disability, also would be eligible for the education, job, or program benefit, with or without a reasonable accommodation. See *Wynne v. Tufts University School of Medicine* (1st Cir. 1992).

The ultimate lack of qualifications occurs when an individual poses a "direct threat" to others in the academic or workplace setting. In *Robertson v. Neuromedical Center* (5th Cir. 1998) *cert. denied*, 526 U.S. 1098 (1999), for example, the Fifth Circuit upheld the termination of a neurologist with ADHD. Holding that there was no duty to accommodate Robertson in his medical practice, the court said:

Robertson posed a "direct threat" to the health and safety of others in the workplace. Robertson's short-term memory problems had already caused various mistakes to be made in patients' charts and in dispensing medicine. Most significantly, Robertson voiced his own concerns about his ability to take care of patients, stating that it was only a matter of time before he seriously hurt someone. In light of this evidence, we agree with the district court's conclusion that any accommodations in this case would be unjustified from the standpoint of the basic medical safety of Dr. Robertson's patients.

See also *McRae v. Potter* (N.D. Ill. 2002); and *Shiring v. Runyon* (3d Cir. 1996).

G.   State Law Definitions of Disability

State laws may differ from federal laws, and, in fact, some state laws have a broader and more inclusive definition of disability than the federal laws. For this reason, it is important to be conversant in state, as well as federal, law in reviewing options.

H.   Summary

The RA and ADA protect individuals who meet the statutory criteria. To invoke the protection of these statutes, individuals must prove that they are individuals with a disability. This requires showing that the person has a physical or mental impairment that substantially limits one or more *major* life activities, such as learning, taking into account the positive and negative effects of any medication and/or compensatory strategies. The limitation must be *substantial*, as compared with the performance of the average person in the general population. The impact of the impairment must be in broad areas of activity and not just in one narrow area. When a substantially limiting impairment has been shown, a disability within the meaning of the RA/ADA has been established. However, there must also be a showing that the person is capable of meeting the essential requirements of the educational program or employment, with or without a reasonable accommodation, and is thus a "*qualified* individual with a disability."

12 RA/ADA: Coverage

A. In General

The rights of individuals with disabilities are governed principally by the Rehabilitation Act of 1973 (RA) and Americans with Disabilities Act of 1990 (ADA). Together these statutes apply to most employers, both public and private, all state and local governmental programs, most places of public accommodation, the executive and congressional branches of the federal government, most federal programs, most government contractors, and all recipients of federal funding. Generally exempt from the disability protections of these laws are personnel on active duty in the armed forces, the federal judiciary, employers of fewer than fifteen employees who do not receive federal financial support, and religiously controlled institutions that do not receive federal funds.

The RA differs from the ADA in one crucial way. The RA generally applies only to the federal government and those who receive money or financial support from it. In a nutshell, the RA follows federal dollars. The ADA, in contrast, applies regardless of federal financial involvement.

B. The RA

The RA prohibits discrimination against individuals with disabilities in federal employment, as well as in government contracts and programs receiving federal financial assistance. It bans discrimination by (1) the U.S. government (29 U.S.C. §791), (2) contractors with the U.S. government (29 U.S.C. §793), and (3) recipients of federal funds (29 U.S.C. §794). The last of these provisions, popularly known as Section 504, covers all federal grant and aid recipients. Most notably, it applies to virtually all elementary, secondary, and postsecondary educational institutions. Section 504 also served as the model for the ADA.

C. The RA Applies to the Federal Government

1. Coverage

Executive Branch

Employment by the executive branch of the federal government is regulated by the Civil Service Reform Act of 1978 (CSRA), 5 U.S.C. §2301(b)(2), which provides that "all employees and applicants for employment should receive fair and equitable treatment in all aspects of personnel management without regard to . . . handicapping condition." Executive branch employment also comes under the RA, 29 U.S.C. §791. In turn, the RA provides that "the standards applied under" the ADA are to be used in deciding "whether this section has been violated." Collectively these statutes prohibit discrimination against individuals with disabilities by the executive agencies, military departments (civilian employees), U.S. Postal Service, Postal Rate Commission, and the Tennessee Valley Authority. The RA also requires affirmative action by those agencies.

Legislative Branch

The ADA specifically provides that the "remedies and procedures" of the ADA "shall be available to any employee of an instrumentality of the Congress" for a violation of the prohibition against "any discrimination based on . . . disability, within the meaning of [the RA and ADA]." This section covers the General Accounting Office, the Government Printing Office, and the Library of Congress. 42 U.S.C. §12209. See generally, *Office of the Senate Sergeant at Arms v. Office of Senate Fair Employment Practices* (Fed. Cir. 1996).

Judicial Branch

The judicial branch currently has no *statutory* duty to refrain from disability-based discrimination. However, the Constitution may impose obligations on the judiciary to make its services accessible to individuals with disabilities. See *Tennessee v. Lane*, 541 U.S. 509 (2004).

2. Basic Policies

The federal government is required by law to be a model employer. To achieve this end, the following basic policies are required:

- Recruitment efforts should be focused on achieving a workforce made up of qualified people from all segments of society, and selection and promotion should be based solely on merit, after fair and open competition.
- All employees and applicants should be treated fairly, without discrimination, and with proper regard for their privacy and constitutional rights.
- Discrimination on the basis of race, color, religion, sex, national origin, age, handicapping condition, marital status, or political affiliation . . . (is prohibited). (An Introduction to the Merit Systems Protection Board, Pages 7–8)

- Each covered agency of the federal government is required to prepare and implement an affirmative action program for the hiring, placement and advancement of handicapped individuals. 29 U.S.C. §791

D. The RA Applies to Most Government Contractors

Each agency of the federal government is required to include clauses in its contracts obligating contractors to prepare and implement an affirmative action program for the hiring and advancement of "qualified individuals with handicaps." 29 U.S.C. §793

E. The RA Applies to Federal Grant and Aid Recipients

1. Statutory Language

The best known of the RA statutory provisions is "Section 504." It provides that recipients of federal funds are prohibited from discriminating against an individual "solely by reason of her or his disability." 29 U.S.C. §794(a). Affirmative action is not required.

29 U.S.C.A. §794(a) provides:

No otherwise qualified individual with a disability . . . shall, solely by reason of her or his disability, be excluded from the participation in, be denied the benefits of, or be subjected to discrimination under any program or activity receiving Federal financial assistance or under any program or activity conducted by any Executive agency or by the United States Postal Service.

2. Grants and Aid are Broadly Defined

The courts have given the nondiscrimination provisions of Section 504 a broad reach by finding the existence of federal financial support and funding in a range of circumstances. In *New York v. Mid Hudson Medical Group* (S.D.N.Y. 1995), the court found that Section 504 applied because of doctors' receipt of Medicare/Medicaid payments, which the court held constituted federal financial assistance. In *Delmonte v. Department of Business & Professional Regulation, Div. of Alcoholic Beverages & Tobacco* (S.D. Fla. 1995), the court held that the Florida Department of Business Regulation was subject to the RA, because the department had "accepted training by several federal law enforcement agencies at no cost."

F. Overview of the ADA

The ADA was passed in July 1990 for the purpose of ending discrimination against individuals with disabilities in the area of employment, education, public accommodations, and licensing of professional and other activities.

The ADA was intended to complement the RA. Together, these laws were intended to extend disability-based civil rights to virtually all segments of society. To some extent, the rights and obligations created by the ADA overlap those of the RA. The simplest way to think of the matter is to remember that the RA follows federal dollars, while the ADA applies directly to *categories* of entities, including employers, private testing entities, licensing authorities, and public and private educational institutions, except for religiously controlled institutions. No lesser standard is contemplated under the ADA compared with the RA.

42 U.S.C. §12201(a) provides:

> Except as otherwise provided in this chapter, nothing in this chapter shall be construed to apply a lesser standard than the standards applied under title V of the Rehabilitation Act of 1973 . . . or the regulations issued by Federal agencies pursuant to such title.

The ADA is implemented by regulations governing employment (EEOC jurisdiction, 42 U.S.C. §12111); public services (Department of Justice jurisdiction, 42 U.S.C. §§ 12131, 12134); and public accommodations (also Department of Justice jurisdiction, 42 U.S.C. §12181). In addition, the ADA/RA standards have been extended to employment by the Congress. 42 U.S.C. §12209; 42 U.S.C.§ 2000e–16b(a)-(b)

The ADA prohibits discrimination in three major areas: employment (Title I); the activities of state and local governments (public schools, public postsecondary institutions, employment, licensing, public programs, etc.) (Title II); and access to privately owned places of public accommodation (private schools, private postsecondary institutions, private testing entities, restaurants, hotels, theaters, etc.) (Title III).

G. ADA, Title I (Employment)

As noted in Chapters 3 and 4, Title I of the ADA is supported by the Commerce Clause of the U.S. Constitution. The basic requirement of Title I is

> No covered entity shall discriminate against a qualified individual with a disability because of the disability of such individual in regard to job application procedures, the hiring, advancement, or discharge of employees, employee compensation, job training, and other terms, conditions, and privileges of employment. (42 U.S.C. §12112[a])

ADA, Title I is not the only federal statute that applies to employment. Sections 791, 793, and 794 of the RA apply to the employment activities of covered entities. In addition Title II of the ADA covers the employment activities of state and local governments.

Under Title I of the ADA, the "term 'covered entity' means an employer, employment agency, labor organization, or joint labor–management committee" 42 U.S.C. §12111(2). An "employer" is "a person engaged in an industry affecting commerce who has 15 or more employees for each working day in each of 20 or more calendar weeks in the current or preceding calendar year, and any agent of such person" 42 U.S.C. §12111(5). This section of the ADA exempts from the term "employer," "the United States, a corporation wholly owned by the government of the United States, or an Indian tribe; or . . . a bona fide private membership club (other than a labor organization) that is exempt from taxation under" . . . the Internal Revenue Code.

H. ADA, Title II (State and Local Governments)

Title II of the ADA prohibits discrimination by state and local governments. This prohibition is valid and enforceable by private right of action where the discrimination is intentional. See *Board of Trustees of the University of Alabama v. Garrett*, 531 U.S. 356 (2001); and *Kiman v. N.H. Department of Corrections* (1st Cir. 2002). The "programs, policies and activities" of state and local governments include public elementary and secondary schools and public colleges, universities, and professional schools. The ADA applies to public, as well as private, educational facilities. The legal principles applicable to public universities are comparable to those applicable to private universities under Title III of the ADA.

Title II provides in pertinent part:

> Subject to the provisions of this subchapter, no qualified individual with a disability shall, by reason of such disability, be excluded from participation in or be denied the benefits of the services, programs, or activities of a public entity, or be subjected to discrimination by any such entity. (42 USC §12132)

The term "public entity" means "any State or local government," as well as "any department, agency, special purpose district, or other instrumentality of a State or States or local government." 42 USC §§12131(1)(A)-(B)

Title II also covers state and local government employment, licensing of professions and trades, courts, prisons, and other activities. State and local prisons are covered by the ADA. In *Pennsylvania Department of Corrections v. Yeskey*, 524 U.S. 206 (1998), the U.S. Supreme Court held that "the plain text of Title II of the ADA unambiguously extends to state prison inmates."

State court systems are "public entities" under Title II and are subject to the ADA's prohibition against discrimination and its corresponding requirement for access. For example, in *Tennessee v. Lane*, 541 U.S. 509 (2004), the U. S. Supreme Court considered Title II of the ADA in a case involving the issue of physical access by persons with paraplegia to the courts. The Court ruled in a 5–4 decision that private parties could sue states for monetary damages under Title II of the ADA where fundamental due process rights, such as access to the courts, are at issue. Applied in this manner, the ADA "is congruent and proportional" to the congressional "object of enforcing the right of access to the courts."

Local governmental activities also are subject to Title II. In *Martinez v. City of Roy* (10th Cir. 1998), a municipal pool employee requested that the Martinez parents, whose children had a skin condition, provide a doctor's verification that the condition was not contagious before permitting the children in the pool. The Martinez parents refused the request and sued under Title II of the ADA. The District Court held that the children were not qualified individuals with disabilities, and the Tenth Circuit affirmed that decision.

I. ADA, Title III (Public Accommodations)

1. General Rule

The ADA prohibition against discrimination by places of public accommodation is simply stated:

> No individual shall be discriminated against on the basis of disability in the full and equal enjoyment of the goods, services, facilities, privileges, advantages, or accommodations of any place of public accommodation by any person who owns, leases (or leases to), or operates a place of public accommodation. (42 U.S.C. §12182[a])

The ADA prohibits discrimination by private entities whose operations as places of public accommodation "affect commerce." 42 U.S.C. §12181(7). The ADA lists the following as "places of public accommodation": inns, hotels, motels, restaurants, bars, theaters, auditoriums, stores, gas stations, lawyers' officers, doctors' offices, hospitals, bus stations, airports, museums, parks, private schools and other educational institutions, day care centers, and gymnasiums. The list simply is illustrative and not comprehensive. 42 U.S.C. §12181(7)

2. Private Schools

The ADA mandates access to the activities of the listed entities in an integrated setting. "Places of education are one of the listed entities." This includes all private elementary, secondary, and postsecondary educational programs, as well as preparatory programs for licensing examinations such as the bar exam and testing entities. 28 C.F.R. §§36.202, 36.203.

3. Hospitals

The list of places of public accommodation in Title III is quite clear. How the ADA applies to the activities of those places is less clear. While there is no doubt that public access to places of public accommodation is mandated, there is a question as to whether such facilities owe nondiscrimination duties to classes of people other than customers. For example, a hospital, as a listed place of public accommodation, clearly owes a duty of nondiscrimination to its patients and guests. But does it owe such a duty to the doctors who have staff privileges at the hospital but are not employees covered by Title I of the ADA? In *Menkowitz v. Pottstown Memorial Medical Center* (3d Cir. 1998), the Third Circuit answered that question in the affirmative.

4. Public Sports Events and Entertainment

Places that host public sports events and entertainment are also places of public accommodation subject to Title III. In *PGA Tour, Inc. v. Martin,* 532 U.S. 661 (2001), the U.S. Supreme Court held that PGA Tour, Inc., a nonprofit corporation that annually sponsors and cosponsors professional qualifying rounds and golf tournaments such as the PGA Tour, was a place of public accommodation subject to Title III of the ADA. PGA Tours, Inc., leased but did not own the golf courses where these events took place.

Martin, a golfer participating in a PGA, Inc., tournament, had a degenerative circulatory disorder that prevented him from walking the golf course. He was substantially limited in the major life activity of walking compared with average people. Therefore he was a person with a disability under the ADA. The court found that allowing Martin to use the golf cart would not fundamentally alter the qualifying golf tournament.

J. Summary

Rights are conferred upon individuals with disabilities by the Rehabilitation Act of 1973 and Americans with Disabilities Act of 1990. Together these statutes apply to most public and private employers, all state and local governmental programs, most places of public accommodation, the executive and congressional branches of the federal government, most federal programs, most government contractors, and all recipients of federal funding. Generally exempt from the disability protections of these laws are personnel on active duty in the armed forces. The RA follows federal dollars, and the ADA applies to categories of entities. However, employers of fewer than fifteen employees are exempted from coverage by Title I of the ADA, and religiously controlled schools are exempted from coverage by Title III of the ADA.

13 RA/ADA Enforcement

A. In General

The RA differs from the ADA in one crucial way. The RA generally applies only to the federal government and those who receive money or financial support from it. In a nutshell, the RA follows federal dollars. The ADA, in contrast, applies regardless of federal financial involvement.

B. Enforcement of the RA

The RA sometimes may be enforced by private civil suit, for example, when intentional discrimination against individuals with disabilities by an entity receiving federal funds can be shown. See generally *Sellers by Sellers v. School Board.* (4th Cir. 1998), *cert. denied,* 525 U.S. 871 (1998). Damages and injunctive relief are available.

> In a suit against a State for a violation of . . . [the RA] . . . remedies (including remedies both at law and in equity) are available for such a violation to the same extent as such remedies are available for such a violation in the suit against any public or private entity other than a State. (42 U.S.C. §2000d-7[a][2]; see also 29 U.S.C. §794a)

Regulations issued under the RA can be enforced in civil suits or administrative proceedings, the purposes of which are to determine whether the federal funding recipient has complied with the grant terms. In cases involving intentional discrimination, private parties may sue. However, whether or not intentional discrimination can be shown, private parties may not recover compensatory damages from the federal government in suits brought under the RA. *Alexander v. Sandoval,* 532 U.S. 275 (2001); *Lane v. Pena,* 518 U.S. 187 (1996)

C. Enforcement of the ADA

The ADA contains various enforcement mechanisms borrowed from the Civil Rights Act of 1964, including actions by the EEOC, Justice Department, and, where the ADA overlaps with the RA, the Department of Labor. Enforcement actions by the federal government are authorized for violations of any Title of the ADA. The Department of Justice, on behalf of an individual, may also pursue fines and penalties. The ADA also encourages the use of alternative dispute resolution (ADR) techniques such as settlement negotiations, conciliation, facilitation, mediation, fact-finding, minitrials, and arbitration to the extent they are "appropriate" and "authorized by law." The act permits civil suits by individuals for relief, including injunctive relief and back pay and as well as compensatory and punitive damages. 42 U.S.C. §12117

Private actions are also allowed and are described below.

1.   Title I

Injunctive Relief
Injunctive relief is available to the EEOC, the Attorney General, or to any person alleging discrimination on the basis of disability in violation of any provision of Title I. The "powers, remedies, and procedures set forth" include injunctive relief.

> If the court finds that the respondent has intentionally engaged in or is intentionally engaging in an unlawful employment practice charged in the complaint, the court may enjoin the respondent from engaging in such unlawful employment practice. (42 U.S.C. §2000e-5[g][1])

Damages
Title I of the ADA prohibits disability discrimination in employment and provides remedies in the form of damages for violations of this Title.

> In an action brought by a complaining party under the powers, remedies, and procedures set forth in . . . [Title I of the ADA] . . . against a respondent who engaged in unlawful intentional discrimination . . . the complaining party may recover compensatory and punitive damages . . . from the respondent. (42 U.S.C. §1981a[a][2])

2.   Title II

Title II does not contain specific enforcement provisions. However, case law makes it clear that damages and injunctive relief are appropriate where the application of Title II is supported by a specific constitutional provision. *Tennessee v. Lane*, 541 U.S. 509 (2004)

3.   Title III

Injunctive Relief
Injunctive relief for violations of Title III is authorized by 42 U.S.C. §12188 (Enforcement).

Damages
The ADA does not authorize damages for violation of this Title.

Finally, 42 U.S.C. §12203 contains prohibitions against retaliation or coercion that would prevent individuals from exercising their rights under the act.

	RA	Title I- ADA	Title II-ADA	Title III-ADA
Private Suit Injunction	Yes	Yes	Limited*	Yes
Private Suit Damages	Yes	Yes	Limited*	No
U.S. Suit Injunction and/or Damages	Yes	Yes	Limited*	Yes

*Limited to those portions of Title II that are specifically supported by the Fourteenth Amendment to the U.S. Constitution.

FIGURE 13.1   Enforcement Provisions of the RA/ADA

D. Attorneys' Fees and Costs

The RA (29 U.S.C.§ 794a) and the ADA (42 U.S.C. §§ 12117, 12133, 12203(c) and 12205) contain substantially the same requirement. Representative of these provisions, 42 U.S.C. §12205 provides:

> In any action or administrative proceeding commenced pursuant to this chapter, the court or agency, in its discretion, may allow the prevailing party, other than the United States, a reasonable attorney's fee, including litigation expenses, and costs, and the United States shall be liable for the foregoing the same as a private individual.

Generally the courts have viewed this provision and its civil rights antecedents as establishing two separate standards for recovery of attorneys' fees and costs. Employees have been required to show that they are the prevailing parties, whereas employers have been required to show that they are prevailing parties and more, for example, that the suit against them was unreasonable or frivolous. *Adkins v. Briggs & Stratton Corp.* (7th Cir. 1998), *Christianburg Garment Co. v. EEOC*, 434 U.S. 412, 421–22 (1978).

In *Bercovitch v. Baldwin School, Inc.*, 133 F. 3d 141 (1st Cir. 1998), discussed earlier, the court reversed a District Court finding that the parents of a student who had been enrolled at the school were entitled to injunctive relief under the ADA/RA. The District Court then considered the Baldwin School's demand for attorneys' fees and costs. The District Court denied the claim for attorneys' fees because the parents' claims were successful in the District Court and were not "frivolous, unfounded or unreasonable." However, the parents were ordered to pay "the school's litigation costs of slightly more than $14,000." *Bercovitch by & Through Bercovitch v. Baldwin Sch.*, 1998 U.S. Dist. LEXIS 16823 (D.P.R. 1998) In *Bercovitch v. Baldwin School, Inc.*, 191 F.3d 8 (1st Cir. 1999), the First Circuit affirmed the District Court's denial of attorneys' fees:

> We hold that attorney's fees may not be awarded to a prevailing defendant under the ADA unless the defendant establishes that the plaintiff's suit was totally unfounded, frivolous, or otherwise unreasonable or that the plaintiff continued the litigation after it clearly became so. The same standard applies to claims under the Rehabilitation Act, given that the language is virtually identical.

The difference between costs and attorneys' fees was addressed in *Walton v. Mental Health Association of Southeastern Pennsylvania* (E.D. Pa. 1999). There the defendant employer in an ADA case was awarded $11,836.51 in costs. The unsuccessful plaintiff argued that she should not have to pay the defendant's costs because (1) she had already had to pay in excess of $10,000 in her own costs, and (2) such an award "puts her at imminent risk of a serious and possibly irreversible mental collapse." Citations omitted. The court held that Federal Rule of Civil Procedure 54 governing the award of costs "has been strictly enforced, and the court has no discretion to make the type of compassionate exception that plaintiff believes is imperative."

E.   Office for Civil Rights (OCR)

The U.S. Department of Education plays a central role in the interpretation and enforcement of the IDEA and the RA and ADA, as the latter two pertain to education. Central to the enforcement of these acts is the Office for Civil Rights (OCR). In its self-described mission, OCR emphasizes access to education and the achievement of excellence through civil rights enforcement.

> Ensuring equal access to education and
> promoting educational excellence
> throughout the nation through
> vigorous enforcement of civil rights.

This section provides an overview of OCR and its activities. More detailed information can be found in OCR publications such as *Annual Report to Congress: Fiscal Year 2003* (Office for Civil Rights, U.S. Department of Education, Washington, D.C., 2004).

The OCR is responsible for enforcing civil rights laws that prohibit discrimination on the basis of race, gender, age, and disability. The agency's rulings apply to 14,859 school districts, 4,197 colleges and universities, and 5,059 institutions conferring certificates below the associate degree level, such as training schools for truck drivers and cosmetologists. This equates to nearly 54.3 million students attending elementary and secondary schools and nearly 16.4 million students attending colleges and universities.

1.   Organizational Structure

OCR is headquartered in Washington, DC. It provides overall leadership, policy development, and coordination of enforcement activities. In addition to the DC headquarters, there are twelve enforcement offices around the nation. The majority of OCR's staff is assigned to the enforcement offices, which are located in Boston,

New York, and Philadelphia (Eastern Division); Washington, DC, Atlanta, and Dallas (Southern Division); Cleveland, Chicago, and Kansas City (Midwestern Division); and Denver, San Francisco, and Seattle (Western Division).

2.   Complaint Resolutions

Complaint resolution is a key method used by OCR to carry out its responsibilities. Persons may file complaints with the appropriate enforcement office if they believe there has been a violation of the civil rights laws enforced by OCR. Fifty-two percent of the complaints received relate to disability-based discrimination.

Generally, the process, as described by OCR, is as follows:

> OCR uses a variety of techniques to resolve complaints, ranging from facilitating voluntary resolutions between parties to negotiating agreements with recipients for voluntary compliance after compliance concerns have been established. If these methods fail, OCR issues violation letters and enters into negotiations to correct those violations. It is only after OCR has advised recipients of their failure to comply with the civil rights laws and has determined that compliance cannot be secured by voluntary means that, as a last resort, OCR seeks compliance through the administrative hearing process or refers cases to the U.S. Department of Justice.

It is interesting to compare this data with the information furnished by the General Accounting Office regarding due process hearings under the IDEA (see Chapter 8). Three of the top six cities shown—San Francisco, Philadelphia, and New York—were among the top six jurisdictions generating due process hearings. Three cities—Atlanta, Dallas, and Boston—were not in the top six. This suggests that in many states, complaints to the OCR are more readily used than due process hearings to resolve disputes.

FY 2003 Complaint Receipts by OCR Enforcement Offices	
Boston	185
New York	203
Philadelphia	232
District of Columbia	123
Atlanta	399
Dallas	306
Chicago	183
Cleveland	160
Kansas City	160
Denver	188
San Francisco	351
Seattle	167
Total	2,657

FIGURE 13.2   Complaint Receipts by OCR Enforcement Offices

3.   Evaluation of the Complaint Resolution Process

The OCR process basically consists of evaluating the submissions of the parties to a dispute. While affidavits and documents may be submitted and reviewed, there is no process for taking testimony, compelling witness attendance, cross-examination of witnesses, or for excluding documents that contain hearsay or are otherwise unreliable. Accordingly, OCR tends to rely heavily on the word of the educational institutions. On a positive note, the process is inexpensive and faster than most other means of litigation and informal disputes resolution.

4.   Compliance Reviews, Monitoring and Technical Assistance

OCR also initiates and conducts compliance reviews whose purpose is to identify civil rights violations, obtain agreement for corrective action, and ensure that the corrective action occurs. For example:

> 1. "Nearly 3,600 students with learning disabilities were excluded by a school district's policy that made only students with certain other disabilities eligible for extended school year services. The school district now makes decisions on extended school year services based on the individual needs of students and not on the category of disability."
>
> 2. "A school system failed to enter a student's achievement test scores into its computer system because he was given extended time to accommodate a disability. After validating modifications for each of its standardized tests, the district developed procedures for recording, maintaining and providing access to scores of all students who take standardized achievement tests."

5.   OCR Case Resolutions

OCR has listed the following examples of its work in the disability area (Descriptions cited from OCR).

Making School Programs Accessible to Students with Disabilities

A school district conducted an annual field trip to an inaccessible theater. Mobility-impaired students were carried from the bus to the second floor of the theater to see the performance and placed in seats or fold-up strollers. Because the theater is a National Historic landmark, structural changes could not be made to provide physical access to the second floor. However, as a result of an on-site investigation, OCR determined there was an accessible first floor dinner theater nearby, and management was willing to relocate performances there. The district agreed to this arrangement, and students can now be taken in their wheelchairs to the accessible theater location.

Eliminating Shortened School Day for Students with Disabilities

Special education students were routinely dismissed earlier than other students in one school district. This resulted in a shorter school week of up to two hours for some disabled students. The district agreed to stop this practice unless early release time is specified in a student's individualized education program.

Providing Auxiliary Aids for Students with Disabilities

A hearing-impaired student alleged that a university denied her the service of note takers and dismissed her after she failed several courses. The university resolved the complaint by reinstating the student and providing free tuition for six credit hours. The university assured that note takers would be provided for all her future classes.

At another university, OCR found that interpreters were routinely 25–35 minutes late for their assigned classes. One student was dropped from class because the interpreter was not present during roll call. Under the resolution agreement, students who use interpreter services will be asked to provide feedback that will determine whether interpreters are retained.

Making Academic Adjustments for Students with Disabilities

A law school student with a disability alleged that the school denied a request for academic adjustments, which resulted in her academic dismissal. The law school resolved the complaint by permitting the student to retake an examination with the necessary academic adjustments. If the student passes the examination, the law school will readmit the student.

OCR received another complaint alleging a state board of regents denied accommodations for its General Educational Development Test for a student with disabilities. The state board resolved the complaint by allowing the student extended time and the use of a calculator.

Providing Transportation Services for Students with Disabilities

One of OCR's enforcement offices received a complaint from a parent alleging that a school district was not providing her daughter, who has a disability, with transportation services from an after-school program as required in her individualized education program (IEP). After being contacted by OCR, the district agreed to provide transportation from after-school activities in accordance with the student's IEP. The district also agreed to reimburse the parent for the expenses she had incurred while transporting her daughter from after-school activities.

Providing Educational Support Services for Students with Disabilities

The parent of a high school student contacted OCR about her son not being provided with the instructional support services that were outlined in his IEP. OCR determined that some teachers were not fully aware of the services that the student was supposed to be receiving and did not know how to raise that issue with school administrators. The school district entered into an agreement that included training teachers on the importance of fully implementing a disabled student's IEP and on the process to follow if they believe that IEP services are not being provided or if they believe that additional or different services are needed.

F.   Department of Justice

The Department of Justice has a similar procedure for evaluating claims of disability discrimination and advising parties concerning the lawfulness of particular courses of conduct.

G.   Summary

Rights are conferred upon individuals with disabilities by the Rehabilitation Act of 1973 and Americans with Disabilities Act of 1990. The RA may be enforced by several federal government departments and sometimes by private suits. The ADA may be enforced by various federal government departments and agencies and sometimes by private suits. Damages and injunctive relief are available remedies under both the RA and the ADA, except that ADA, Title III, does not provide for damages as a remedy for violations of that title.

14 Elementary and Secondary Education

A. In General

We have already considered in some detail the IDEA and its application to elementary and secondary education. In this chapter we discuss in greater detail the application of the RA/ADA to elementary and secondary education and explore differences between those laws and the IDEA. In discussing the RA/ADA, we define "individual with a disability" as a person who "has a physical or mental impairment which substantially limits one or more of such person's major life activities." (See also discussion in Chapter 11.)

The RA/ADA approach to education is fundamentally the same, whether considering elementary, secondary, or postsecondary. *Discrimination* against individuals with disabilities is prohibited, and *qualified individuals* with disabilities are entitled to *reasonable accommodations* in meeting the *essential requirements* of the educational program.

B. Discrimination

1. Basis for Public Education

Elementary and secondary education in the United States is required and provided by state laws. The right to equal education is viewed as a "fundamental right." *Brown v. Board of Education,* 347 U.S. 483 (1954). The "equal fundamental rights" view of *Brown* closely parallels similar expressions used in state constitutions and education laws.

Following are examples of views on education set forth in various state constitutions and laws:

California

SECTION 1. A general diffusion of knowledge and intelligence being essential to the preservation of the rights and liberties of the people, the Legislature shall encourage by all suitable means the promotion of intellectual, scientific, moral, and agricultural improvement. . . .

SEC. 5. The Legislature shall provide for a system of common schools by which a free school shall be kept up and supported in each district at least six months in every year, after the first year in which a school has been established. California Constitution, Article 9

Massachusetts
Wisdom, and knowledge, as well as virtue, diffused generally among the body of the people, being necessary for the preservation of their rights and liberties . . . it shall be the duty of legislatures and magistrates, in all future periods of this commonwealth, to cherish the interests of literature and the sciences, and all seminaries of them. Massachusetts Constitution: Chapter V, Section II

New York
The New York State Constitution requires that "[t]he legislature shall provide for maintenance and support of a system of free common schools, wherein all the children of this state may be educated" (Art. XI, §1) cited in *Reform Educational Financing Inequities Today (R.E.F.I.T.) & C. v. Mario M. Cuomo, Governor of the State of New York*

Vermont
§ 1. RIGHT TO EQUAL EDUCATIONAL OPPORTUNITY
The right to public education is integral to Vermont's constitutional form of government and its guarantees of political and civil rights, . . . Therefore, it is the policy of the state that all Vermont children will be afforded educational opportunities which are substantially equal although educational programs may vary from district to district. Vermont Statutes, Title 16; Ch. 1

The common theme among these examples is that the basic education of all children is important for society. Therefore the state government has the obligation to provide to its citizens a free basic public education. In all the states, education is viewed as a basic right. In contrast, there is no federal right to education, as such. Rather the only federal requirement is that whatever education the states choose to provide must be made available, without discrimination, to everyone, including individuals with disabilities and other protected categories.

2.   FAPE under the RA

The RA requires that the states make available a "free appropriate public education" (FAPE) to individuals with disabilities, because a free public education is available to individuals who do not have disabilities.

Free appropriate public education.
(a) General. A recipient that operates a public elementary or secondary education program or activity shall provide a free appropriate public education to each qualified handicapped person who is in the recipient's jurisdiction, regardless of the nature or severity of the person's handicap.
(b) Appropriate education.
    (1) For the purpose of this subpart, the provision of an appropriate education is the provision of regular or special education and related aids and services that (i) are designed to meet individual educational needs of handicapped persons as adequately as the needs of nonhandicapped persons are

met and (ii) are based upon adherence to procedures that satisfy the requirements of §§104.34, 104.35, and 104.36.

(2) Implementation of an Individualized Education Program developed in accordance with the Education of the Handicapped Act is one means of meeting the standard established in paragraph (b)(1)(i) of this section. 34 C.F.R. §§ 104.33(a)-(b). The key requirement is the mandated provision of "regular or special education and related aids and services" that are "designed to meet individual educational needs of handicapped persons as adequately as the needs of nonhandicapped persons are met." Also note that all public schools are subject to the more general requirements of the regulations which implement Title II of the ADA, i.e., schools must comply with Title II, whether or not they receive federal funds.

The basic requirements under the RA are as follows:

The basic requirements common to those cases, to the [IDEA], and to this regulation are (1) that handicapped persons, regardless of the nature or severity of their handicap, be provided a free appropriate public education, (2) that handicapped students be educated with nonhandicapped students to the maximum extent appropriate to their needs, (3) that educational agencies undertake to identify and locate all unserved handicapped children, (4) that evaluation procedures be improved in order to avoid the inappropriate education that results from the misclassification of students, and (5) that procedural safeguards be established to enable parents and guardians to influence decisions regarding the evaluation and placement of their children. (Appendix A to Part 104—Analysis of Final Regulation)

In a word, the Section 504 regulations require that individuals with disabilities covered by the RA receive a "free appropriate public education." Compliance with the IDEA is one, but only one, means of providing FAPE in public school.

The components of FAPE are defined, as well.

Section 104.33(b) concerns the provision of appropriate educational services to handicapped children. To be appropriate, such services must be designed to meet handicapped children's individual educational needs to the same extent that those of nonhandicapped children are met. An appropriate education could consist of education in regular classes, education in regular classes with the use of supplementary services, or special education and related services. Special education may include specially designed instruction in classrooms, at home, or in private or public institutions and may be accompanied by such related services as developmental, corrective, and other supportive services (including psychological, counseling, and medical diagnostic services). (Appendix A to Part 104—Analysis of Final Regulation)

The Department of Education says that for elementary and secondary education programs, a qualified person with a disability is a person with a disability who is:

1. of an age during which it is mandatory under state law to provide such services to persons with disabilities;

2. of an age during which persons without disabilities are provided such services; or

3. a person for whom a state is required to provide a free appropriate public education under the Individuals with Disabilities Education Act (IDEA). (Free appropriate public education for students with disabilities: requirements under section 504 of the rehabilitation act of 1973, Office of Civil Rights, U.S. Department of Education [July 1999];)

In general all school age children who have disabilities are entitled to FAPE.

Students are *qualified* to attend school because they are *required* to attend school. That simple fact means that the RA, as it applies to public elementary and secondary schools, must be interpreted differently from the law as it applies in other circumstances. Basically, *if children are required to attend school, the school has an obligation to attempt to educate them when they get there.* The process of providing education to a child with a severe disability might require a fundamental alteration in the form and content of the educational program offered to other students. The public school system is required to educate, as "qualified" students, children who might not be qualified if they were to apply to a typical private school.

The Department of Education also addressed appropriate public education for students with disabilities similar to the memorandum cited above:

> An appropriate education will include:
> 1. educational services designed to meet the individual educational needs of students with disabilities as adequately as the needs of nondisabled students are met;
> 2. the education of each student with a disability with nondisabled students, to the maximum extent appropriate to the needs of the student with a disability;
> 3. nondiscriminatory evaluation and placement procedures established to guard against misclassification or inappropriate placement of students, and a periodic reevaluation of students who have been provided special education or related services; and
> 4. establishment of due process procedures that enable parents and guardians to receive required notices, review their child's records and challenge identification, evaluation and placement decisions and that provide for an impartial hearing with opportunity for participation by parents and representation by counsel, and a review procedure.

Note that the education services required under the RA as a "free appropriate education" may, in some cases, be quite similar to education services required by the IDEA.

3. Comment on the RA Regulations

The RA requirement for a "free appropriate public education" is not the same as the requirement under the IDEA, despite the similarity in language. First, the RA applies to individuals who have impairments that substantially limit major life activities compared with the average member of the population. In contrast, the standard under the IDEA refers to children "with mental retardation, hearing impairments (including deafness), speech or language impairments, visual impairments (including blindness), serious emotional disturbance . . . orthopedic impairments, autism, traumatic brain injury, other health impairments, or specific learning disabilities" who "by reason thereof, need[s] special education and related services." To be covered by the IDEA, a child must have a listed condition and need special education and related services to address it.

To illustrate the possible difference in coverage: A student with severe dyslexia who is highly intelligent and compensates well might be determined to have a specific learning disability that requires special education and related services, which would qualify the student for services under the IDEA. However, the student might not be limited in learning compared with average people because of his overall performance in academics, including reading. In such a case, the child would not be disabled under the RA, because there would be no substantial limitation in the major life activity of learning. Note that, while we are discussing the RA, the same definition of disability exists in the ADA.

Similarly the provision of special education and related services can entail fundamental modifications in the course materials or their method of presentation. Generally fundamental modifications are not required by the RA/ADA, which require only reasonable accommodations.

Most students who have the disabilities listed under the IDEA and who also require special education and related services would be considered to be substantially limited in a major life activity and therefore covered by the RA. However, these students are entitled to reasonable accommodations under the RA and not to the broader and more comprehensive services provided under the IDEA.

The Department of Education explained the statutory relationships this way:

> The fact that a school district has found a student to need special education and related services under IDEA because of a listed condition creates a strong, although rebuttable, presumption that the condition, with any mitigating measures used, is an impairment that substantially limits a major life activity such as learning or reading.

See Memorandum to OCR Staff, from Norma V. Cantu, Assistant Secretary for Civil Rights, Subject Internal Guidance Document Entitled "Sutton Investigative Guidance: Consideration of 'Mitigating Measures' in OCR Disability Cases" dated September 29, 2000.

4. Private Schools

Private preschool, elementary, and secondary education programs that accept federal aid are covered by the RA/ADA. There are some differences between private and public programs, which we cover later in this chapter. The RA states that:

> (a) A recipient that provides private elementary or secondary education may not, on the basis of handicap, exclude a qualified handicapped person if the person can, with minor adjustments, be provided an appropriate education, as defined in §104.33(b)(1), within that recipient's program or activity.
> (b) A recipient to which this section applies may not charge more for the provision of an appropriate education to handicapped persons than to nonhandicapped persons except to the extent that any additional charge is justified by a substantial increase in cost to the recipient. 34 C.F.R. §104.39

The private school requirements are explained further in Appendix A to Part 104—Analysis of Final Regulation:

> Paragraph (a) of Sec. 104.39 is intended to make clear that recipients that operate private education programs and activities are not required to provide an appropriate education to handicapped students with special educational needs if the recipient does not offer programs designed to meet those needs. Thus, a private school that has no program for mentally retarded persons is neither required to admit such a person into its program nor to arrange or pay for the provision of the person's education in another program. A private recipient without a special program for blind students, however, would not be permitted to exclude, on the basis of blindness, a blind applicant who is able to participate in the regular program with minor adjustments in the manner in which the program is normally offered.

The ADA covers private schools that are not religiously controlled. In general Title III requires that each "nursery, elementary, secondary, undergraduate, or postgraduate private school, or other place of education," including "a day care center," complies with the ADA's mandate that:

> No individual shall be discriminated against on the basis of disability in the full and equal enjoyment of the goods, services, facilities, privileges, advantages, or accommodations of any place of public accommodation by any person who owns, leases (or leases to), or operates a place of public accommodation. 42 U.S.C. §12182(a)

In brief, Title III requires that the covered schools (1) not discriminate against persons with disabilities on the basis of disability, (2) make reasonable modifications to their policies and practices, where required to avoid discrimination, and (3) provide appropriate auxiliary aids and services needed for effective communication with students unless doing so would constitute a fundamental alteration in the program or constitute an undue burden. Each of these will be explored at greater length in the next chapter.

5.   Testing

The duty to avoid discrimination includes designing tests and examinations to ensure that they are not discriminatory. Tests and examinations must therefore be structured in such a way that their results accurately reflect the individual's aptitude or achievement level or whatever other factor the examination legitimately purports to measure. Test modifications may be required for a student with a disability, provided those modifications do not alter the fundamental nature of the program or create an undue hardship. See 34 C.F.R. §§104.35(b)

C.   Otherwise Qualified

1.   Public Schools

The 504 Regulations define the terms "qualified" and "otherwise qualified" as they pertain to public elementary and secondary schools.

> As used in this part, the term. . .
>
> (l) Qualified handicapped person means . . . [w]ith respect to public preschool elementary, secondary, or adult educational services, a handicappped person (i) of an age during which nonhandicapped persons are provided such services, (ii) of any age during which it is mandatory under state law to provide such services to handicapped persons, or (iii) to whom a state is required to provide a free appropriate public education under [the IDEA]. (34 C.F.R. §104.3[L][2])

Note the emphasis on the mandatory education requirements.

2. Private Schools

The §504 Regulations also define the terms "qualified" and "otherwise qualified" as they pertain to private elementary and secondary schools.

> As used in this part, the term . . . Qualified handicapped person means:
>
> (3) With respect to postsecondary and vocational education services, a handicapped person who meets the academic and technical standards requisite to admission or participation in the recipient's education program or activity;
>
> (4) With respect to other services, a handicapped person who meets the essential eligibility requirements for the receipt of such services. (34 C.F.R. §§104.3[1][3]-[4])

Therefore, to be qualified for a private school, a student must meet "the essential eligibility requirements for the receipt of such services." In *Bercovitch v. Baldwin School, Inc.*, 133 F.3d 141 (1st Cir. 1998), for example, the U.S. Circuit Court of Appeals for the First Circuit reversed the District Court holding and held that Jason, a student with ADHD, was not entitled to "be exempted from the normal operation of the school's disciplinary code" as a reasonable accommodation under either the ADA or the RA. Comparing the RA/ADA with the IDEA, the court found that "the ADA imposes no requirement on Baldwin to devise an individualized education plan such as the IDEA requires of public schools. The district court order comes perilously close to confusing the obligations Congress has chosen to impose on public schools with those obligations imposed on private schools."

In *Axelrod v. Phillips Academy, Andover* (D. Mass. 1999), the U.S. District Court for Massachusetts considered the case of Nicholas, a student with ADHD, who had exhibited years of marginal performance and fell below the school's academic standards. He was placed on academic probation. His parents requested two accommodations: waiver of the foreign language and math requirements. The school granted the first but denied the second. The school also offered a tutor, which offer was rejected, and recommended that Nicholas spend less time on the phone and on his computer. Nicholas received unsatisfactory grades for failure to complete his work. He was then forced to withdraw two semesters before graduation.

The court held that ADHD is an impairment under the ADA. However, the court found that Nicholas failed to prove he was otherwise qualified, that is, with reasonable accommodations he could meet the school's academic standards, and that the request for the math waiver was not supported with documentation of a math learning disability. Indeed the evidence showed that his math score on the Scholastic Aptitude Test (SAT) was 640 out of a possible 800, or the 88th percentile. The court then found that there is no reasonable accommodation a school can make to ensure that students apply themselves to their work in a timely manner.

Schools and semiprivate athletic organizations may not discriminate against qualified individuals with disabilities. In *Bingham v. Oregon School Activities Association*, 37 F. Supp. 2d 1189 (D. Or. 1999), a student repeated the tenth grade due to a specific learning disability and ADHD which impacted his use of written language. An Oregon School Activities Association (OSAA) rule prohibited students from playing sports for more than eight consecutive semesters commencing in ninth grade. OSAA normally waived its rule for students who have extended schooling due to drugs, emotional problems, broken homes, and juvenile delinquency. However, OSAA would not waive its rule for disabilities, and therefore denied the student a waiver because of his learning disability and ADHD. The court ruled for the student, finding that he was substantially limited in learning. Then the court held that he was entitled to a waiver, stating, "It is unreasonable to grant hardship exemptions for 5th year seniors who present a basis for waiver that does not amount to a disability, while refusing even to consider a waiver on the basis of a disability under the ADA."

D. Summary

Education for children is a fundamental right created by state constitutional provisions and education laws. The New York Constitution, for example, requires that "the legislature shall provide for maintenance and support of a system of free common schools, wherein all the children of this state may be educated." The RA and ADA require that this affirmative obligation to provide public education to children also include children with disabilities. The RA and ADA also contain antidiscrimination provisions for private schools, except that the RA applies only to schools that accept federal funds, and the ADA does not cover religiously controlled schools.

15 Postsecondary Education

A. In General

The RA applies to postsecondary educational institutions that receive federal funds. The receipt of federal money, not the nature of the institution, determines whether the RA applies. Therefore, if the educational institution does not receive federal funds, it is not subject to the RA.

In contrast, under the ADA, the nature of the institution, rather than the receipt of federal funds, is the decisive factor. All public educational institutions are governed by ADA, Title II, whether or not they receive federal funds. All private educational institutions, except those that are religiously controlled, are governed by Title III.

Postsecondary institutions are affected by the RA and ADA in three principal areas: (1) testing (for admissions, evaluation of academic performance, and graduation), (2) the delivery of course materials, and (3) nonacademic benefits of campus life, for example, sports, dormitory living, and so on.

In this chapter, as in prior chapters, we use the following definition of an individual with a disability (see also Chapter 8). An "individual with a disability" is a person who "has a physical or mental impairment which substantially limits one or more of such person's major life activities."

The RA/ADA approach to postsecondary education is fundamentally the same as in other areas: *discrimination* against individuals with disabilities is prohibited, and *qualified individuals* with disabilities are entitled to *reasonable accommodations* in meeting the *essential requirements* of the educational program.

B. Duty of Nondiscrimination

1. The Long Arm of the RA in Education

Generally the obligations created by the RA may be imposed only on the recipient of the federal funding. The RA provides:

> No otherwise qualified individual with a disability . . . shall, solely by reason of her or his disability, be excluded from the participation in, be denied the benefits of, or

be subjected to discrimination under any program or activity receiving Federal financial assistance or under any program or activity conducted by any Executive agency or by the United States Postal Service. (29 U.S.C.A. §794[a])

The phrase "program or activity" is most broadly defined where postsecondary institutions are concerned. The term "program or activity" means "all of the operations of . . . a college, university, or other postsecondary institution, or a public system of higher education; or . . . a local educational agency . . . system of vocational education, or other school system. 29 U.S.C.A. §§794(b)(2)(A)-(B)

In other words, if any part of an educational institution, whether public or private, receives federal funds, the provisions of the RA apply to all of its operations. We are concerned with the part of those "operations" that consist of the delivery of educational services. Thus, federal funds received by *one* department of a university would impose the obligation of nondiscrimination on *all* departments of the institution.

2.   General Duty under the RA/ADA

In general there is no obligation under either the RA or ADA that a postsecondary institution design an individualized course of study for an individual with a disability. However, a postsecondary institution must provide equal access to classroom and other educational materials. This duty is described in the regulations as an obligation to provide course and testing modifications, as well as auxiliary aids and services.

The general duties of educational institutions under the ADA were addressed in a letter from the Civil Rights Division of the Department of Justice to James R. Judge, Esq. (May 13, 1994). The letter discussed the exemption of religiously controlled schools under the ADA:

> Title III of the ADA prohibits discrimination on the basis of disability by any private entity that owns, leases, leases to, or operates a place of public accommodation. A private school, as a place of education, would ordinarily be regarded as a place of public accommodation subject to title III. However, a religious entity, i.e., a religious organization or an entity controlled by a religious organization, is exempt from the requirements of title III. The exemption is intended to have broad application; it applies to both religious and secular activities of a religious entity. Therefore, a private school controlled by a religious entity is exempt from coverage under title III.

C.   Otherwise Qualified

To receive the protection of the RA/ADA, a student with a disability must also be "qualified" for the educational program. Students in postsecondary education, unlike students in public elementary and secondary school who are presumed to be "qualified," must be "otherwise qualified" for their educational programs in order to be protected under the ADA and RA. In addition, they must establish that they have a disability, as defined under the law, and that the proposed accommodation does not fundamentally alter the course program or test. Cases concerning disability status and the "otherwise qualified" requirement under the ADA and RA are discussed in Chapter 16. In this section, we examine academic accommodations.

The Section 504 regulations define the terms "qualified" and "otherwise qualified," as follows:

> As used in this part, the term . . . Qualified handicapped person means:
>
> (3) With respect to postsecondary and vocational education services, a handicapped person who meets the academic and technical standards requisite to admission or participation in the recipient's education program or activity;
>
> (4) With respect to other services, a handicapped person who meets the essential eligibility requirements for the receipt of such services. (34 C.F.R. §§104.3[l][3]-[4])

The same standards are required by the ADA. Under both the ADA and RA, an "individual with a disability" must also be "otherwise qualified." "Otherwise qualified" individuals are persons who, although they have a disability, would be eligible for the education, or program benefit, with or without a reasonable accommodation. *See Wynne v. Tufts University School of Medicine* (1st Cir. 1992).

An educational institution has no obligation to alter the fundamental requirements of its programs as an accommodation under the RA/ADA. A student who cannot comply with the essential course requirements is not otherwise qualified to be in the program. Students who are not otherwise qualified may be expelled, even if they have a disability. For example, in *Ellis v. Morehouse School of Medicine* (N.D. Ga. 1996), an individual with dyslexia requested and received a decelerated first-year curriculum and double time to complete his examinations. The medical school refused to provide a decelerated program for the third and fourth years, which consisted of clinical rather than classroom programs, on the grounds that the accommodations would require modification of the essential nature of the clinical programs. The court held this to be proper. The student was not qualified to be a doctor. See also *Doe v. Vanderbilt University* (6th Cir. 1997), and *Zukle v. Regents of the University of California* (9th Cir. 1999).

In *Powell v. National Board of Medical Examiners* (2nd Cir. 2004), the court held that, under Title III of the ADA or Section 504, a medical student with learning disabilities was not entitled to extra test time on the medical licensing examination, because she was not a person with a disability and was not qualified to be in medical school. The court further found that there was no evidence of discrimination against the student. She was not entitled to continue in medical school after failing the first licensing test. The school had the authority to decide that students must pass the first licensing test to continue in the program. The medical school had provided her with tutors, had excused her from an honor code violation, and had allowed her to remain enrolled without paying tuition. Despite all of this, the student subsequently failed the test, and the school was not obligated to accommodate her further.

D.   Reasonable Accommodations

1.   Testing and Fundamental Academic Requirements

A postsecondary institution must provide equal access to classroom and other educational materials. This duty is described in the ADA regulations as an obligation
to provide testing modifications together with auxiliary aids and services. That includes a selection of nondiscriminatory methods of testing and nondiscriminatory
administration of selected tests.

Each examination must be:

> . . . selected and administered so as to best ensure that, when the examination is ad-
> ministered to an individual with a disability that impairs sensory, manual, or speak-
> ing skills, the examination results accurately reflect the individual's aptitude or
> achievement level or whatever other factor the examination purports to measure,
> rather than reflecting the individual's impaired sensory, manual, or speaking skills
> (except where those skills are the factors that the examination purports to measure).
> (28 CFR §36.309[b])

Test Selection
Standardized testing for admission to educational programs is permissible. The
ADA and RA do not require higher education institutions to discontinue the use of
standardized tests in the admissions process.

Testing that relies on a single criterion is unlawful, where that criterion can be
shown to be an inaccurate predictor of performance and the use of that criterion has
no compelling justification. The issue of testing was considered in *Stutts v. Freeman*
(11th Cir. 1983). Under the RA, the court found discriminatory the use, as a single
criterion for employment as a heavy equipment operator apprentice, of a written
test that could not be shown to be an accurate predictor of performance.

Through a review of its educational program, an institution should be able to
identify those features of the program which are essential and those which are not.
At the postsecondary level, accommodations are required only for those features of
a program that are nonessential. For example, a student with dyslexia would not be
entitled to additional test time in a speed-reading test. Time in that case is essential.

When challenged, an educational institution may be required to validate testing constraints and methods that it considers essential.*Wynne v. Tufts University
School of Medicine* (1st Cir. 1992). In *Guckenberger et al. v. Boston University*, 974 F.
Supp. 106 (D. Mass. 1997), the U.S. District Court for Massachusetts ruled that the
use of substitute courses in place of foreign language courses could be a reasonable modification to Boston University's requirements for a liberal arts degree if
the course substitutions would not alter the fundamental nature of the liberal arts
program. When "an academic institution rationally, without pretext, exercises its deliberate professional judgment not to permit course substitutions for an academic
requirement in a liberal arts curriculum, the ADA does not authorize the courts to
intervene even if a majority of other comparable institutions disagree."

Test Administration

Tests must be administered in a manner that does not discriminate against students with disabilities, including provision of reasonable testing accommodations. *Morisky v. Broward County* (11th Cir. 1996). Examinations and courses must be offered in a "place and manner accessible to persons with disabilities or [through] other alternative accessible arrangements for such individuals." 28 CFR § 36.309(a). Examinations must be structured in such a way that their results "accurately reflect the individual's aptitude or achievement level or whatever other factor the examination purports to measure." 28 CFR § 36.309(b). The examinations may not reflect "the individual's impaired sensory, manual, or speaking skills" unless (1) the purpose of the test is to measure those factors and (2) the measurement of those factors has a valid educational purpose. See generally, *Morisky v. Broward County* (11th Cir. 1996); *Wynne v. Tufts University School of Medicine* (1st Cir. 1992). In *Letter of Findings issued to Educational Testing Service (1993),* the Office for Civil Rights (OCR) of the Department of Education concluded that the Educational Testing Service could not arbitrarily limit extended time to double time, but rather must give consideration to a documented request for triple time.

Examinations tailored to individuals with disabilities must be administered in facilities that are "accessible" to those individuals. The examinations are generally required to be modified "in the length of time permitted for completion" and in the "manner in which the examination is given." 28 CFR §36.309(b)(2)

Auxiliary aids and services must be provided in testing. Modifications are not required where they would alter the fundamental nature of the course or pose an undue hardship. Auxiliary aids in examinations "may include taped examinations, interpreters or other effective methods of making orally delivered materials available to individuals with hearing impairments, Brailled or large print examinations and answer sheets or qualified readers for individuals with visual impairments or learning disabilities, transcribers for individuals with manual impairments, and other similar services and actions." 28 CFR §36.309(b)(3)

Alternative accessible arrangements, including "provision of an examination at an individual's home with a proctor," may be utilized if accessible facilities are not available. 28 CFR §36.309(b)(4). These modifications and auxiliary aids must be provided to those individuals with disabilities who require them.

In Stern v. University of Osteopathic Medicine and Health Sciences (8th Cir. 2000), the court considered a request for accommodation by a medical student with dyslexia. The student asked permission to supplement multiple choice answers by essay or responses to oral questioning. The medical school refused but gave the student a private room, extended time, and multiple choice tests on tape. Nonetheless, the student failed, was expelled, and sued under the RA. At trial, the student's own expert witness testified that the accommodations given by the school were all that was necessary to address his dyslexia. The student offered no evidence that the accommodations he proposed were related to his disability and would provide him with a benefit not otherwise available. The court found for the medical school.

The U.S. District Court for the Southern District of New York held that a bar admissions applicant was an "individual with a disability" because she was substantially limited in the major life activities of reading and working. The court held that she was entitled to reasonable accommodations in taking the New York Bar Examination, including extended test time and a large print exam. *Bartlett v. New York State Board of Law Examiners* (S.D.N.Y. 2001)

In *Detroyer v. Oakland Community College* (Mich. Ct. App. 2001), a Michigan court found that the college had reasonably accommodated a student with a learning disability and ADD under the Michigan disability law. The college allowed the student to use Spell Check and to take tests outside the classroom. The court rejected the student's argument that the instructor must ignore her spelling mistakes for grading purposes, noting that colleges do not have to lower their grading standards.

Test Modifications

Testing modifications are required for a qualified individual with a disability if they will not alter the fundamental nature of the program being offered or create an undue burden.

> (3) A private entity offering an examination covered by this section shall provide appropriate auxiliary aids for persons with impaired sensory, manual, or speaking skills, unless that private entity can demonstrate that offering a particular auxiliary aid would fundamentally alter the measurement of the skills or knowledge the examination is intended to test or would result in an undue burden. (28 CFR §36.309[b][3])

Fundamental Academic Requirements

Postsecondary institutions are not required to lessen the quality of the education they provide. In *Letter of Findings Issued to Golden Gate University* (1996), a student with a learning disability (identified as "C") registered for a graduate-level seminar that required extensive reading. "C" requested a take-home examination as an accommodation and was told that all students would have a take-home examination. On receiving the final, a take-home examination, "C" for the first time requested that the examination format be modified from "open ended" questions to "more pointed" ones. "C" alleged this was necessary because of difficulty with questions "that require the test taker to be capable of mental recall." OCR found that the accommodation request was properly denied because use of the open-ended question is a proper means of measuring graduate-level understanding of materials.

"C" also argued that the low grade in the seminar was indicative of discrimination because "C" otherwise received A's. To this argument, OCR replied:

> C appears to be under the misapprehension that the duty to provide academic adjustments includes a responsibility to provide such adjustments until a certain outcome is achieved, e.g., a grade of A. This is not what was contemplated by the OCR regulations. The objective is to create equal opportunity, not equal outcomes. Tests are modified to achieve greater validity not higher grades.

Postsecondary institutions also are not required to permit course substitutions where the required course is considered essential. *Letter of Findings Issued to Wingate University* (1996). See also *Guckenberger v. Boston University* 974 F. Supp. 106 (D. Mass. 1997).

Undue Burden or Hardship

The U.S. Department of Education has stated that, in making undue hardship determinations, the primary consideration will be the size and budget of the institution compared with the cost of the requested aids, and not the amount of tuition paid by the student. *Letter from W. Smith, Acting Assistant Secretary for Civil Rights, U.S. Department of Education, to Neill Stern, Executive Vice President, Parker College of Chiropractic* (March 6, 1990)

2.   Delivery of Classroom and Other Educational Materials

A postsecondary institution must provide equal access to classroom and other educational materials, described in the regulations as an obligation to provide course modifications and auxiliary aids and services.

The institution offering the course:

> . . . must make such modifications to that course as are necessary to ensure that the place and manner in which the course is given are accessible to individuals with disabilities. . . .
>
> Required modifications may include changes in the length of time permitted for the completion of the course, substitution of specific requirements, or adaptation of the manner in which the course is conducted or course materials are distributed. (28 CFR §§ 36.309[c][1],[2])

Auxiliary aids and services in the presentation of the course also are required. The institution offering the course "shall provide appropriate auxiliary aids and services for persons with impaired sensory, manual, or speaking skills, unless the private entity can demonstrate that offering a particular auxiliary aid or service would fundamentally alter the course or would result in an undue burden." 28 CFR § 36.309(c)(3)

The auxiliary aids and services must "recognize individual communications needs" and must provide "contemporaneous communication" of the entire educational experience being offered, including class participation. Selection of auxiliary aids and services must be guided by an interactive process involving the student and the institution.

Auxiliary aids in courses "may include taped texts, interpreters or other effective methods of making orally delivered materials available to individuals with hearing impairments, Brailled or large print texts or qualified readers for individuals with visual impairments and learning disabilities, classroom equipment adapted for use by individuals with manual impairments, and other similar services and actions." 28 CFR § 36.309(c)(3)

Alternative accessible arrangements, including videotaped lectures, cassettes, and prepared notes, may be utilized. 28 CFR § 36.309(c)(5). As with aids in examinations, auxiliary aids in courses must be provided to those individuals with disabilities who require them. Ordinarily, students with disabilities who require aids in examinations and courses would request those aids and would provide appropriate supporting documentation.

3.   Selecting the Appropriate Accommodation

Students must request appropriate accommodations. In order to obtain an accommodation (known as "academic adjustments" and "auxiliary aids and services"), the individual must contact the appropriate university office and follow the procedure for documenting the disability and the need for particular accommodations. Failure to comply with reasonable procedures will bar the student's claim. *Letter of Findings Issued to Highline Community College (1996).* The OCR said:

> In order to provide the necessary academic adjustments, recipients may require students to provide evidence of the disability and to notify the appropriate personnel that such academic adjustments are necessary for the student to access a recipient's program. At the post-secondary level, Section 504 does not require recipients to provide such academic adjustments or accommodations if they are not requested by the student.

A timely request for accommodation, in compliance with institutional procedures is essential. See *Letter of Findings Issued to University of California, Los Angeles (1996); Letter of Findings Issued to Philadelphia College of Optometry (1996).*

The process of selecting the appropriate academic adjustment or accommodation is similar to the process in the employment setting. In *United States v. Becker C.P.A. Review* (D.D.C. 1994), the U.S. District Court issued an order, reflecting the agreement of the parties, that the ADA requires educational institutions to provide auxiliary aids and services which ensure "effective communication" of the educational experience, among all participants, in a manner that can be understood by each individual student. The aids and services must be selected with a view to recognizing "individual communication needs." Consequently an interactive evaluation process was required.

While this Consent Order is not, strictly speaking, a legal precedent, the courts have reached the same result in cases that do constitute precedent. See *Beck v. University of Wisconsin* (7th Cir. 1996), discussed in the next chapter. The Consent Order is instructive because it makes clear three points: (1) a place of public accommodation may not, alone, determine which aids and services are appropriate for a student with a disability; (2) the aids and services provided must be "effective" in achieving "contemporaneous communication" of the "educational experience, among all participants, in a manner that can be understood by each individual" and that allows for "equal participation in the educational experience" offered by the institution; and (3) effectiveness is determined primarily by specific consideration of the needs of the students affected.

When accommodations have been properly requested, justified, and agreed on, they must be supplied in a timely fashion. A failure to do so violates both the RA and ADA. *Letter of Findings Issued to California State University, Sacramento (1996).*

4. Accommodations Must Be Requested

Accommodations are required only for individuals with disabilities who request them. In *Letter of Findings Issued to St. Louis Community College at Meramec (1992)*, the Department of Education held that any student with ADHD who met admissions criteria was a qualified individual with a disability. When the student requested additional time for tests, but did not request the rights to use loose-leaf sheets for laboratory note taking and to transcribe those notes into the lab book, an educational institution was permitted to lower his laboratory grades for failure to comply with the requirement that all notes be entered directly during the laboratory session. An institution is not obligated to provide assistance that has not been requested! Accord: *Letter of Findings Issued to Almont Community School District (1996).*

In *Letter of Findings Issued to Temple University (1995)*, OCR ruled that a student who failed to follow reasonable procedures for provision of academic adjustments is not entitled to them. As the OCR put it: "It is lawful for a University to establish reasonable standards and procedures to obtain academic adjustments."

5. Documentation Requirements

Applicants and students who are seeking to obtain accommodations must present reasonable documentation to support the request. In *Dubois v. Alderson-Broaddus College, Inc.* (N.D.W.Va. 1997), the court considered the case of a student who was granted accommodations (oral rather than written exams) but was required to give a forty-eight-hour notice of his need for these accommodations. The student objected and sued under the ADA. The court held that the student had not established that he was an individual with a disability because his only documentation consisted of a psychologist's report which stated that he "might suffer from a specific learning disability." The student had also refused to take a WAIS (Wechsler Adult Intelligence Scale) to confirm the diagnosis. *Letter of Findings Issued to State University of New York (1993).* See also *Letter of Findings Issued to Frostburg State University (1995).*

Two important disability documentation issues are addressed in *Guckenberger v. Boston University*, 8 F. Supp. 2d 82 (D. Mass. 1998). The court articulated how current the testing must be and what credentials the institution may require of evaluators. Boston University (BU) had imposed a new requirement that students with learning disabilities be retested every three years. After the commencement of the litigation, BU changed its policy to permit waiver of the retesting if the student's evaluator deemed such retesting medically unnecessary.

The court ordered that BU end its policy of requiring that, to be eligible for accommodations, students with learning disabilities, who have current evaluations conducted by trained professionals with at least master's degrees and sufficient experience, be retested by professionals with PhD or MD credentials. The court applied a different standard for evaluation of students with ADHD.

The court's order states:

1. The Court orders BU to cease and desist implementing its current policy of requiring that students with learning disorders (not ADD or ADHD) who have current evaluations by trained professionals with masters degrees and sufficient experience be completely retested by professionals who have medical degrees, or doctorate degrees, or licensed clinical psychologists in order to be eligible for reasonable accommodations.

The court approved the then current BU policy of requiring this level of expertise for the diagnosis of ADHD because these "conditions are primarily identified through clinical evaluations rather than through standardized testing, and a well-trained eye is essential for proper diagnosis."

The court further concluded that BU breached its contract with three of the named plaintiff students "by failing to honor the express representations of its representatives about the students' ability to document their disabilities and to receive accommodations from the university." The court ordered that judgment be entered in the aggregate amount of over $29,000 in favor of six named student plaintiffs.

In *Letter of Findings Issued to State University of New York (1993)*, OCR ruled that the university was entitled to refuse to provide an accommodation where a student requested that exam formats be modified to utilize essay rather than multiple choice questions. The student was asked to and did provide medical documentation, including a neuropsychological evaluation, but the documentation contained nothing to substantiate that essay questions rather than multiple choice questions were required.

6.   Specific Accommodations

Course Substitutions

Some individuals with learning disabilities and/or ADHD may request course substitutions in foreign language or mathematics. Generally, if the institution follows a deliberative process and reasonably concludes that the course requirement is fundamental to its program, then the institution properly may deny the requested course substitution. *Guckenberger v. Boston University*, 8 F. Supp. 2d 82 (D. Mass. 1998)

In *Letter of Findings Issued to Bellevue Community College* (June 13, 1995), OCR ruled that Bellevue Community College violated the RA/ADA when it refused to permit a course substitution for a required mathematics course, solely on the ground that mathematics was mandatory at four-year universities. Accordingly, the college failed to show that mathematics is essential.

In *Letter of Findings Issued to Mt. San Antonio College* (1997), OCR ruled that Mt. San Antonio College was not justified in pursuing a policy of refusing substitution for mandatory courses, unless the student has taken and failed the course twice using all available resources and the failing grades were on the student's transcript.

Temporary Accommodations

An educational institution is required to provide accommodations only in response to a properly supported request. Some institutions provide temporary accommodations to students pending receipt of final and appropriate documentation. While these good faith actions are commendable, generally temporary accommodations are not legally required.

In *Letter of Findings Issued to University of Southern Mississippi* (1996), OCR ruled that the university (USM) was not required to provide accommodations until the request for them was supported by reasonable documentation. USM had temporarily provided accommodations pending receipt of the documentation. OCR said:

> The evidence reveals that USM provided "good faith" temporary accommodations to the complainant until the necessary documentation could be submitted by the complainant or a psychologist even though they were not required by Section 504 or Title II.

7. Required Accommodations Are Free

The ADA prohibits separate and additional charges for the costs of providing course and examination modifications and auxiliary aids.

> (c) Charges. A public accommodation may not impose a surcharge on a particular individual with a disability or any group of individuals with disabilities to cover the costs of measures, such as the provision of auxiliary aids, barrier removal, alternatives to barrier removal, and reasonable modifications in policies, practices, or procedures, that are required to provide that individual or group with the nondiscriminatory treatment required by the Act. (28 CFR §36.301[c])

The provision of professional services such as psychiatric counseling or career counseling, which are normally billed at an hourly rate, are not affected by this provision. However, if institutions provide such services as part of the regular tuition, then surcharges based on the additional effort necessary to address an individual's disability are not permitted.

In *University of Arizona*, OCR Docket No. 09-91-2402; 2 NDLR ¶ 285, OCR found that the University of Arizona was required under the RA to provide certain academic adjustments and educational auxiliary aids, including taped texts, at no additional charge and in a timely manner to a student with learning disabilities. See also *Letter of Findings Issued to Mitchell College* (1994), and *United States v. Board of Trustees for the University of Alabama* (11th Cir. 1990).

In order to satisfy OCR that the services are in fact free, the institution may be required to develop "accounting practices" which will "identify the costs involved for each service" provided to students with learning disabilities. These accounting practices must "demonstrate that fees are not charged for auxiliary aids and academic adjustments." *Letter of Findings Issued to Hofstra University* (1996)

8. Programs for Students Who Are Not "Qualified"

Programs intended to increase the skills of students who would not be qualified for admission to regular programs are viewed in a different manner. In *Halasz v. University of New England* (D. Me. 1993), the court considered two programs maintained by the University of New England: (1) the Individual Learning Program (ILP), which offered specific support services for students with learning disabilities in a university setting and (2) the First Year Option (FYO) program for first year students who did not have the credentials for admission to a degree program. Students in the FYO program could take one or two courses with ILP support and apply for admission after the first year provided they made acceptable grades. There was a separate and potentially more expensive fee structure for FYO students. The court held, among other things, that the university did not violate the RA by maintaining a separate and potentially more expensive fee structure for its FYO program. The court reasoned that the FYO program was available for students who were not qualified to earn a degree even with the reasonable accommodations required by the RA. Since the program afforded an opportunity for unqualified students to obtain skills they lacked, the university had no legal obligation to offer the program and so properly could charge fees for the program.

E.   Summary

The RA (Section 504) bans discrimination by all federal grant and aid recipients and applies to most postsecondary educational institutions. The ADA applies to public postsecondary institutions (Title II) and to private postsecondary institutions that are not religiously controlled (Title III). Under these laws, qualified students with disabilities are entitled to reasonable accommodations in courses and testing. Under the RA and ADA, most higher education institutions must make programs, including courses and examinations, accessible to qualified individuals with disabilities.

Students must show that they have a disability and are qualified for the program. Institutions are not required to make modifications in courses or examinations that would alter the essential nature or constitute an undue hardship on the institution. The accommodation requested by the student must be both reasonable and necessary because of the particular disability. Institutions generally have no duty to identify students with disabilities, but rather must respond to disclosure of a disability and requests for specific accommodations.

Specific accommodations that generally are required of institutions to which the ADA applies, where documentation supports the need in particular cases, include extended test time, individual room for tests, and large print exams.

Specific accommodations that may not always be legally required include foreign language waiver or course substitution and mathematics waiver or course substitution. Educational institutions that can justify the need for mastery of a foreign language or mathematics in a particular program would be able to require the same of students with disabilities.

Specific accommodations that generally are not legally required include (1) modification in type of test, for example, short answer rather than multiple choice, pointed questions rather than open ended questions, and the right to supplement multiple choice answers; (2) extended time on a practical exercise, such as giving a physical exam as part of a physician's assistant program; and (3) extended time to complete the practical part of a program, such as three years to complete the two-year clinical part of medical school.

16 Employment

A. In General

In Chapter 15 we considered the application of the RA/ADA to postsecondary education. In this chapter, we consider the application of those laws to employment.

Employees with disabilities are protected by the RA and ADA in all aspects of employment. In this chapter, we use the definition of an individual with a disability we developed in Chapter 11, that is, a person who "has a physical or mental impairment which substantially limits one or more of such person's major life activities."

The RA/ADA approach to employment is fundamentally similar to other areas. *Discrimination* against individuals with disabilities is prohibited, and *qualified individuals* with disabilities are entitled to *reasonable accommodations* in meeting the *essential requirements* of the employer.

B. Basic Requirement

The RA applies to three classes of employer: (1) the federal government, except the judiciary and armed forces; (2) most government contractors, by virtue of their contracts; and (3) recipients of federal funds. Under the ADA, the nature of the institution, not the receipt of federal funds, is the decisive factor. Employers are governed primarily by ADA, Title I.

Title I of the ADA applies to private employers, state and local governments, employment agencies, and labor unions, and covers employers with fifteen or more employees. Regulations for Title I are found in 29 C.F.R. Part 1630. State and local governments also fall under ADA, Title II, without regard to the number of individuals they employ.

The basic requirement of Title I is that:

No covered entity shall discriminate against a qualified individual with a disability because of the disability of such individual in regard to job application procedures, the hiring, advancement, or discharge of employees, employee compensation, job training, and other terms, conditions, and privileges of employment. (42 U.S.C. §12112[a])

C.   The Major Life Activity of Working

The ADA protects qualified individuals with disabilities and contains the same definition of "individual with a disability" that is found in the RA. Under both laws there are special problems that must be addressed when individuals seek to show that they are substantially limited in the major life activity of working. Working is treated differently from all other major life activities for purposes of considering whether an individual with an impairment is substantially limited. In order to determine whether a substantial limitation on working exists, the impairment must bar the individual from significant classes of jobs, and not just a particular job. Only disabilities with the former, and broader, impact are considered substantially to limit working. See *Wernick v. Federal Reserve Bank of New York* (2d Cir. 1996); *Dutcher v. Ingalls Shipbuilding* (5th Cir. 1995); *Gilbert v. Storage Technology Corporation* (10th Cir. 1996); *Burke v. Virginia* (E.D. Va. 1996); *aff'd,* 1997 U.S. App. LEXIS 13388 (4th Cir. 1997).

D.   Otherwise Qualified

1.   Basic Rule

The ADA does not protect all individuals with disabilities. It applies only to a "qualified individual with a disability." For example, the law provides:

> (8) Qualified individual with a disability
>   The term "qualified individual with a disability" means an individual with a disability who, with or without reasonable accommodation, can perform the essential functions of the employment position that such individual holds or desires. (42 U.S.C. §12111)

2.   Essential Job Requirements

Individuals with disabilities must prove that they are able to meet the essential requirements of a job, with or without a reasonable accommodation. If the record shows that a person cannot perform without a reasonable accommodation, that individual must prove that a particular accommodation would enable him to perform. See *Bombard v. Fort Wayne Newspapers, Inc.* (7th Cir. 1996).

Just what are the "essential job requirements"? The courts have devoted a significant effort to answering that question. Essential requirements include (1) prerequisite qualifications, such as physical, mental, academic, and work experience requirements (see *McDaniel v. Allied Signal, Inc.* [W.D. Mo. 1995]); (2) hard-core job skills (*Di Pompo v. West Point Military Academy* [2d Cir. 1992]); and (3) requirements for cooperativeness and good citizenship in the workplace. *Dazey v. Department of the Air Force 54 M.S.P.R. 658* (M.S.P.B. 1992); *Mancini v. General Electric Co.* (D. Vt. 1993)

Some persons with impairments may be required to take medications in order to ameliorate the effects of the condition. While the beneficial effects of medications may render them qualified for the job, the individuals also have the duty to manage those medications. See *Siefken v. Village of Arlington Heights* (7th Cir. 1995) wherein an individual with a disability may have a duty to manage that disability in order to remain qualified for the job.

E. Testing

Employment-related testing under the ADA must comply with the same rules applicable to postsecondary education discussed in Chapter 11. Specifically, testing must be justified, where necessary, and modified to accommodate reasonably an individual with a disability.

The ADA prohibits an employer from inquiring whether an individual has a disability or the extent of the disability. The ADA also prohibits medical examinations and inquiries, absent a showing that such inquiries are job related and consistent with business necessity. *Steven L. Karracker et al. v. Rent-A-Center, Inc.*, Docket No. 02C2026 (7th Cir. 2005) involved personality testing to screen for promotion with the company. The test included over 500 questions from the Minnesota Multiphasic Personality Test (MMPI). The court found that the MMPI measures conditions such as depression, paranoia, and mania, and is used in diagnosing psychiatric disorders. Accordingly, the court held that the MMPI is a medical examination or inquiry, and therefore is not permitted under the ADA for routine use in preemployment or prepromotion screening.

F. Reasonable Accommodations

There are three general types of reasonable accommodations for individuals with disabilities. The first type ensures equal opportunity in the job application process; the second enables individuals to perform the essential features of a job; and the third enables them to enjoy the same benefits and privileges as those available to individuals without disabilities. The most common of the three types are accommodations that enable an individual with disabilities to perform the essential features of a job.

G. Selecting the Accommodation

The Seventh Circuit has established an interactive process of selecting a reasonable accommodation in which the employer and employee must be responsive to reasonable inquiries from each other. *Beck v. University of Wisconsin* (7th Cir. 1996). In that case, the employee and employer did not communicate adequately, leaving the university to try to ascertain what actions it should take to accommodate the employee and the employee feeling that she had not been adequately accommodated. The court held that "because the University was never able to obtain an adequate understanding of what action it should take, it cannot be held liable for failure to make 'reasonable accommodations.'"

H.   Limitations on the Duty to Accommodate

Employers are not required to change a job feature if doing so would create an "undue hardship." Such accommodations would be unreasonable. In addition, employers do not have to provide accommodations to an employee who is a danger to others. Again, such accommodations would be considered unreasonable.

I.   Individualized Inquiry

Legitimate job-related safety requirements may operate to bar an individual with disabilities from some employments. *Ward v. Skinner* (1st Cir. 1991), *cert. denied; Ward v. Secretary of Transportation*, 503 U.S. 959 (1992). The ADA and the RA allow proper and reasonable restrictions where safety is concerned. In general, both laws require that each person with a disability be accorded an individualized inquiry to ensure that any rule that would limit activities has a reasonable basis. *School Board of Nassau County v. Arline* 480 U.S. 273 (1987); *Traynor v. Turnage*, 485 U.S. 535 (1988) (*Note:* Both these cases have been superseded by statutes; however, they are still appropriate for the points made in this text.) See also *Chandler v. City of Dallas* (5th Cir. 1993), *cert. denied*, 511 U.S. 1011 (1994).

J.   "By Reason Of"

For an action to be discriminatory under the ADA and RA, the action must be because of the disability and not for another valid reason. In *Ross v. Beaumont Hosp.* (E.D. Mich. 1988), a hospital terminated the privileges of a surgeon who suffered from narcolepsy, despite the fact that her condition was largely controlled through medication. However, the surgeon also engaged in verbal abuse of nurses over a seven-year period, and there was no evidence that the abuse was related to the narcolepsy. Accordingly the termination was held to be lawful under the RA, because it was based in major part on her unacceptable conduct, rather than her disability. In *Shartle v. Motorola, Inc.* (N.D. Ill. 1994), the firing of a security guard with dyslexia was found proper because the reason for the firing was insubordination and not dyslexia.

K.   Constructive Discharge and Hostile Work Environments

Usually there is no ambiguity as to whether an employee has been fired from a job, but occasionally an employer may decide to make employment so unpleasant that the employee will quit. Under certain circumstances, such conduct is considered a constructive discharge. In *Sinopoli v. Albert Regula*, Docket No. 97-7229 (2d Cir. October 9, 1997), the court said that to "establish a constructive discharge, a plaintiff must show that the employer deliberately ma[de his] working conditions so intolerable that [he was] forced into an involuntary resignation."

The Third and Fourth Circuits have enunciated a five-factor test in establishing a "hostile work environment" claim under the ADA. The test requires that the plaintiff show that "(1) he is a qualified individual with a disability; (2) he was subjected to unwelcome harassment; (3) the harassment was based on his disability; (4) the harassment was sufficiently severe or pervasive to alter a term, condition, or privilege of employment; and (5) some factual basis exists to impute liability for the harassment to the employer." *Fox v. General Motors*, 247 F.3d 169 (4th Cir. 2001); *Flowers v. Southern Regional Physician Services, Inc.*, 247 F. 3d 229 (5th Cir. 2001.

The type of evidence required is proof of a "hostile work environment" which in turn "requires a showing that the workplace is permeated with discriminatory intimidation, ridicule and insult, that is sufficiently severe or pervasive to alter the conditions of the victim's employment." *Harris v. Forklift Systems*, 510 U.S. 17 (1993).

L. Disclosure

No employee has an obligation to disclose a disability, and no employer has an obligation to provide accommodations for a disability which has not been disclosed. See *Morisky v. Broward County* (11th Cir. 1996). To invoke the ADA, individuals must disclose their disability to the persons who have decision-making authority. Disclosure is appropriate only when the individual seeks to invoke the RA/ADA and not otherwise.

M. Confidentiality

Confidentiality of disability information is protected by law but is subject to various exceptions on a need-to-know basis.

1. Preemployment Inquiries

A prospective employer who is subject to the ADA "shall not conduct a medical examination or make inquiries of a job applicant as to whether such applicant is an individual with a disability or as to the nature or severity of such disability." 42 U.S.C. §12112(d)(2)(A). However, the prospective employer may "make preemployment inquiries into the ability of an applicant to perform job-related functions." 42 U.S.C. §12112(d)(2)(B). After a prospective employer makes an offer, but before the start of employment, he may require an "employment entrance examination" if (1) "all entering employees are subjected to such an examination regardless of disability," (2) certain confidentiality restrictions (discussed below) are observed, and (3) the "results of such examination" are used only in accordance with the ADA. 42 U.S.C. §12112(c)

2. Medical Examinations

The postoffer, preemployment medical examination must meet the requirement that information obtained regarding the medical condition or history of the applicant is collected and maintained on separate forms and in separate medical files and is treated as a confidential medical record, except that (1) "supervisors and managers" may be "informed regarding necessary restrictions on the work duties of the employee and necessary accommodations," (2) first aid and safety personnel "may be informed, when appropriate, if the disability might require emergency treatment," (3) government officials may have access to the information for the purposes of ensuring compliance with the ADA (42 U.S.C. §12112[d][2]-[3]), (4) state workmen's compensation offices may be provided with the medical information, and (5) insurance companies may have access where the firm requires a medical examination to provide health or life insurance to employees.

3. Performance-Based Medical Examinations

Job performance problems may trigger an employer's demand that the employee obtain a medical evaluation by the employer's staff physician or psychiatrist. The scope of the employee's obligation to comply with such a demand depends on the circumstances. In *Yin v. California* (9th Cir. 1996) *cert. denied*, 519 U.S. 1114 (1997), the court held that California may compel an employee with a prolonged and egregious history of absenteeism and a record of on-the-job illnesses to undergo a fitness-for-duty medical examination. The ADA was held to pose no barrier to the requirement.

4. Job Accommodation Information

An employer may require a medical examination to confirm the existence of a claimed disability and the appropriateness of a proposed reasonable accommodation.

5. Drug Testing Information

Under the ADA, an employer or prospective employer may test for the illegal use of drugs. These tests may, of course, identify the lawful use of prescription medications, such as Dexedrine or Ritalin, as well as illegal drugs. The EEOC believes that if the results of a drug test indicate the presence of a lawfully prescribed drug, such information must be kept confidential, in the same way as any other medical record. *Note:* the use of "suspicionless" searches by governmental agencies has been curtailed by the Supreme Court. *Chandler v. Miller*, 520 U.S. 305 (1997)

6. Admissions

Disclosure brings with it the possibility of an admission that the employee is not otherwise qualified. "I have a learning disability and that's why I am always late" is an example. Such a statement may suggest that the disability may prevent the individual from achieving regular timely attendance, an essential requirement of any job. As we have learned earlier, an individual who cannot meet the essential requirements of a job is not otherwise qualified and is not protected by the RA/ADA.

Admissions can also occur when an individual seeks inconsistent remedies. For example, individuals who seek to establish that they are qualified individuals with disabilities under the ADA and are therefore protected by the ADA may be unable, at the same time, to show that they are permanently disabled and entitled to

Social Security. The statements made for the two different claims may be used to defeat each other. *Cleveland v. Policy Management Systems Corp.*, 526 U.S. 795 (1999)

N. Summary

The ADA protects qualified individuals with disabilities from discrimination in most private sector and state and local government employment. The RA/ADA approach to employment is fundamentally the same as in other areas. *Discrimination* against individuals with disabilities is prohibited, and *qualified individuals* with disabilities are entitled to *reasonable accommodations* in meeting the *essential requirements* of the employer.

Employees with disabilities who are qualified for their jobs may be entitled to reasonable accommodations in the workplace. In many cases it is difficult for employees, especially where cognitive impairments are involved, to establish that they are both substantially limited in a major life activity and at the same time qualified for the job at issue.

The accommodations sought must be reasonable, and reasonableness depends on the nature of the particular job. For example, flex time may be reasonable in some jobs but not in others. A request by an employee with ADHD was found by a court to be unreasonable because of the senior level of the employee. The accommodations requested were nondistracting workplace, multistaged tasks, written instructions, intermediate deadlines, a single supervisor, and assistance in setting up a time management system. The court found that senior level employees must be able to exercise independent judgment and juggle tasks when necessary. Such accommodations may be reasonable for junior level employees.

The accommodation must be specific and not vague. For example, an employer is not required to provide reduced stress in the workplace because the employer would not be able to control all of the factors that produce stress, and compliance by the employer would depend on the employee's assessment of his or her stress level at any given time.

There must be a need for the accommodation based upon the disability and not just a desire for the accommodation. For example, the employee cannot insist upon the day shift rather than the night shift simply because the employee prefers the day shift.

Over 95 percent of ADA cases are won by employers. Because of the difficulties often present in seeking to establish that the employee is substantially limited but qualified for the job and in seeking to show that requested accommodation is reasonable, it is important for employees to carefully evaluate their legal position and to consider the possibility of working out with the employer a solution that is acceptable to both. Many employers are quite agreeable to reasonable requests by an employee that are likely to improve the performance of the employee. In the event legal action is pursued, generally, professional documentation of the disability and the need for accommodation will be of great importance.

CHAPTER 17

Other Legal Issues

A. No Child Left Behind

1. Overview

On January 8, 2002, President Bush signed the No Child Left Behind Act, the most recent amendments to the Elementary and Secondary Education Act of 1965. This statute, dubbed "an historic agreement to improve the educational opportunities for every American child," has profound implications for special education. Like the IDEA, NCLB conditions the receipt of federal funds on state agreement to implement the program required by its provisions. In describing the objectives of this unique law, the Department of Education said, *No Child Left Behind* is based on stronger accountability for results, more freedom for states and communities, proven education methods, and more choices for parents."

These principles are referred to as "The Four Pillars of the NCLB."

2. Stronger Accountability for Results

Under *No Child Left Behind*, the goal is to close the achievement gap and make sure all students achieve academic proficiency, regardless of the reasons that they have had difficulty in the past. According to the Department of Education:

> Annual state and school district report cards inform parents and communities about state and school progress. Schools that do not make progress must provide supplemental services, such as free tutoring or after-school assistance; take corrective actions; and, if still not making adequate yearly progress after five years, make dramatic changes to the way the school is run.

3. More Freedom for States and Communities

NCLB provides a great deal of flexibility to states and school districts in how they use federal education funds. For example, most school districts have the option to transfer up to 50 percent of the NCLB formula grant funds among specified programs under the act without separate federal approval. This allows districts to direct funds to their most pressing needs, such as hiring new teachers, increasing teacher pay, and improving teacher training and professional development.

4. Proven Education Methods

The NCLB emphasizes "scientifically based instruction programs in the early grades" with a view to ensuring that student learning and achievement in reading is improved. The NCLB "puts emphasis on determining which educational programs and practices have been proven effective through rigorous scientific research."

5. Options for Parents

In schools that are deficient as measured by state standards, the parents have options. Parents may transfer their children to a better-performing public school. "Also, students who attend a persistently dangerous school or are the victim of a violent crime while in their school have the option to attend a safe school within their district." Students from low-income families attending schools that fail to meet state standards for at least three years are "eligible to receive supplemental educational services, including tutoring, after-school services, and summer school."

6. Report Cards

The NCLB is enforced by report cards. Based on "annual statewide assessments," schools are required to show their progress, or lack of it, toward NCLB goals. The report cards serve as the basis for determining whether the schools are deficient, a finding that triggers the rights described earlier.

7. Just Education

The NCLB is intended to ensure that all children become educated, a process that begins with reading competence. The theory is that reading deficiencies must be remediated whether they result from learning disabilities, language difficulties, or economic disadvantage. This may result in more children's needs being addressed in general education, rather than through IDEA services. The ultimate goal is help the child to read, whether through general or special education.

8. Cases Filed

The NCLB has been challenged in the courts by two major suits.

The State of Connecticut (CT) brought suit on August 22, 2005, against the U.S. Department of Education (USDOE), asking a federal court to require that U.S. Secretary of Education Margaret Spellings provide an additional $42 million to the state or exempt it from some of the terms of the NCLB. CT contends that yearly testing and school improvement requirements of the NCLB will cost CT far more than the $70.6 million the state currently is receiving under the NCLB. CT refers to assurances in the NCLB that states and school districts would not have to use their own money to pay for complying with the NCLB requirements.

The *Wall Street Journal* (August 23, 2005) reported that CT Education Commissioner Betty Sternberg said that the additional costs result from the USDOE's refusal to let Connecticut test students in alternate years, rather than every year, and its refusal to loosen the testing requirements for English language learners and disabled children. Further, most states have asked the USDOE for exemptions from one or more sections of the law. The USDOE has refused requests to allow states to do alternate year testing. Maine is considering a suit similar to CT's.

The case was heard by the U.S. District Court for the District of Connecticut in September 2006. This followed several amendments to the original complaint. The causes of action raised in that complaint were that Secretary Spellings is (1) violating the NCLB, (2) exceeding her authority under the U.S. Constitution's Spending Clause and the Tenth Amendment, and (3) violating the Administrative Procedure Act. The relief requested included essentially an order that CT is not required to expend its own funds to comply with the USDOE interpretation of the NCLB, an order declaring that CT's failure to comply would not provide a basis for withholding federal funds and would enjoin the USDOE from controlling the allocation of CT resources.

Note that the Constitution's Spending Clause empowers the United States to "provide for the common Defense and general Welfare of the United States." The Tenth Amendment provides essentially that powers not delegated to the United States in the Constitution "are reserved to the States respectively, or to the people." The CT position is that the USDOE interpretation of the NCLB—giving USDOE broad power to order CT to test in a particular way, and soon, and to use state funds to do so—exceeds the federal government authority to spend its own money for the general welfare and violates the Tenth Amendment reservation of powers (not otherwise delegated in the Constitution to the federal government) to the states.

The District Court judge dismissed three of the four claims in the lawsuit, largely on procedural grounds. The judge said, in dismissing the claim regarding unfunded mandates and annual testing, that he could not make a "pre-enforcement declaration." That is, since the state has continued to comply with the act to avoid any penalties, including possible loss of federal funds, any action on the court's part would be premature since the secretary has not taken any enforcement actions against the state.

The judge also dismissed the state's claim that it had been denied a waiver, stating it was "arbitrary and capricious" under the federal Administrative Procedure Act. The Spending Clause claim was also dismissed.

Despite all of this, the judge kept alive the state's claim that USDOE had acted "arbitrarily and capriciously" in denying CT's requests to plan amendments regarding compliance with testing provisions for students with limited English proficiency and with disabilities. The judge stated that a ruling on that claim would require a review of the administrative record, and he also gave the parties time to file additional information.

The second suit was filed in April 2005 by a number of school districts and educational associations essentially seeking a court ruling that school districts do not have to spend non-NCLB funds to comply with the NCLB. *Pontiac v. Spellings* was filed by the National Education Association, nine of its state affiliates, and nine school districts. The plaintiffs sought the following relief:

1. A declaratory judgment determining that "states and school districts are not required to spend non-NCLB funds to comply with the NCLB mandates, and

that a failure to comply with the NCLB mandates for this reason does not provide a basis for withholding any federal funds to which they are otherwise entitled under the NCLB."

2. An injunction prohibiting the defendant and any other officer or employee of the Department of Education (ED) "from withholding from states and school districts any federal funds to which they are entitled under the NCLB because of a failure to comply with the mandates of the NCLB that is attributable to a refusal to spend non-NCLB funds to achieve such compliance."

3. Reimbursement by defendant of plaintiffs' attorneys' fees and costs.

Plaintiffs' argument was based first on NCLB language that states and school districts shall not be mandated by the NCLB "to spend any funds or incur any costs not paid for under this Act." This language is different from IDEA language.

Plaintiffs, secondly, and more broadly, contended that Congress has an obligation, under the Spending Clause of the U.S. Constitution, to provide the funds promised under the NCLB funding and authorization formulas. Specifically, the complaint alleges that by "requiring states and school districts—including plaintiff school districts to comply fully with all of the NCLB mandates even if the federal funds that they receive are insufficient to pay for such compliance, defendant Spellings is violating the Spending Clause by changing one of the conditions pursuant to which states and school districts accepted funds under the NCLB."

In November 2005, the lower court dismissed the NEA's claim that the federal government is in violation of the NCLB "unfunded mandate" provision. The case has been appealed to the Sixth District Court of Appeals for the Sixth District, which heard oral arguments in late November 2006. A decision is expected some time in 2007.

B. FERPA

The Family Educational Rights and Privacy Act of 1974 (FERPA), 20 U.S.C.A. Section 1232g, sometimes known as the Buckley Amendment, provides that federal funds will not be made available to state educational agencies or institutions that fail to comply with specified provisions of FERPA. Under FERPA, parents have the right to inspect and review their child's educational records. The parents also have the right to challenge the accuracy of those records. Further, educational records may not be released to third parties without the written consent of the parents, except for release to specified categories of persons, such as school officials and accrediting organizations.

When a student reaches age eighteen or is attending a postsecondary educational institution, the rights accorded the parents under FERPA become the rights of the student. The student must consent to release of records, rather than the parents. In fact, the consent of the student is required in order for the educational institution to release the student's records to the parents.

When an educational agency no longer needs to maintain a student's records, the agency must notify the parents, or the student, if the student is age eighteen or older. The parents or student, depending on the age of the student, may request that the records be destroyed. If the records are destroyed, the educational agency may retain, as a permanent record, basic information concerning the student, including name, contact information, attendance, grades, and final year of school completed.

The Supreme Court has ruled on what constitutes an educational record protected under FERPA. In *Owasso Independent School District No. I-011 v. Falvo*, 534 U.S. 426 (2002), the Supreme Court considered whether the practice of "peer grading" violated FERPA.

Under the practice of "peer grading," students grade one another's papers. After the students receive back their own papers, the students call out their grades to the teacher or walk to the teacher's desk and reveal the grade to the teacher in confidence. The mother of three children in the school district objected to the practice, which she said "severely embarrassed her children by allowing other students to learn their grades." When the school district refused to change its practices, she filed a class action suit under federal law, including FERPA, seeking court orders prohibiting the practices.

In a unanimous decision, the U.S. Supreme Court held that the school district was correct. The court found that, while the student's papers do contain information directly related to a student, they are not records under FERPA because they were not maintained as such by an educational institution or by a person acting on behalf of such agency or institution. FERPA, therefore, did not prohibit the practice of peer grading. The court noted that the mother's interpretation of FERPA would

> force teachers to abandon other customary practices, such as group grading of team assignments. Indeed, the logical consequences of respondents view are all but unbounded. At argument, counsel for [Falvo] seemed to agree that if a teacher in any of the thousands of covered classrooms in the Nation puts a happy face, a gold star, or a disapproving remark on a classroom assignment, federal law does not allow other students to see it.

C.   Civil Liability of Educators

1.   Overview

When can teachers and administrators be sued? What civil liability might they incur? These are important questions. This chapter provides basic information on various kinds of civil wrongs, called torts, for which one person may be sued by another person.

2.   Tort

The term tort refers to various civil wrongs for which a person may sue another and seek a remedy, such as monetary damages. Tort liability generally arises out of a tradition of law called the common law. Tort liability may also arise out of the U.S. Constitution.

A tort is different from a crime. In the case of a crime, the state charges a person with a particular criminal offense and seeks in a court trial to impose a penalty, such as imprisonment. Sometimes one act committed by a person may give rise to both criminal and civil liability. For example, if one person assaults and harms another person, the assault may be a crime for which a penalty will be imposed in criminal court and also a tort for which money damages may be awarded in civil court.

Tort liability is also different from contract liability. In contract liability, the right asserted by one person against another person arises out of the agreement between the two individuals. For example, one person may sue another in civil court for breach of contract. The remedy may be to perform the contract or to pay money damages for the failure to perform.

3.   Common Law Torts

Common law torts fall into two categories: intentional interference and negligence.

Intentional Interference

As the term suggests, the perpetrator must perform an act and intend that act to harm the interest of the person toward whom it is directed. Two acts of intentional interference are (1) assault and battery and (2) false imprisonment.

Assault and Battery.   Common acts of intentional interference are assault and battery. A battery involves a physical touching, but an assault involves the threat of physical harm, even though no physical touching has occurred. Assault and battery often occur together, but may exist independently of each other. A few examples will illustrate the relationship between assault and battery. If a person raises his hand, threatens to strike another person and does strike that person, then both assault and battery have occurred. If a person threatens another with harm while brandishing a weapon, an assault has occurred, but no battery. If a person strikes another from behind by surprise, the act is battery but not assault.

How may teachers be accused of assault and/or battery? Such accusations most often arise in connection with punishment of a student that is alleged to be excessive, malicious, or in violation of school rules. Keep in mind that teachers do have the authority to discipline students under a legal doctrine called *in loco parentis*. In other words, the teacher during the school day has some authority that a parent has with respect to the student. An example of appropriate teacher action would be where a teacher physically separates and restrains children who were physically harming each other in a fight. While there is physical touching and some display of force, the amount of force is appropriate and in support of the teacher's duty to maintain order and safety. An example of inappropriate teacher action would be if a teacher were to strike a student in anger, causing injury and significant physical bruising.

False Imprisonment.   Another tort that could be alleged is false imprisonment. An action for false imprisonment must show (1) restraint of physical liberty and (2) unlawfulness of that restraint. Certain categories of people are permitted to restrain others because of a particular relationship. Law enforcement officers are permitted to restrain others. Teachers, acting in loco parentis, are permitted to place reasonable restraints on the physical liberty of students. Reasonable restraint might be placing a student in after-school detention for a brief period of time. Even if the teacher incorrectly concluded that the student's conduct merited detention, the restraint would not constitute false imprisonment so long as the teacher was acting in good faith, without malice, and the detention conditions and time period were reasonable. On the other hand, locking a student in a closet for hours would not be reasonable and would be false imprisonment.

Negligence

Not all torts are intentional. Some involve only negligence. Negligence is unintentional conduct that falls below an applicable standard of conduct and results in harm to another person.

Standard of Conduct. Teachers have education and training to perform their duties. As a result, in some court cases teachers have been required to meet the higher standard of the "reasonably prudent teacher" in similar circumstances and not merely the standard of the "reasonable prudent person."

Teachers have a higher duty toward students than the average person has toward others. This higher duty results from the in loco parentis role. Thus, teachers may have a duty to act to protect students in some situations, so that a failure to act may be negligence. Note that people in the general population do not have a duty to protect others, absent a special relationship that creates a higher duty.

The duty to act, however, does not impose an unreasonable obligation. A teacher may have a duty to separate two first-grade students who are fighting but would not have a duty to physically intervene in a struggle between two members of the high school football team. See *Kim v. State*, 62 Hawaii 483, 616 P. 2d 1376 (1980).

Where the risk of injury to the student is greater, the duty of the teacher is greater. For example, the duty of the physical education teacher would be greater than the duty of the French teacher. Learning French is not inherently risky, whereas playing football involves some risk of physical injury.

Suppose a teacher does commit an unintentional act that falls below that applicable standard of conduct. Is the teacher liable? The answer is that there also has to be a "harm" caused by the negligent act. Otherwise, there is no tort.

Harm and Causation. Legally speaking, the act of negligence must be the proximate cause of the harm. A proximate cause is a logical, sequential cause of the harm. A few examples will illustrate when an act is the proximate cause of a harm. Where a teacher observes elementary students fighting on the school playground at recess, leaves to make a personal telephone call, and returns to find that one of the students has been injured, the teacher's failure to perform a duty to intervene would be the proximate cause of the harm. The injury that occurred was foreseeable. On the other hand, the teacher's conduct would not be the proximate cause of harm where the teacher leaves the classroom for a few minutes to go to the principal's office, and, in those few minutes, a student from another class enters the room with a small knife and cuts one of the students. In this example, there was no student conduct requiring the teacher's intervention at the time the teacher left the room, and the injury that occurred was not foreseeable by the teacher.

Defenses Against Allegations of Negligence

If a civil action is brought against a teacher for negligence, what are the possible defenses? Some defenses are arguments that no tort occurred. Such arguments include that there was no negligent act, that there was no harm, or that the negligent act was not the proximate cause of the harm.

Even if there is a negligent act that is the proximate cause of a harm, there are a number of tort defenses that may be raised: (i) contributory negligence, (ii) last clear chance, (iii) comparative negligence, (iv) assumption of risk, (v) natural elements (sometimes referred to as acts of God), and (vi) immunity.

Contributory Negligence.   Contributory negligence refers to negligence on the part of the injured party that contributed to the injury. If a student's negligence contributed to his or her own injury, the teacher may be found not to have committed a tort.

Can a child be negligent? The answer is yes. However, a child is not held to the standard of care applicable to an average person, but, rather, to the standard of care for a child of the same age, physical characteristics, and educational level. Since children by nature do not always exercise good judgment and are sometimes careless, it is not easy for teachers to establish contributory negligence where a child is involved, especially a young child.

Last Clear Chance.   The legal concept of "last clear chance" is that the injured party had a last clear opportunity to avoid the harm and did not do so. Given the elevated duty of teachers to students, it would be rare that the last clear chance defense would be useful to a teacher.

Comparative Negligence.   Some states have statutes providing for comparative negligence. The concept of comparative negligence is that, where both the injured person and the allegedly negligent perpetrator have some degree of fault for the injury, the injured person may recover a portion of the damages based upon the portion of responsibility that is borne by the alleged perpetrator. This approach of partial recovery is in contrast to the contributory negligence and last clear chance approaches, which bar any recovery by the injured party if the injured party contributed to or could have avoided the injury.

Assumption of Risk.   The assumption of risk defense is essentially that the injured party agrees to assume the risk inherent in the activity in which he or she is involved. A key element of assumption of risk is knowledge of the risk involved in the activity. Some examples will illustrate the application of the assumption of risk defense.

A teacher, upon seeing lightning, instructs students to proceed inside the school. A boy in ninth grade runs toward the school entrance while looking back at friends. Instead of running through the door, he crashes into an adjacent glass panel, sustaining an injury. The teacher would not be liable for negligence. The student assumes the risk of adverse weather conditions and the risks of proceeding from place to place on school grounds. Further, he was aware of the location of the doors and of the adjacent glass panel. Students are generally held to have assumed ordinary risks in playing sports, such as being hit by a puck while playing field hockey.

On the other hand, a student would not be considered to have assumed the risk of being directed to perform activities that are clearly inappropriate for his particular circumstances. For example, a student with physical disabilities who was required to participate in sports activities despite his physical limitations would not have the risk of injury from such an activity.

Natural Elements.   While teachers should take actions to protect students from anticipated natural events, such as lightning, teachers would not be held liable for injuries resulting from an unexpected lightning strike.

Immunity.   Certain entities and persons have immunity from liability. For example, state governments generally have sovereign immunity from tort liability, unless the state government consents to be sued or the immunity is abrogated. A school district is part of the state and so can have immunity. Teachers and administrators do not have immunity.

Some states have enacted "save harmless" laws that provide that, in the event of a judicial determination that a teacher owes damages to a student, the school district will pay up to a certain amount of the damages that the teacher otherwise would be obligated to pay.

4.   Constitutional Torts

A constitutional tort essentially is the extension of personal liability to an official, such as a teacher, who violates the constitutional rights of another person. The Civil Rights Act of 1871, Title 42 U.S.C. Section 1983, provides for such personal liability in the civil rights context. Some types of officials, such as elected state officials, have either absolute immunity or qualified immunity.

Fourteenth Amendment Equal Protection of the Law

Teachers, under some circumstances, may be held liable for money damages for violation of the rights of students. In *Doe v. Withers, 20 IDELR 422* (W.Va. Cir. 1993), a teacher who deliberately refused to comply with a provision of a student's IEP was held liable for monetary damages to the student in the amount of $10,000. In this case, the student's right was expressly and clearly stated, and the teacher's refusal was deliberate and without any basis. Teachers acting in good faith but on a mistaken belief as to the right of the student generally would not be personally liable for damages. (See Section C.5 for the facts of this case.)

Fourth Amendment Search and Seizure

Another issue that may arise for teachers concerns when and whether a search of a student's person, belongings, or locker is justified. The Fourth Amendment to the

Constitution provides essentially for a right of privacy and prohibits unreasonable searches and seizures. Must teachers meet the same test as police in order to conduct a valid search? The answer is no. Because of the doctrine of in loco parentis and the duty to provide security for students in general, schools and teachers need not meet the standard of "probable cause" for searches that would be applicable to the police. Rather, school personnel may search if they have reasonable suspicion. Ordinarily, the reasonable suspicion must be in an individual context, justifying the search of one or several individuals as opposed to a search of all students or all lockers. Note that the use of metal detectors, a noninvasive method, may be applied to all students.

There are varying degrees of privacy, depending on what is being searched. School lockers and desks involve a relatively lower degree of privacy, as there should not be the same expectation of privacy that would exist for the student's own backpack or automobile. Searches of the person involve a relatively higher degree of privacy. Searches of a student's pockets have been upheld. However, strip searches by school personnel generally are not permitted.

What are the possible consequences if the teacher engages in an unreasonable search and infringes on the constitutional right of privacy of a student? A student could bring an action for damages under the Civil Rights Act of 1871, 42 U.S.C. 1983. Generally, the teacher would not be liable if acting in good faith in performing the unreasonable search but could be liable if maliciously violating the privacy right of the student.

5. Cases

In *Doe v. Withers* (W.Va. Cir. 1993), a ninth-grade student with a specific learning disability was receiving education under an IEP, which required oral testing. All teachers, except Withers, his American History teacher, complied with the IEP requirements. Withers repeatedly and deliberately refused to administer oral tests and required the student to take a written test on the first semester history materials. The student failed the test. A second teacher administered a second semester oral American History test, which the student passed. The student and his family sued under federal civil rights laws for injunctive relief with respect to his first semester grade and for damages. The court issued an injunction requiring that the first semester American History test be administered orally, but declined to require that the school award the student a passing grade for the first semester simply because the test had initially been given in violation of the IEP. In addition, the jury awarded the student and his family $5,000 in compensatory damages and $10,000 in punitive damages against the history teacher personally.

The Withers case does not represent the only means by which personal liability might be incurred. In *Armijo by and Through Chavez v. Wagon Mound Public School,* (10th Cir. 1998), the U.S. Court of Appeals for the Tenth Circuit considered the question of whether school officials might be personally liable for the suicide of a student covered by the IDEA. The Court of Appeals noted that public officials, though generally liable only for their own acts, are liable for the violent acts of third parties where there is a special relationship because "the state assumes control over an individual sufficient to trigger an affirmative duty to provide protection to that individual," and where the state created the danger that harmed the individual.

To show that the state created the danger, Armijo's parents had to demonstrate that (1) Armijo was "a member of a limited and specifically definable group"; (2) conduct of the school officials put Armijo at "substantial risk of serious, immediate and proximate harm; (3) the risk was obvious or known; (4) school officials "acted recklessly in conscious disregard of that risk"; and (5) "such conduct, when viewed in total, is conscience shocking."

The court believed that the parents might be able to meet these standard because "Armijo was a member of a limited and specifically definable group—special education students who have expressed threats of suicide" and ordered the case to trial.

See also *Pamela McCormick ex re. Eron McCormick v. Waukegan School District et al.*, Docket No. 02-1538 (7th Cir. July 7, 2004) (Chapter 5).

D. High Stakes Testing

Many states have imposed standardized exit examinations, which must be completed successfully by students prior to graduation. Typically, these tests are in addition to regular classroom tests required to pass particular courses. In *Rene v. Reed* (Ind. App. June 20, 2001), the Indiana Court of Appeals considered and rejected a series of challenges to these "high stakes" tests. Indiana adopted a general qualification examination (GQE) for tenth-grade students as part of a comprehensive system of statewide testing. All students, including those with disabilities, were required to take the test. The Indiana schools were required to provide extensive remediation for those who were unsuccessful.

Meghan Rene was a high school student with a disability who received special education and related services under IDEA. Prior to the GQE requirement, she had always been excused from standardized testing. Her IEP provided that she was in the diploma program and that, if she completed all her course work and complied with her IEP, she would receive a diploma. The IEP specifically required that all tests should be read to her and that she be permitted to use a calculator on all tests. However, Indiana did not permit accommodations for "cognitive disabilities" that could "significantly affect the meaning and interpretation of the test score." Accordingly, Meghan was denied accommodations required by her IEP, took the GQE, and failed it. She filed a class action suit to enjoin Indiana from requiring that she and others pass the GQE as it then existed in order to graduate. They sued and lost in the trial court.

The Indiana Court of Appeals affirmed the trial court, holding that (1) the implementation of the GQE did not deny the students due process because they were sufficiently exposed (three to five years) during their schooling to the material tested on the GQE; (2) they had adequate notice of the requirement and adequate time to prepare for the GQE; and (3) the Indiana remediation program was an adequate remedy for any due process violation that might have occurred.

The court ruled that the IDEA had not been violated by Indiana's prohibition of Rene's mandated IDEA accommodations, specifically a reader and the use of a calculator. The court said that "the State need not honor certain accommodations called for in the Students' IEPs where those accommodations would affect the validity of the test results," specifically, those accommodations for "cognitive disabilities" that can "significantly affect the meaning and interpretation of the test score." The court drew these distinctions:

> For example, the State permits accommodations such as oral or sign language responses to test questions, questions in Braille, special lighting or furniture, enlarged answer sheets, and individual or small group testing. By contrast, it prohibits accommodations in the form of reading to the student test questions that are meant to measure reading comprehension, allowing unlimited time to complete test sections, allowing the student to respond to questions in a language other than English, and using language in the directions or in certain test questions that is reduced in complexity.

The court concluded that "an accommodation for cognitive disabilities provided for in a student's IEP" need not "necessarily be observed during the GQE." For example, in a test of ability to calculate, a student would not be permitted a calculator as an accommodation.

However, there have been two class action settlements in which states have agreed to special accommodations for students with disabilities on high stakes tests. Most recently, in August 2004, Alaska agreed that students who qualify as disabled would receive special accommodations, such as extended time, on the Alaska High School Qualifying Exam. In addition, students who fail the initial exam could take a modified exam. Finally, for severely disabled students who still are unable to pass, experts could judge their work to determine whether that work meets state standards.

Under California law, members of the class of 2004 must pass the California High School Exit Examination (CAHSEE). Students with learning disabilities sued under the IDEA and the RA to require that reasonable accommodations be provided on the test. The U.S. District Court issued a preliminary injunction providing that:

1. Students may take the CAHSEE with all accommodations, modifications, alternative testing provided for that test in their IEPs or 504 plans.
2. Students whose IEPs or 504 plans do not specifically address CAHSEE may use all accommodations, modifications, and alternative testing their plans provide for standardized testing.
3. Students whose IEPs or 504 plans do not specifically address CAHSEE or standardized testing may use all accommodations, modifications, and alternative testing their plans provide for general classroom testing.
4. "An 'appropriate accommodation' is any accommodation necessary to render a student's score on the CAHSEE a meaningful measure of that student's academic achievement." *Chapman v. California Department of Education,* 229 F.Supp. 2d 981 (N.D. Cal. 2002)

The court ruled that "an 'appropriate accommodation' is any accommodation necessary to render a student's score on the CAHSEE a meaningful measure of that student's academic achievement." *Chapman v. California Department of Education,* 229 F.Supp. 2d 981 (N.D. Cal. 2002)

However, after protracted litigation, the court became convinced that portions of the relief requested were premature, because, as the court recognized, the development of the CAHSEE is a "highly dynamic process," not sufficiently complete to permit a determination as to whether it violated applicable law. *Note:* On appeal, the case was titled *Smiley v. California Department of Education,* 53 Fed. Appx. 474 (9th Cir. 2002).

The significance of high stakes testing will continue to grow for the foreseeable future.

E. Summary

There have been a series of new areas of concern for the special educator. No Child Left Behind promises to expand the efforts made to assist all children in achieving academic skills. FERPA confers certain rights regarding educational records of students in educational institutions that receive federal funds. These rights include a right of privacy and a right to inspect records. FERPA has been interpreted to preclude parental suits to enforce FERPA regulations.

Under some circumstances, courts impose civil liability on educators. An example of a circumstance that would expose a teacher to civil liability would be deliberate mistreatment of a student.

High stakes testing is growing in significance and generating challenges on behalf of students with disabilities who seek test accommodations.

INDEX

A

Aaron B. v. *El Paso Independent School District*, 77
Ability Center of Greater Toledo v. *City of Sandusky*, 20
Academic adjustments, 141
Accommodations
  course substitutions, 160
  for employment, 165
  free, 161
  job information, 168
  requesting, 159
  selection of, 158–59
  temporary, 160–61
Accountability, No Child Left Behind and, 171
Adarand Constructors v. *Pena*, 14
Adkins v. *Briggs & Stratton Corp.*, 137
Administrative decisions
  contesting federal court, 103–12
  contesting state court, 112
  exhaustion of remedies, 104–5
  litigation, 103
  states, immunity from suit and, 103–4
Administrative litigation, 3
Administrative review, 101
Admissions, 168–69
aff'd, Fennell v. *Cortines*, 105
African Americans, Reconstruction Civil Rights Act and, 12
Agency interpretations, 4
Albertsons, Inc. v. *Kirkingburg*, 122, 123
Alexander v. *Sandoval*, 9, 19–20, 135
Alexis v. *Board of Education for Baltimore County Public Schools*, 67
Alternative dispute resolution (ADR), 3, 87
  agreement to use, 87
  settlement agreement, 87–88

Alternative educational placement (AEP), 77
Alternative education program (AEP), 82
Amendments, constitutional
  Eleventh, 13
  Fifth, 11, 12–13
  Fourteenth, 7, 8, 11
  Tenth, 7
Americans with Disabilities Act (ADA), 3, 5, 11, 26, 41
  attorney fees and costs, 137–38
  cases, no duty to identify under, 46–47
  coverage, 127–33
  discipline, 84
  enforcement of, 135–42
  impairments covered, 121
  individual with disability and, 119–26
  interpretation of, 16
  major life activities, 124–25
  Office for Civil Rights and, 138–41
  relationship among RA and IDEA, 26–31
  Section 504, 11
  sovereign immunity and, 14
  status of regulations, issue of, 19–21
  statutory language, 120–21
  substantially limits, 121–23
  Title I, 130–31, 136
  Title II, 131–32, 136
  Title III, 132–33, 136
Analysis of Comments and Changes, 40, 41, 70, 74
Andersen v. *Apfel*, 123
Andrea G. v. *Community Independent School District*, 80
Aphasia, developmental, 38

Appellate courts, 1
  federal, 2
  opinions, 4
Applied behavioral analysis (ABA), 56, 66
Arbitration, 85–86
Armijo by and Through v. *Wagon Mound Public School*, 180
Armijo v. *Wagon Mound Public School*, 55
Arons v. *New Jersey State Board of Education*, 58, 98
Arons v. *Office of Disciplinary Counsel*, 58
Asperger's syndrome, 38, 40–43, 64
Assault and battery, 176
Association for Retarded Children (ARC), 24
Assumption of risk, 178–79
Attention deficit hyperactivity disorder (ADHD), 40–43, 64, 68, 80
  diagnosis of, 41
  private education and, 27–28
  private schools and, 62, 149–50
  as specific learning disability, 42
Attorney fees
  costs and, 113–18
  defining prevailing party, 113–14
  determination of, 117
  educational agency as prevailing party, 114–15
  limiting recovery of, 114
  in mediation, 91
  nonreimbursable activities, 117
  RA and ADA, 137–38
  recovery of, 115–18
  unproductive litigation and, 116–17
  unreasonable rates and hours, 117–18

Authority, 75
Autism, 34, 41, 64
Autism Unit (AU), 63
Auxiliary aids, 157
    providing, 141
Axelrod v. *Phillips Academy, Andover,*
    149

B
Banks ex rel. Banks v. *Danbury Board
    of Education,* 68
Barnes v. *Gorman,* 9
Bartlett v. *New York State Board of
    Law Examiners,* 124, 156
Beck v. *University of Wisconsin,* 158,
    165
Behavioral intervention plan (BIP),
    97
Bercovitch v. *Baldwin School, Inc.,* 27,
    73, 115, 137, 149
Berger v. *Medina City School District,*
    67
Beth V. v. *Carroll, Jr.,* 106
Bill of Rights, 13
Bingham v. *Oregon School Activities
    Association,* 150
*Board of Education of Baldwin Union
    Free School District* v. *Sobel,* 64
Board of Education of Harford County
    v. *Bauer,* 62
*Board of Education of Hendrick Hud-
    son School District* v. *Rowley,* 52
*Board of Education of the Pawling Cen-
    tral School District* v. *Schulz,* 37
Board of Education v. *Rowley,* 11, 30,
    52, 60, 63, 67
*Board of Trustees of the University of
    Alabama* v. *Garrett,* 15, 131
Bombard v. *Fort Wayne Newspapers,
    Inc.,* 164
Bradley ex rel. Bradley v. *Arkansas
    Dep't of Educ,* 13
Bradley v. *Simon,* 12
Bragdon v. *Abbott,* 16
Braille instruction, 58
Brennan v. *Mercedes Benz USA, Uni-
    versal Technical Institute,* 55
Brillon v. *Klein Independent School
    District,* 65
Brown v. *Board of Education,* 143
Buckhannon Board & Home Care, Inc.
    v. *W.Va. Department of Health &
    Human Resources,* 113, 114
Buckley Amendment, 174–75
*Bucks County Department of Mental
    Health/Retardation* v. *Pennsylv-
    ania,* 52–53, 68

Burden of proof, 99
Burilovich ex rel. Burilovich v. *Board of
    Education,* 56, 57
Burke v. *Virginia,* 125, 164

C
California High School Exit Exami-
    nation (CAHSEE), 106, 107, 182
Capistrano Unified School District v.
    Wartenberg, 66
Capistrano Unified School District v.
    *Wartenberg by & Through
    Wartenberg,* 42, 47
Captioned Films Act, 24
Case law, federal, 4
*Cedar Rapids Community School Dis-
    trict* v. *Garret F.,* 10, 30, 36, 50,
    52, 62
*cert. denied, Bexley City School Dis-
    trict* v. *Knable,* 111
cert. denied, Ward v. *Secretary of
    Transportation,* 166
Chandler v. *City of Dallas,* 166
Chandler v. *Miller,* 168
Chapman v. *California Department of
    Education,* 107, 182, 183
Child find, 43
Child with disability, 37–38, 44
Christianburg Garmet Co. v. *EEOC,* 137
Christopher S. v. *Stanislaus County of
    Education,* 106
City of Cleburn, Texas v. *Cleburn Liv-
    ing Center, Inc.,* 15
City of Rancho Palos Verdes v.
    Abrams, 12
Civil disputes, 3
Civil liability, of educators, 175–81
    common law torts, 176–79
    constitutional torts, 179–80
    tort, 175–76
Civil Rights Act, 19, 180
CJN v. *Minnesota. Minneapolis Public
    Schools, Special School District
    No. 1,* 61
*Cleveland Heights-University Heights
    City School District* v. *Boss 144
    F.3d 391,* 67
Cleveland v. *Policy Management Sys-
    tems Corp.,* 169
Clyde K. v. *Puyallup School District
    No. 3,* 64
Code of Federal Regulations (CFR),
    4, 27
Coen v. *Riverside Hospital,* 125
College Sav. Bank v. *Florida Prepaid
    Postsecondary Educ. Expense
    Bd.,* 14

Commerce Clause, of Constitution, 7
Common law torts, 176–79
    intentional interference, 176–77
    negligence, 177–79
Comorbidity, problem of, 47–48
Comparative negligence, 178
Compensatory education, 53–54
Complaints, due process, 94–96
Conduct disorder, 47
Confidentiality
    agreement, 90–91
    in employment, 167–69
    mediation, 90
    medical examinations, 167–68
    preemployment inquiries, 167
Connors v. *Mills,* 58, 98
Constitution, 1, 7–21
    Commerce Clause, 7
    due process, 12–13
    federal system and, 2
    Fourteenth Amendment, 7, 8
    intentional discrimination
        barred, 15–18
    principles, 7–8
    rational basis review, 13–15
    Spending Clause, 7
    state regulations, 18–20
    statutory measures, 8–12
    Tenth Amendment, 7
Constitutional provisions, 4
Constitutional torts, 179–80
    Fourteenth Amendment equal
        protection of law, 179
    Fourth Amendment search and
        seizure, 179–80
Constructive discharge, 166–67
Continued services, 82–83
Contributory negligence, 178
Corine R., B/N/F Rick & Stacey R. v.
    *Marlin Independent School Dis-
    trict,* 35
Council for Exceptional Children, 5
Counseling
    rehabilitation, 49
    services, 49
*County School Board of Henrico
    County* v. *Palkovics,* 60
Course substitutions, 160
Court opinions
    appellate, 4
    district court, 4
    Supreme, 4
Court proceedings, 103–12
    contesting administrative deci-
        sions in federal court, 103–12
    contesting administrative deci-
        sions in state court, 112

Courts
  federal, 2
  organization of, 2
  state, 1–2
  Supreme, 1
Crimes, 79–80
Cypress Fairbanks Independent School District v. Michael F., 64

D

Daubert v. Merrell Dow Pharms., 100
Davidson v. Midelfort Clinic, 125
Davis v. Monroe County Board of Education, 18, 29, 73, 78
Dazey v. Department of the Air Force 54 M.S.P.R. 658, 164
D.B. v. Craven County Board of Education, 60
D.D. v. New York City Board of Education, 107
Deaf-blindness, 34
Deal v. Hamilton County Board of Education, 42, 56, 57, 111
Delmonte v. Department of Business & Professional Regulation, Div. of Alcoholic Beverages & Tobacco, 129
Department of Education v. Cari Rae S., 45
Department of Justice, 141
Detroyer v. Oakland Community College, 156
Developmental aphasia, 38
Developmental delay, 34
Developmental Test of Visual Motor Integration (VMI), 39
DiBuo v. Board of Education, 60
Di Pompo v. West Point Military Academy, 164
Disability
  severity of, 122
  state law definitions, 126
Discipline, 73–84
  continued services, 82–83
  disputes, 83–84
  as fundamental requirement, 73
  IDEA approach to, 74–75
  relationship to RA/ADA, 84
  school code violations, 75–79
  serious criminal misconduct, 79–82
Disclosure, 167
Discrimination, 143–48
  intentional, 15–18
  Rehabilitation Act and, 8
Disputes, 83–84

District court
  evidentiary proceedings, 110
  opinions, 4
Documentation, requirements, 159–60
Doe v. Arizona Department of Education, 106
Doe v. Vanderbilt University, 153
Doe v. Withers, 54, 179, 180
Donald B. v. Board of School Commissioners of Mobile County, Alabama, 63
Douglas W. v. Greenfield Public Schools, 67
Drinker v. Colonial School District, 110
Drug testing information, 168
Dubois v. Alderson-Broaddus College, Inc., 159
Due process, 12–13
  contesting, 45
  procedural, 13
  protection, 13
  resorting to, 105
  substantive, 12–13
Due process hearing, 93–101
  administrative review, 101
  behavior, 98
  burden of proof, 99
  complaint and response, 94–96
  decision, 100
  document introduction, 99
  evidence of facts, 99–100
  judicial review, 101
  key document, disclosure of, 96
  notice and prehearing matters, 93
  opening statement, 99
  opinion evidence, 100
  preparing for, 97
  representation, 98
  requirement, 93–94
  resolution conference, 96
  right to, 96–97
  rules governing, 99
  statute of limitations, 98
  time and location, 98
Dutcher v. Ingalls Shipbuilding, 125, 164
Duty to evaluate, 43–48
Dyslexia, 38, 68, 155

E

Economic Opportunities Amendments, 24
Education
  elementary, 143–50
  postsecondary, 151–62
  secondary, 143–50

Educational materials, delivery of, 157–58
Educational support services, 141
Education for All Handicapped Children Act, 9, 23, 33
Education of the Handicapped Act, 145
Educators, civil liability of, 175–81
EEOC v. J.B. Hunt Transport, Inc., 125
Eileen T. v. Northside Independent School District, 81
E.J. v. Matula, 87
Elementary and Secondary Education Act, 24
Elementary education, 143–50
  discrimination in, 143–48
Eleventh amendment, 13
Elida Local School District Board of Education v. Erickson, 40
Ellis v. Morehouse School of Medicine, 153
Emma C. v. Eastin, 60
Emotional disturbance, 34
Employment, 163–69
  basic requirements, 163
  confidentiality, 167–69
  constructive discharge, 166–67
  disclosure, 167
  discrimination and, 166
  essential job requirements, 164–65
  hostile work environments, 166–67
  individualized inquiry, 166
  limitations on duty to accommodate, 166
  major life activities, 164
  otherwise qualified, 164–65
  reasonable accommodations, 165
  testing, 165
Equal Employment Opportunity Commission (EEOC), 125
Equal protection
  intentional discrimination barred, 15–18
  rational basis review required, 13–15
Eric H. ex rel. Gary H. v. Judson Independent School District, 38
E.S. v. Independent School District No. 196, 67
Evaluation
  child find, 43
  comment on duty to, 45–47
  comorbidity, 47–48
  content of, 44

Evaluation (*cont.*)
duty to, 43–48
failure or refusal, 45
initial, 44
Evidence
of facts, 99–100
opinion, 100

F
Failure to evaluate, 45
False imprisonment, 176–77
Family Educational Rights and Privacy Act (FERPA), 90, 174–75
Federal case law, 4
Federal Circuit Courts of Appeal, 29
Federal courts, 2
contesting administrative decisions in, 103–12
Federal grant and aid recipients, RA and, 129
Federal law, 4
Federal Register, 4
Federal Rules of Civil Procedures (FRCP), 108
FEDLAW, 4
Fick v. *Sioux Falls*, 60
Fifth Amendment, 11
due process, 12–13
Florence County School District Four v. *Carter*, 52, 53, 66, 67
Flour Bluff Independent School District v. *Katherine M.*, 65
Flowers v. *Southern Regional Physician Services, Inc.*, 167
Ford v. *Long Beach Unified School District*, 39
Fourteenth Amendment, 7, 8, 11
equal protection of law, 179
IDEA and, 9–10
intentional discrimination and, 15
rational basis and, 14–15
Fourth Amendment, search and seizure, 179–80
Fox v. *General Motors*, 167
Free appropriate public education (FAPE), 9, 19, 23, 29, 49–71
basic rule, 52–53
Board of Education v. *Rowley*, 52
compensatory education, 53–54
definition of, 51–55
denying, 60
failure to furnish, 52–55
personal liability, 54–55
under RA, 144–46
related services, 62–63
statutory language, 51–52

Fundamental academic requirements, 156–57
Fundamental right, 16–18
right of freedom, 16–17
right to be free from cruel and unusual punishment, 17
right to meaningful access to public education, 17–18
Funding, IDEA working through, 37

G
Garcia v. *State University of N.Y. Health Sciences Center*, 18
Gebser v. *Lago Vista Independent School District*, 18, 78
General Accounting Office (GAO). *See* Government Accountability Office (GAO)
George S. v. *Webb Consolidated Independent School District*, 82
Gerstmyer v. *Howard County Public School*, 66
Gilbert v. *Storage Technology Corporation*, 164
Gonzaga University v. *Doe*, 19
Government Accountability Office (GAO), 94
Greenbush School Committee v. *Mr. and Mrs. K., Civ.*, 51
Greenland School District v. *Amy N.*, 67
Guckenberger et al v. *Boston University*, 154, 157, 159, 160

H
Halasz v. *University of New England*, 161
Hammond v. *Hartford School District*, 67
Handicapped Children's Early Education Assistance Act, 24
Harm and causation, 177–78
Harris v. *Forklift Systems*, 167
Hartmann v. *Loudoun County Board of Education*, 64, 65
Hearing impairments, 34
Henrico County Public Schools v. *Spielberg*, 56
Hessler v. *State Board of Education*, 61, 66
High stakes testing, 181–83
Hope v. *Cortines*, 105
Hospitals, Title III, ADA, 132
Hostile work environments, 166–67

I
Immunity, 179
sovereign, 13, 103

Impulsive acts, 81–82
Inclusion, 63–66
Individualized education program (IEP), 9, 17, 23, 47, 52, 55–61
components of, 58–59
defects, 60–61
document, 58–60
due process hearing and, 97
planning for meeting, 57–58
2004 reauthorization, 61, 69–71
services in, 49
team, 55–57
violation of, 54
Individualized family service plan (IFSP), 53
Individualized inquiry, 166
Individuals with Disabilities Education Act (IDEA), 3, 5, 9–11, 13, 23–26
accomplishments, 25–26
approach to discipline, 74–75
coverage, 33–48
evaluations, 43–44
Fourteenth Amendment and, 10
free appropriate public education, 9, 23, 49–71
funding and, 29–31, 37
inclusion, 63–66
individualized education plan, 9, 23
least restrictive environment, 9, 23, 63
mediation under, 88–89
philosophy of, 35–36
placement, 61–62
purposes of, 25, 49
reauthorization of, 36–37, 61
related services, 49
relationship among RA and ADA, 26–31
statutory language, 37–43
supportive services, 49
Individual transition plans (ITP), 97
Infants, with disabilities, 53
Initial evaluation, 44
Injunctions, 109
In loco parentis, 176
Intentional discrimination
ADA, interpretation of, 16
barred, 15–18
denial of right, 18
fundamental right, 16–18
RA, interpretation of, 16
Intentional interference, 176–77
assault and battery, 176
false imprisonment, 176–77
Irving Independent School District v. *Tatro*, 50

J

Jackson v. *Birmingham Board of Education*, 19

Jacob A. v. *San Antonio Independent School District*, 81

James C. v. *Corpus Christi Independent School District*, 63

Jason D.W. v. *Houston Independent School District*, 116

J.C. v. *Regional School District 10*, 79, 114

Jeremy H. v. *Mount Lebanon School District*, 105

Job accommodation information, 168

John Doe v. *Board of Education of Oak Park & River Forest High School District 200*, 81

Johnson ex rel. Johnson v. *Olathe District School*, 57

Johnson v. *Clearfield Area School District*, 117

J.P. ex rel. Popson v. *West Clark Community Schools*, 42, 68

Judicial review, 101

Judicial system, 1–5
  administrative litigation, 3
  alternative dispute resolution, 3
  federal courts, 2
  law, sources of, 3–5
  state courts, 1–2

K

Kammueller v. *Loomis, Fargo & Co.*, 31

Kennedy, Edward, 10, 24

Key documents, disclosure of, 96

Kiman v. *N.H. Department of Corrections*, 131

Kimel v. *Florida Board. of Regents*, 14, 15

Kim v. *State*, 177

Kings Local School District v. *Zelazny*, 60

King v. *Floyd County Board of Education*, 108

Knable ex rel. Knable v. *Bexley City School District*, 111

Kumho Tire Co. v. *Carmichael*, 100

L

Lane v. *Pena*, 135

Language impairments, 34

Lapides v. *Bd. of Regents*, 14

Larson v. *Independent School District No. 361*, 60

Last clear chance, legal concept, 178

Laughlin v. *Central Bucks School District*, 42

Law
  constitutional provisions, 4
  federal, 4
  federal case, 4
  regulations and, 4
  sources of, 3–5
  state, 4, 31–32
  statutes, 4

L.B. v. *Nebo School District*, 66

Learning, 124

Learning Disabilities Association of America, 5

Learning disabilities (LD), diagnosis, 25

Least restrictive environment (LRE), 9, 23, 63, 64, 65, 70

Leisen v. *City of Shelbyville*, 124

Letter of Findings Issued to Almont Community School District, 159

Letter of Findings Issued to Bellevue Community College, 160

Letter of Findings Issued to Educational Testing Service, 155

Letter of Findings Issued to Golden Gate University, 156

Letter of Findings Issued to Highline Community College, 158

Letter of Findings Issued to Hofstra University, 161

Letter of Findings Issued to Mitchell College, 161

Letter of Findings Issued to Mt. San Antonio College, 160

Letter of Findings Issued to Philadelphia College of Optometry, 158

Letter of Findings Issued to St. Louis Community College at Meramec, 159

Letter of Findings Issued to Temple University, 159

Letter of Findings Issued to University of California, Los Angeles, 158

Letter of Findings Issued to University of California, Sacramento, 159

Letter of Findings Issued to University of Southern Mississippi, 161

Letter of Findings Issued to Wingate University, 157

Letter of Findings to Frostburg State University, 159

Letter of Findings to State University of New York, 159, 160

Leukemia, as OHI, 40

Limited English proficiency, 44

Litigation
  administrative, 3
  cost of, 3

Local education agency (LEA), 23, 39

Loren H. v. *Royal Independent School District*, 78

Lovaas-trained therapists, 53

Lunceford v. *D.C. Board of Education*, 29

Lyons v. *Smith*, 42, 121

M

MacRae v. *Potter*, 126

Major life activities, 124–25
  concentration and thinking, 125
  learning, 124
  reading, 124
  working, 124–25
  of working, 164

Mancini v. *General Electric Co.*, 164

Mandatory medication, 62

Manifestation determinations, 76–77
  consequences of, 78–79
  deliberate conduct and, 80–81
  impulsive acts as, 81–82
  procedural failures in, 82

Mark R. v. *Board of Education*, 50, 67

Martinez v. *City of Roy*, 131

Matrix Analogies Test (MAT), 40

Matthew Head v. *Glacier Northwest*, 124, 125

M.C. v. *Central Regional School District*, 54

McArdle's disease, 54

McDaniel v. *Allied Signal, Inc.*, 164

McGuiness v. *University of New Mexico School of Medicine*, 124

McLaughlin v. *Holt Public School Board of Education*, 65

Mediation, 85–92
  arbitration, 85–86
  attorney fees in, 91
  civil and statutory rights, 87–88
  confidentiality, 90
  confidentiality agreement, 90–91
  congressional preference, 88
  ending, 89
  under IDEA, 88–89
  impartial mediators, 89
  improper use of, 88
  mediator selection, 89–90
  notice of hearing, 89
  parental decision, 89
  process, 89–91
  proper subjects of, 88
  scheduling, 89
  settlement agreement, 91
  state educational agency complaint, 86–87

Medical examinations, 167–68
  performance-based, 168
Medical services, 50
Menkowitz v. *Pottstown Memorial Medical Center*, 132
Mental retardation, 34
Metro. Government v. *Cook*, 111
Miller, George, 10, 24
Mills v. *Board of Education of the District of Columbia*, 24
Minnesota Multiphasic Personality Test (MMPI), 165
Misty S. v. *Northside Independent School District*, 77
MM v. *School District*, 110
Monahan v. *Nebraska*, 29
Monticello School District No. 25 v. *George L.*, 111
Montoy v. *Kansas*, 31
Morisky v. *Broward County*, 155, 167
Mrs. B. v. *Milford Board of Education*, 48
Muller v. *The East Islip Union Free School District*, 48
Multiple disabilities, 34
Murphy v. *Arlington Central School District Board of Education*, 105
Murphy v. *United Parcel Service, Inc.*, 122, 123
Muscular dystrophy (MD), 54

N
Natural elements, 179
Negligence, 177–79
  assumption of risk, 178–79
  comparative, 178
  contributory, 178
  defenses against allegations of, 178–79
  harm and causation, 177–78
  immunity, 179
  last clear chance, 178
  natural elements, 179
  standard of conduct, 177
Nevada Department of Human Resources v. *Hibbs*, 15
New Paltz Central School District v. *St. Pierre*, 45
New York State Constitution, 32
New York v. *Mid Hudson Medical Group*, 129
N.L. v. *Knox County Schools*, 28
No Child Left Behind Act (NCLB), 9, 37, 171–74
  accountability, 171
  freedom for states and communities, 171

parent options, 172
  proven educational methods, 172
  report cards, 172
Nondiscrimination, duty of, 151–52
Notice of hearing, 89

O
Office for Civil Rights (OCR), 27, 45, 138–41
  complaint resolution, 139–41
  organizational structure, 138–39
  test administration and, 155
Office of Special Education and Rehabilitative Services, 40
Olmstead v. *L.C. by Zimring*, 16, 24
Opinion letters, 5
Orthopedic impairments, 34
Other health impairments (OHI), 33, 34, 40, 64
  leukemia, 40
Owasso Independent School District No. I-011 v. *Falvo*, 175

P
Pace v. *Bogalusa City School Board*, 11, 104
Pack v. *Kmart Corp.*, 125
Pamela McCormick ex rel. Eron McCormick v. *Waukegan School District*, 54, 108, 181
Parental reimbursement, limitations on, 68
Pasatiempo v. *Aizawa*, 45
Peck v. *Lansing School*, 69
Peer grading, 175
Pennsylvania Association of Retarded Citizens v. *Commonwealth*, 24
Pennsylvania Department of Corrections v. *Yeskey*, 131
Personal liability, 54–55
Pervasive developmental delay (PDD), 53
PGA Tour, Inc. v. *Martin*, 133
Placement, 61–62
  private school, 66–71
Polera v. *Board of Education*, 105
Pontiac v. *Spellings*, 173
Postsecondary education, 151–62
  nondiscrimination, duty of, 151–52
  otherwise qualified, 152–53
  reasonable accommodations, 154–62
Powell v. *National Board of Medical Examiners*, 153
Powers v. *Indiana Department of Education*, 108

Prevailing party
  defining, 113–14
  educational agency as, 114–15
Price v. *The National Board of Medical Examiners*, 124
Private organizations, 5
Private schools, 27–28, 66–71
  otherwise qualified, 149–50
  parental reimbursement, 68
  placement, 61–62, 66–69
  public services in, 69–71
  RA and, 147–48
  Title III, ADA, 132
Procedural due process, 13
Professional Group for Attention and Related Disorders, 41
Public education, 27
  basis for, 143–44
  otherwise qualified, 148–49
Public entity, 16
Public sports events and entertainment, Title III, ADA, 133

Q
Qualified immunity, 12

R
Rairdan v. *Salanco School District*, 67
Rational basis review, 13–15
  principles, 13
  sovereign immunity, 14
Reading, 124
re Arons, cert. denied, Arons v. *Office of Disciplinary Counsel*, 98
Reasonable accommodations, 154–62
  delivery of educational materials, 157–58
  documentation requirements, 159–60
  free, 161
  programs for non-qualifying students, 161–62
  requesting, 159
  selecting, 158–59
  specific, 160–61
  testing and fundamental academic requirements, 154–57
Reconstruction Civil Rights Act, 12
  qualified immunity, 12
Reed v. *Mokena School District No. 159*, 108
Rees v. *Jefferson School District*, 18, 78
Reform Educational Financing Inequities Today v. *Mario M. Cuomo, Governor of State of New York*, 144

Refusal, to evaluate, 45
Regulations, 4
  RA, 146–47
  Section 504, 46
  status of, 19–21
  Title II, 20
Rehabilitation Act (RA), 5, 8–9, 26, 28, 41
  cases, no duty to identify under, 46–47
  coverage, 127–33
  discipline, 84
  in education, 151–52
  enforcement of, 135–42
  FAPE under, 144–46
  federal government and, 128–29
  federal grant and aid recipients and, 129
  government contractors and, 129
  impairments covered, 121
  individual with disability and, 119–26
  interpretation of, 16
  major life activities, 124–25
  Office for Civil Rights and, 138–41
  regulations, 46, 146–47
  relationship among ADA and IDEA, 26–31
  Section 504, 26
  sovereign immunity and, 14
  status of regulations, issue of, 19–21
  statutory language, 120–21
  substantially limits, 121–23
Rehabilitation counseling, 49
Reid v. *District of Columbia*, 54
Related services, 62–63
  mandatory medication, 62
Rene v. *Reed*, 181
Report cards, 172
Resolution conference, 96
Ridgewood Board of Education v. *N.E. for M.E.*, 51
Right of Freedom, 16–17
Right to Be Free From Cruel and Unusual Punishment, 17
Right to Meaningful Access to Public Education, 17–18
Risk, assumption of, 178–79
Ritalin, 63
Robertson v. *Neuromedical Center*, 125
Roberts v. *Pennsylvania Department of Public Welfare*, 16
Roe v. *Cheyenne Mt. Conf. Resort*, 46
Roe v. *Nevada*, 55

Roland M. v. *Concord School Committee, cert. denied*, 31, 97, 111
Ross v. *Beaumont Hospital*, 166
R.R. v. *Fairfax County School Board*, 109
Rules of procedure, 110

S
S. v. *Attica Central Schools*, 106
Sacramento City Unified School District, Board of Education v. *Rachel H. by & Through Holland*, 64
Scalia, Justice Antonin, 14
Schaffer v. *Weast*, 99
Scholastic Aptitude Test (SAT), 150
School Board of Nassau County v. *Arline 480*, 166
School codes, 75
School code violations, 75–79
  basic rule, 75–76
  cases on, 77–78
  children with disabilities and, 79
  manifestation determinations, 76–77, 78–79
  school codes, 75
School Committee of Burlington v. *Department of Education*, 31, 54, 97, 110
School nurse services, 49
Schultz v. *Spraylat Corp.*, 124
Seattle School District, No. 1 v. *B.S.*, 45
Seawright v. *Charter Furniture Rental, Inc.*, 115
Secondary education, 143–50
  discrimination in, 143–48
Section 504, 8, 11, 23, 26, 50, 83, 148
  regulations, 46
Sellers by Sellers v. *School Board*, 46, 135
Sellers v. *School Board of Manassas*, 28
Seminole Tribe v. *Florida*, 14
Serious criminal misconduct, 79–82
  consequences of, 80–82
  crimes, 79–80
  deliberate conduct, 80–81
  impulsive acts, 81–82
Settlement agreements, 87–88
  from mediation, 91
Severe discrepancy, 38–40
Shartle v. *Motorola, Inc.*, 166
Shepard v. *Irving*, 18
Sherman v. *Mamaroneck Union Fee School District*, 59
Shiring v. *Runyon*, 126

Shore Regional High School Board of Education v. *P.S.*, 60
Shortened school days, eliminating, 140
Siefken v. *Village of Arlington Heights*, 165
Single state supreme courts, 1
Sinopoli v. *Albert Regula*, 166
Smiley v. *California Department of Education*, 107, 183
South Carolina v. *Katzenbach*, 15
Sovereign immunity, 13, 103
Special Education Expenditure Project (SEEP), 94
Special education population, 33–35
Specific learning disabilities, 34, 38, 39, 47
  ADHD as, 42
Speech impairments, 34, 64
Spending Clause, of Constitution, 7, 24
  IDEA and, 11
  Rehabilitation Act and, 9
Spielberg v. *Henrico County Public Schools*, 56
Spilsbury v. *District of Columbia*, 62
Springer v. *The Fairfax County School Board*, 47
Standardized testing, 154, 182
Standard of conduct, 177
State courts, 1–2
  appellate, 1
  contesting administrative decisions in, 112
  single state supreme, 1
  trial, 1
State educational agency (SEA), 39
  complaint, 86–87
State law, 4, 31–32
  definitions of disability, 126
Status of regulations, issue of, 19–21
Statute of limitations, 108–9
  due process hearing, 98
Statutes, 4
  ADA, 26
  IDEA, 23–26
  overview, 23–32
  RA, 26
  RA/ADA and IDEA, relationships among, 26–31
  state law, 31–32
Statutory language, 37–43
  ADA, 120–21
  ADHD and Asperger's syndrome, 40–43
  child with a disability, 37–38
  FAPE, 51–52

Statutory language (*cont.*)
RA, 120–21, 129
severe discrepancy, 38–40
specific learning disability, 38, 39
Statutory measures, 8–12
Americans with Disabilities Act, 11
Individuals with Disabilities Education Act, 9–11
Reconstruction Civil Rights Act, 12
Rehabilitation Act, 8–9
Stay-put provisions, 109–10
Stephen N. Roth, M.D. v. Lutheran General Hospital, 124
Stern v. University of Osteopathic Medicine and Health Sciences, 155
Steven L. Karracker et al. v. Rent-A-Center, Inc., 165
Strict scrutiny, 14
Substantive due process, 12–13
Supportive services, 50
Supreme Court, 1
Americans with Disabilities Act and, 3
IDEA and, 10
impact of rulings, 123
medical services and, 50
opinions, 4
Susan N. v. Wilson School District, 42
Susquenita School District v. Raelee S., 110
Sutton v. United Air Lines, Inc., 122, 123

T
Taylor v. Corinth Public School District, 64
Teacher of the Deaf Act, 24
Temporary accommodations, 160–61
Tennessee v. Lane, 13, 15, 131, 136
Tenth Amendment, 7
Testing, 148, 154–57
drug, 168
employment-related, 165
high stakes, 181–83
modifications, 156
standardized, 154, 182
test administration, 155–56
test selection, 154

Test of Auditory Perceptual Skills (TAPS), 40
Title II regulations, 20
T.N. v. Bridge City Independent School District, 78
Toddlers, with disabilities, 53
Tort, 175–76
common law, 176–79
constitutional, 179–80
Toyota Motor Manufacturing, Kentucky, Inc. v. Williams, 122–23
Training of Professional Personnel Act, 24
Transportation services, providing, 141
Traumatic brain injury (TBI), 34, 41
Traynor v. Turnage, 166
Treatment and Education of Autistic and Related Communication-Handicapped Children (TEACCH), 56
Trial courts, 1
federal, 2
T.S. v. Independent School District No. 54, Stroud, Oklahoma, 61
Tunstall v. Bergeson, 83
The 24th Annual Report to Congress on the Implementation of the IDEA, 35

U
Undue burden or hardship, 157
Unified School District No. 1 v. Connecticut Department of Education, 83
United States v. Becker C.P.A. Review, 158
United States v. Board of Trustees for the University of Alabama, 161
United States v. Georgia, 15, 17
United States v. Virginia, 15
Unproductive litigation, attorney fees and, 116–17
Urban v. Jefferson County School District R-1, 60
U.S. Department of Justice, 5

V
vacated and remanded, N.Y. State Board of Law Examiners v. Bartlett, 124

Veronica P. v. Evolution Academy Charter School, 82
Veronica P. v. Garland Independent School District, 45
Virginia Department of Education v. Riley, 37, 108
Visual Aural Digit Span Test (VADS), 39
Visual impairments, 34

W
Wagner v. Board of Education of Montgomery County, 109
Wallace v. County of Comal, State of Texas et al, 12
Walter K. v. Goliad Independent School District, 65
Walton v. Mental Health Association of Southeastern Pennsylvania, 138
Ward v. Skinner, 166
Warner v. Independent School District No. 625, 114
Weber v. Cranston School Committee, 105
Wernick v. Federal Reserve Bank of New York, 164
White v. Ascension Parish School Board, 60
Wide Range Assessment of Memory and Learning (WRAML), 40
Wolfe v. Taconic-Hills Central School District, 62
Wong v. Regents of the University of California, 121, 124
Woodcock-Johnson Revised (WJ-R), 40
Working, 124–25
Wright v. Universal Maritime Service Corp., 3, 87
Wynne v. Tufts University School of Medicine, 125, 153, 154, 155

Y
Yaris v. Special School District of St. Louis County, 61–62
Yin v. California, 168

Z
Zobrest v. Catalina Foothills School District, 69
Zukle v. Regents of the University of California, 153
Zvi D. v. Ambach, 110